The World's Oldest Health Plan

The World's Oldest Health Plan

STARBURST PUBLISHERS

P.O. Box 4123, Lancaster, Pennsylvania 17604

To schedule Author appearances write:
Author Appearances, Starburst Promotions, P.O. Box 4123
Lancaster, Pennsylvania 17604 or call (717) 293-0939

Credits:
Cover art by Bill Dussinger

First Printing, March 1994

ISBN: 0-914984-57-8
Library of Congress Catalog Number 93-85138
Printed in the United States of America

Dedication

To my husband *Rich,*
who believes the information in this book saved
his hearing, his posture, and his mind.

Acknowledgment

Special Thanks to . . .

Sharon Purdy, Ruth Kelly, and the late Dan Manley, who encouraged me with faith, loving words, and sometimes sharp words. I am grateful to Lyn Nowicki, Canon Philip Wainwright, and Mary Lynn for their kind words of editoral nature. I am indebted to Stephen Yu, David Cohlmeyer, Dr. David Jenkins, Dr. David Copeland, Dr. Carolyn Dean, Dr. Jerry Green, Dr. Zolton Rona, Dr. "Bill" Dean, the Rev. Bill and Linda Reisberry, and Bishop Reed who have given me either inspiration or encouragement over the years that I have been working on this book. Special thanks to Jane at the St. Vincent's Hospital library for her tireless effort to dig up research material for me.

Table Of Contents

Metric Equivalents

These equivalents are only approximate, as are all measures used in cooking. If a recipe calls for 'g' meaning grams, you may either weigh it or use the conversion chart. I believe that metric measures should be weights for solids, not volume as listed here, but this is not my choice. Most countries that have recently changed to metric have opted for the volume measures. All U.S. measures are standard unless otherwise noted.

1 cup 8 oz.	= 250 mL
3/4 cup 6 oz.	= 200 mL
1/2 cup 4 oz.	= 125 mL
1/4 cup 2 oz.	= 75 mL
2/3 cup	= 160 mL
1/3 cup	= 75 mL
1 Tablespoon	= 15 mL
1 teaspoon	= 5 mL
1/2 teaspoon	= 2 mL
1/4 teaspoon	= 1 mL

225°F	= 110°C
250°F	= 130°C
275°F	= 140°C
300°F	= 150°C
325°F	= 170°C
350°F	= 180°C
375°F	= 190°C
400°F	= 200°C
425°F	= 220°C
450°F	= 230°C
475°F	= 240°C

Introduction

There are many sources for diet information both ancient and modern. There is only one healthy diet that modern medicine agrees upon. That is a high fiber, low fat diet. This diet is the one that year after year is proven to be the healthiest through scientific research and practical usage. It is this diet that I will focus on in *The World's Oldest Health Plan*. This same diet can be found in many ancient health, medical, and religious texts.

I have taken my reference material from two sources: The Christian versions of the Bible and published medical and health material. Many will claim that the Bible is not the world's oldest source material that speaks about diet, and I will agree. However, it is the *diet and health secrets* contained therein that are the World's Oldest Health Plan, not the references in the Bible. I do not intend to get into a philosophical argument as to which text is the oldest source of health information. I intend only to show that the healthiest diet known to us today has been in the Bible all along. I have stayed away from using any of the modern findings in the Dead Sea Scrolls or other newly discovered manuscripts. Rather, I have kept within the material that we have had at our fingertips for the last 1,500 years or so. This is the same Bible that our grandparents and great grandparents read.

In the last fifty years North Americans and Europeans have shown an increasing interest in matters of health and diet. Reading *The World's Oldest Health Plan* will stimulate and increase your desire to change your eating habits to this sensible plan taken from the Bible and agreed upon by modern science.

Don't you know that you yourselves are God's temple and that God's Spirit lives in you? If anyone destroys God's temple, God will destroy him; for God's temple is sacred, and you are that temple. 1 Corinthians 3:16 & 17 (NIV)

I

The World's Oldest Health Plan

Basic Lifestyle–Food Guide
Meal Planning
The Well-Equipped Pantry

The Basic Lifestyle

The basic lifestyle involved with the World's Oldest Health Plan is very simple: Eat healthy, nourishing foods at the right times to sustain your body. Drink water and exercise according to your lifestyle. Spend some time each day in spiritual pursuits and learn to relax. Love your neighbor and yourself, forgive your neighbor and yourself, and ask for forgiveness as needed.

The World's Oldest Health Plan is designed from information in the Bible to be the healthiest way to keep your body (temple) from being destroyed. In other chapters we will explore how certain foods and habits build up health and why. We will also explore how certain habits can destroy your body, some slowly and some quickly.

3 MEALS A DAY

Three meals a day are enough for most people. If you have blood sugar problems, or some other health reason you need to eat more often, then do so. This is especially true if you are a child or a teenager. You will need to eat more often since you will be expending more energy. When doing heavy work or sports, it is essential to eat more carbohydrates and still have protein for the energy you need to keep going without wearing out your body.

EAT A VARIETY OF FOODS

Every day it is important to eat a variety of foods. This includes all vegetables, especially dark green leafy vegetables, yellow vegetables or fruits, beans (including tofu and tempeh), whole grains and whole grain products, and as many raw or nearly raw foods as you can eat. If you eat raw vegetables you will get enough vitamin C and you will not *need* to eat fruit for its vitamin C content. Raw dark green leafy vegetables also contain the highest amount of folic acid, so essential for having healthy babies. If you are treating any fungus or yeast-related problem or blood sugar problem you may not want to eat fruit for a while. (We will talk about this in greater detail in Chapter V—Special Treats.) You will survive. In the summer you might want to eat more fruit when it is picked fresh and ripe.

It is not essential that you eat meat or dairy products so long as you eat lots of beans, grains, and dark green leafy vegetables. Meat, eggs, and dairy products should be treated as condiments in your diet. That is, eaten in small amounts. Animal products do not have to be eaten daily for survival. Many peoples of the world never eat animal products and they survive very well. As you will see in the following chapters, those people who eat very little or no animal products are the healthiest. This is similar to the diet followed by most people in the Bible.

FOLLOW BIBLE PRINCIPLES

It is possible for us to have good health if we follow the principles set out in the Bible; that is to eat small amounts of dairy products in the form of cheese or yogurt, but not necessarily daily. Eat small amounts of animal flesh, mainly fish from cold waters, organically-grown chicken or turkey, or eggs, also not on a daily basis. Reserve eating meat like lamb, beef, pork, etc. for special occasions or when you are out to dinner. Eat mostly grains, vegetables, beans, sea vegetables, fruits, olives, and fish. If you eat meat or cheese eat "bitter herbs" with it.

BALANCE FATS

Balance animal fats with vegetable fats. Don't eat mostly animal fats like butter, lard, dairy products, ice cream, cream, bacon fat, cheese, or cream cheese. Use vegetable source fats in your diet.

These include olives & olive oil, canola oil (also called rapeseed oil), sesame seeds & tahini, almonds & almond oil, walnuts & walnut oil, avocado & avocado oil, flax seeds & flax seed oil, hazelnuts & hazelnut oil, sunflower seeds & sunflower seed oil, pistachio, and brazil nuts. Fats of all kinds should not be more than 5–10% of your diet. Protein should be another 5–15% of your daily diet. This means that no more than 20% of your daily food intake should be fat/protein foods. Twenty years ago this was considered a radical health food diet. Today, in the 90's, it is considered a sensible and healthful diet.

COUNT THE FATS

In the beginning it will be essential for you to count the fats in your current diet and start to figure out how to reduce the total percentage of fats in your diet to less than 30% of the calories for the day. (15–20% is preferable.) Follow the instructions in Chapter VI for determining the total fats in your daily diet. Determine the total for the day, not for each meal. It is OK to eat a whole grain bagel or English muffin with cream cheese or butter for breakfast so long as the total daily fat calories total less than 30% of the total calories. Even a cheese omelet can be balanced out with more carbohydrates and less fat for the rest of the day. Use your common sense, plan ahead, be in charge of your own lifestyle and your own health.

POOR FAT HABITS

Using margarine is the worst fat habit that I can think of, it even ranks higher than eating a steak once in a while. Using shortening for cooking is a very bad habit. Eating whipped toppings and coffee whiteners are also bad habits. These are man-made fat products, they are not what our bodies were intended to eat or live on. My number one rule is: **If God made it, eat it, if man made it, leave it alone!** Please stay away from "artificial" fats. Reduce your taste for fats by eating less fats; don't substitute man-made ones that we can't be sure of.

Eating high fat meats cooked well-done with the fat still on is another bad food habit. If you must eat meat, buy a lower fat cut, broil it after trimming off the visible fat. And don't cook it past medium.

Stay away from processed meats and cheeses, even if they say they are low-fat. They contain ingredients that can disturb your fat balance without even being obvious. Things like MSG, salt, sugar, hydrogenated fats, palm kernel oil, or coconut oil are not acceptable to someone who desires the best of health.

FAT AND BITTER HERBS

Always eat bitter herbs when you eat any fat foods. Fat Foods include cheese, mayonnaise, cream, meats, or avocado. Look at Chapter III under Bitter Herbs for the reasons, and a list of the foods that are bitter herbs.

SAMPLE MEAL

If you eat 100 grams (3 1/2 ounces) of meat, always eat a dark green leafy salad with no dressing, or lemon juice as a dressing or an olive oil based dressing. Eat sprouts, parsley, watercress, mint, dandelion greens, etc. in the salad and two servings of vegetables, one should be a dark yellow or orange vegetable, and a whole grain roll or crackers without butter. Have fresh fruit for dessert. Voila! You will have balanced the fats to a healthy level.

MAYONNAISE AND CHOLESTEROL

Mayonnaise is made from 1 egg and 1 cup of good oil. With the lemon juice and/or vinegar in it you end up with 1 1/2 cups of mayonnaise. If you use 2 tablespoons on a sandwich you will be getting 1/12th of an egg yolk since there are 24 tablespoons in 1 1/2 cup. If you are eating a roast beef sandwich you will be eating between 100 and 170 mg of cholesterol in the beef if it is lean and you only have 3 1/2 ounces. The 2 tablespoons of mayonnaise has less than 16 mg of cholesterol in it. Which would be better left out? If you make the mayonnaise with virgin olive oil you will be using mono-unsaturated fat that can help balance the saturated fats. If you eat less meat and more lettuce and use whole grain low-fat bread, you can still eat the mayonnaise. See how easy it is? Don't listen to advertising that tries to sell you something that is not logical like no-cholesterol mayonnaise or salad dressing or no-fat salad dressings. If you want to reduce cholesterol or fats in your meals reduce the meats, cheeses, dairy products, and fried foods.

WHY EAT 3 MEALS A DAY?

Food is the fuel for your body. Without fuel your body will not run efficiently or will not run at all. It is just that simple. Compare the human body to a car. Would you consider running a car without gas? Don't ask your body to function without food. Would you consider running your car without oil? Don't ask your body to run without oxygen. Would you consider driving your car without water? Don't ask your body to work without water.

TIMING OF MEALS

The length of time it takes to digest a meal is around four hours. The length of time between meals is around four hours. When you eat, eat enough food/fuel to keep you going for about four hours. When it is used up you will be hungry and it will also be time to eat. It is so sensible, why have we forgotten it? Why do we eat too much, go without food and fatigue our body, become so hungry that we stuff ourselves with food that we aren't going to use for energy, but will store as fat? Why? When eating three regular meals is so easy, so loving, so caring to ourselves? We were given bodies that can function efficiently and beautifully, if they are fed the right fuels at the right times. How can we be content with abusing them?

We were given the responsibility to take care of our body, mind, and spirit. We were even given the tools to use to do this. And yet, many still do not want to accept our God-given responsibility towards ourselves. If you don't take care of your body and then become ill or addicted, don't just pray for healing of the "dis-ease." Pray for the strength to take care of yourself! To take responsibility for yourself! Would you run a car without gas and oil and then, when it breaks down, pray for it to be repaired? No, of course not. You would take it to a mechanic to repair the damage. When you don't take care of your body, then take it to the doctor for him or her to fix it, you are doing the same thing. Please don't waste the doctor's time with things that you can prevent with a healthy lifestyle. Leave his time for more serious things like accidents, floods, epidemics, and true emergencies.

The Israelites were much better at taking care of themselves than we are today. Then, again, they didn't have junk food, refined foods, nutritionless foods, cigarettes, "hurryitis," "get-ahead" fever, or TV and radio advertising to entice them away from being natural. The World's Oldest Health Plan is a return to the responsibility of being grown up, of being fully responsible for your own health. We were given this choice. Do you choose life? Or do you choose a slow death from false lifestyle choices?

THE MOST IMPORTANT MEAL

Breakfast is the most important meal of the day. We have gone without eating for 6 to 8 hours, a kind of mini fast. This is why the first meal of the day is called "break-fast." We need to give our body some fuel to do the morning work. Complex carbohydrates are energy-giving and should be eaten at breakfast. This includes whole grains, potatoes, corn, lima and other beans, and fruit. You could even have a salad and a roll if you wish.

Sugar is a simple carbohydrate. This means that it simply won't last long enough in your system to give you energy for 4 hours. Simple carbohydrates are used up fast and need to be replaced fast or you won't have any energy. This is why, when you eat something sweet for breakfast, you need to eat again in only 1 or 2 hours. Otherwise, you might find yourself fatigued, yawning, irritable, or unable to concentrate. You might even feel that you need more sugar or even caffeine to perk you up. This kind of "quick start" fuel is not very long lasting and should be avoided.

Complex carbohydrates come from whole grains, fruits, and vegetables. They burn slowly because they are more complex. Slow burning fuel will keep your body supplied with energy for a longer period of time than quick burning fuel. This is explained more fully in Chapter II—Our Daily Bread.

WHAT SHOULD I EAT FOR BREAKFAST?

Cooked whole grains such as oatmeal, barley, buckwheat, millet, rice, wheat, or corn with flaxseeds and, perhaps, oat bran, are a good breakfast meal. Add vegetables, such as corn, lima or other beans, carrots, sweet potato, cauliflower, mushrooms, etc, while the grains are cooking. Once the grains are cooked, you can add fresh raw seasonings like parsley, basil, chives, pressed garlic, green onions, and so on. This can be eaten as is or soy sauce (tamari or shoyu) can be added. Often, I add a small amount of olive oil or flaxseed oil. Sometimes I get carried away and add small bits of cheese. (This is when I know that I am having a no-fat lunch.) The grains can be cooked as grains or twice as much water can be added to make porridge.

Muffins made with Ezekiel-type blended flour and fruit or grated carrots are great for breakfast, since they contain vegetable protein and complex carbohydrates. Nowadays most muffins are low in fat and sweeteners and make excellent breakfasts. When they are made with whole grains and high fiber flours they give the lasting power and energy needed to start the day.

Buckwheat noodles cooked with broccoli stems, sweet potatoes, arame, onions, and slices of fresh ginger is one of my favorite breakfasts. Add the broccoli flowers just before serving so that they are still bright green. I like to add pressed garlic before serving. Serve with tamari or shoyu, if desired. This can be drained and served as a bowl of noodles or it can be served as a thick soup with the broth. Top it with fresh parsley. If you don't have time for all this cooking you can find whole grain ramen with vegetable seasoning packets that cook in three minutes. There are also instant boil-in-bag brown rice with vegetables or beans "dinners" that you can cook for breakfast. There are many different whole grain instant meals that you just add water to or add water and microwave for a few seconds. These are great for breakfast if they are all natural and have no MSG and contain whole grains. (I am not fond of using a microwave, but if this is the only way you can make breakfast, use it.)

Scrambled tofu with vegetables is great for breakfast with whole grain toast. See *The World's Oldest Health Plan Recipe Companion* for recipes and more ideas on what to eat for breakfast.

SNACKS

Snacks between meals are acceptable if you are hungry or need energy. Often the snack can be part of the regular meal that you save away and eat later. Fresh fruit is a good snack. If you are worried about calories, just have the fruit for a snack rather than with breakfast. If you know you will be hungry in the afternoon, plan your snack and have it with you so you won't be tempted to eat something sugary, salty, or filled with caffeine. Unroasted nuts and seeds are good snacks; popcorn with herbs and no butter is an excellent snack. You can even fix it at work. Low-fat, low sodium crackers are great to have for snacks. Vegetable sticks are excellent. A can of low-sodium vegetable juice cocktail is great for a snack and you can keep it in your desk or car for just such times. If you have a sandwich for breakfast or lunch save half for a snack later. You will feel better and have the same amount of calories.

Children and teenagers need to eat more often than adults since they use up the energy in physical activity and during growth. So long as they are active, give them snacks between meals. It generally is not true that if you give children snacks they will not eat their meals. Give them snacks of wholesome foods like whole grain muffins or crackers, fruit, lettuce or celery and nut butter, vegetables, or vegetable juice drinks at the right times. If they are hungry after school this is the time to give them a snack, hours before supper so they can work it off. If you wait until just before dinner when their blood sugar is so low from not eating, they may not want to eat dinner for two reasons. One, they will be full, and two, they will have raised their blood sugar enough to not want to eat.

If you let them go too long without eating, they might eat too much when they do eat. That teaches them to binge eat or stuff themselves. If a person gets too hungry, his or her reasoning powers will be almost nonexistent and the need for fuel will be so great anything that will give a quick fix will do. That might be fruit, but most of the time it will be something with sugar. This will turn them into "sugarholics": people who use the quick fix of sugar to try to get energy all the time. (Caffeine, colas, chocolate, coffee all produce the same kind of results—the quick fix.) This is very exhausting for the body, since the body needs real food to function, not just a quick jolt. This can lead to being more susceptible to stress as well as being addicted to the quick/instant answer.

SNACKING LOWERS CHOLESTEROL

A study reported in the October 5, 1989 *New England Journal of Medicine* showed that men who ate their regular food in 17 snacks a day instead of three meals, had an 8.5% reduction in cholesterol and a 13.5% reduction in LDL cholesterol levels. They ate the same amount of foods and the same 2700 kilocalories as the control group who ate it in three meals a day and showed no changes in any cholesterol levels.

BEDTIME SNACKS

When I was a child, I spoke like a child, I thought like a child, I reasoned like a child; when I became a man, I gave up childish ways. 1 Corinthians 13:11 (RSV)

Since food is eaten to give energy for the body to do something, it is not reasonable to eat before going to bed. What will you be doing that will require that energy? Nothing! If you find that you want a bedtime snack you may be out of balance in your diet and lifestyle. Perhaps you desire to eat before bed because you were put to bed as a baby with a bottle, and you developed this habit. Take the advice of Paul and grow up. You no longer need to think or act like a child. When you are grown up, be done with childish ways. If you find this difficult, you may need counseling. This might be nutrition counseling, spiritual counseling, or co-dependency counseling. It is time to look at your habits and take charge of your life; don't let your habits and addictions rule you. Wait until you have read this book through thoroughly before you go for counseling. You might find the solution and change your diet to change your life.

Ho! Everyone who thirsts, come to the waters; and you who have no money, come, buy and eat. Yes, come, buy wine and milk without money and without price. Why do you spend money for what is not bread, and your wages for what does not satisfy? Listen carefully to Me, and eat what is good, and let your soul delight itself in abundance. Isaiah 55:1,2 (NKJV)

HOW TO TELL WHEN TO MAKE A CHANGE

There are so many recommendations of how much food to eat, when to eat it, what to eat, and so on, that it might be difficult to sort it all out. Here is my food guide that has worked for thousands of people.

It doesn't matter what you eat so long as:

1. you get up early in the morning feeling wide awake and do some exercise,
2. you have enough energy to spend with your family after work and on weekends,
3. you only need 6-8 hours of sleep at night,
4. you feel great without taking stimulants such as coffee, tea, sugar, alcohol, or tobacco,
5. you never lose your temper or get angry,
6. you always have time for spiritual pursuits,
7. you have no more than one headache or cold a year,
8. you enjoy activities that are aerobic like swimming, hiking, bicycling, tennis, dancing, or family or group sports,
9. you can say no to temptations,
10. you are guided by your own knowing of what is right or wrong rather than being led by a begging child or competitive neighbor,
11. you have time to help someone who needs you.

The World's Oldest Health Plan is designed to bring you in control of your life, your choices, your health, and your ability to be relaxed and express love. Food alone will not do this. But the proper diet will help you have the strength to be able to be in control of your life. If you spend some time in the beginning planning out a healthy lifestyle, you will spend less time later on trying to overcome the effects of a bad one.

Food Guide

Eat 2–3 servings or more of whole grains every day. This can be in the form of cereal, whole grains, noodles, bread, or crackers.

Eat 3–4 servings or more of vegetables every day. At least one serving should be raw, more if possible. Eat dark green leafy vegetables &/or orange vegetables daily.

Eat 1–2 servings of protein a day. The best sources are whole grains with nuts and seeds, beans with grains, soy bean products such as tofu or tempeh, and sprouted seeds and grains. Whole eggs can be eaten twice a week. If they are used in cooking, like muffins or binders in loaves, then you may eat that in addition to the servings of eggs, since each serving would contain a fraction of an egg. Or you may wish to only eat eggs used in cooking; that is acceptable. No more than six servings of dairy products a week in all forms, excluding butter. You may wish to eliminate dairy products altogether and you may do so if you eat beans, whole grains, and dark green leafy vegetables daily. Eat fish or seafood from cold waters no more than twice a week. Any other sources of protein can be eaten once a week if desired. Remember that animal based proteins are not essential to life if you are eating the other foods recommended. When you eat meat, use it as an addition to other foods, not as the main event of a meal. If you eat a roast turkey or chicken, for example, only serve 1–3 ounces to each person. This is more than enough for the entire day's worth of protein if you are eating whole grains, legumes, and dark green leafy vegetables.

Eat 1–2 servings of fruit. This is optional if you are eating raw vegetables twice a day.

This may seem radical, but if you read the other chapters in this book you will see why this is the best diet. This is the diet that the

Hebrews followed, the ancient Chinese and Japanese followed, and even our ancestors in Europe and Africa followed. This is also the diet outlined in the new Food Pyramid/Food Guide in the US.

Meal Planning

Meal planning is essential for your health, well-being, budget, and time. Plan a menu for a week or a month. The entire family should be involved in planning the meals, snacks, and treats. They should also be involved in the shopping and preparing of the foods. We all eat, we are all responsible for our own body and mind, we should all learn to do it as early as possible. This will eliminate a lot of friction later. If children know they are going to have a snack at a certain time they can relax, if they know what it will be they can also relax. They will not be going on their own whims at the time, but will be following a plan and demonstrating discipline. This will save a lot of begging, whining, and other humiliating behaviors from occurring.

Once you have planned the meals and snacks, get out the recipes so whoever is in charge of the meals that day can look at them ahead of time. List the foods needed on the basic shopping list. Buy the foods listed. This way you will not be tempted to buy something not on the list when you are in the store. You can also explain to children that this is the way it is so that they will not have to bother begging for something that is not on the list. If they want something not on the list ask them to discuss this at the next meal planning meeting. If it is not nutritious it should be voted down after a short discussion of the facts. After a few months on a healthy lifestyle if you do succumb to eating sugary foods ask each person to be in charge of assessing his behavior after he has eaten the item. Chances are there will be a very different dynamic in the family that even the smallest pre-schooler can understand and wish to do away with.

Some foods will be on the staples list. If so, look for them in the cupboard, determine if there is enough for the week or month and cross it off the list.

In smaller families, shop for the basic staples once a month or less often. Each week shop for fresh fruits, vegetables and baked goods, if you don't make your own.

Once a month or less have a family baking day and bake breads, muffins, crackers, etc. to last for the allotted time. Freeze some of it to keep it fresh.

If you have a family-sized freezer you may want to make entrées to freeze for later to save time and energy. Things like vegetable pot pies, fruit pies, casseroles, and sauces can be made ahead and frozen. During fresh tomato season I often make and "put up" spaghetti and pizza sauce for later use. (See *The World's Oldest Health Plan Recipe Companion* for recipes.)

A family party of making a large amount of whole wheat pizza dough that can be rolled out and then frozen is a great idea. This will give young children something they can make for dinner with very little trouble. All they would need to do is put on the canned sauce from the cupboard, add some vegetables, grate cheese and mix with tofu if desired, sprinkle it on and bake it. Even packages of pre-grated cheese can be frozen in serving portions for later use. Always buy the low-fat, natural type, not the processed type. This can often save money if a bulk amount is bought at a wholesaler. Served with a green salad or vegetable sticks it is a perfect meal. Children as young as 6 can learn to use a knife properly, and they should be taught and supervised.

Small individual pizzas can be made for them to have as snacks which they can heat up themselves. They will be more responsible if they are part of the meal planning, shopping, and cooking, and can serve themselves. It is important that they also are responsible for putting things away and cleaning up, just like an adult. Agree ahead of time what the rules are, then stick with them.

IS THIS ALL THERE IS?

The World's Oldest Health Plan includes food and water, exercise, spiritual pursuits, relaxation, loving your neighbor and yourself, and forgiveness. These are the basic principles for a healthy life. Chapters II through VII will deal with the food aspects of a healthy life. It is my belief that when your body is not healthy, neither is your mind. Remember this from grade school, "A healthy body is a healthy mind, and a healthy mind is a healthy body?" This still holds true for people of all ages.

Chapter VIII will deal with the remaining aspects of good health. Please read this book through before you decide to make any changes in your life or pass judgment on the World's Oldest Health Plan.

The Well-Equipped Pantry

Staple Foods To Keep On Hand

GRAINS
- barley
- brown rice, long and/or short grain, basmati
- buckwheat
- corn meal
- millet
- rolled oats
- oat bran
- oat groats
- popping corn
- rye
- wheat bran
- wheat groats

FLOUR PRODUCTS
- whole grain pasta: fettuccine, elbow macaroni, soba, lasagna noodles, fusilli, etc.
- whole grain ramen
- whole wheat bread flour (keep refrigerated or frozen)
- whole wheat pastry flour (keep refrigerated or frozen)
- Ezekiel-type blended flour

BEANS—dried or in jars or cans without salt, EDTA, or MSG
- chick peas
- kidney, red and/or white
- baby limas
- lentils
- mung
- great northern
- navy
- pinto
- romano

DRIED HERBS & SPICES (I keep them in jars on a shelf in alphabetical order.)
- allspice
- anise seeds

basil
bay leaves
caraway seeds
cardamom–ground & whole
celery seeds–ground & whole
chile peppers–ground, whole, & chopped
chives
cinnamon-ground & whole
coriander seeds–ground & whole
cumin seeds–ground & whole
cloves–ground & whole
curry powder–mild or hot
dill seeds
dill weed
garlic powder
ginger powder
marjoram
mint leaves
mustard seeds–ground & whole
nutmeg–whole with grater or ground
oregano
pepper corns & grinder
paprika
rosemary
savory
summer savory
thyme
turmeric
wasabi (Japanese 'mustard' powder)

BAKING SUPPLIES

almond extract
arrowroot starch
baking powder (no aluminum)
baking soda
carob powder
corn starch
cocoa, unsweetened
coconut, grated, unsweetened
honey
milk powder, non-instant

peppermint extract
sea salt
vanilla extract

FRESH HERBS
arugula
basil
celery
chives
coriander, also known as cilantro
dill
garlic
ginger
green onions
onions
parsley
rosemary

REFRIGERATED SUPPLIES
almond butter
almond oil
apple cider vinegar
barbeque sauce
butter
canola oil
catsup
Dijon mustard
lemons or limes
mayonnaise
olive oil
olives, green
olives, black
peanut butter–nitrogen-sealed only
peanut oil
salsa
tahini
tamari or shoyu
tofu in aseptic packs

REFRIGERATED SNACKS
almonds
apricots
brazil nuts
cheese, low-fat or goat milk
concentrated fruit juices
currents
dates
figs
flax seeds
juice drinks, unsweetened in aseptic packs
mineral water
pecans
pumpkin seeds
raisins
sunflower seeds
trail mix–no peanuts
vegetable sticks
walnuts

DRY SUPPLIES & MIXES
arame
carob drink
cocoa, unsweetened
falafel mix
fajita mix
fruit tea for children to drink hot or cold
grain 'coffee'
hijiki
kombu
macaroni & cheese mix, etc., from natural market
mint tea
nori
pasta salad mix, etc., from natural market
salsa mix
spice tea
tofu burger mix
veggie burger mix

CANS OR JARS

beans, no salt or MSG
chili
lentils
olives
crushed pineapple in own juice
sardines in water or soy oil
soup, no MSG
spaghetti or pizza sauce
stews
tomato paste
tuna in water
whole tomatoes in own juice

When David came to Mahanaim, Shobi son of Nahash from Rabbah of the Ammonites, and Makir son of Ammiel from Lo Debar, and Barzillai the Gileadite from Rogelim brought bedding and bowls and articles of pottery. They also brought wheat and barley, flour and roasted grain, beans, and lentils, honey and curds, sheep, and cheese from cows' milk for David and his people to eat. For they said, "The people have become hungry and tired and thirsty in the desert." 2 Samuel 17:27-29 (NIV)

II

Our Daily Bread
Whole Grains & Fiber

What Are The Whole Grains?

Whole grains grow on plants. Grains are grown in all kinds of different climates, soil, and terrains. Many of them are protected by a hull or a coarse outer layer. The grains ripen and are allowed to dry on the plant. Then they are harvested and winnowed. This allows the hull to be removed easily, in most cases. For most grains this was done with a screen, tray, large bowl, or sheet. The grain was gently tossed into the air and the hulls that had become loosened would blow off in the breeze leaving the grain, which was heavier, to drop back into the container. Sometimes the grain was rubbed or stepped on to loosen the hulls first. This seed or grain just as it comes from the plant is called a whole grain. It is the real grain, just as it was grown.

Whole grains contain all the essential nutrients that sustained the Children of Israel in their daily lives. Grains are called the staff of life because they can support life. This is the reason they should be eaten as our daily bread. Whole grains are an essential part of a healthy and wholesome diet. I wish I could say that by eating whole grains instead of processed fractionated grains you would have perfect health, reduce your visits to the doctor, and reduce your medicine. I can't. But it will help you be healthy, have more energy, and feel better. However, there is more to health and happiness than bread alone.

Whole grains contain protein, which is composed of smaller units called amino acids. Amino acids are the building blocks of the cells of our body. Grains also contain starch or carbohydrate, B vitamins, fiber, and, in some cases, vitamin E. The fiber and B vitamins are necessary for the utilization of the starch in the grains.

RESEARCH ON WHOLE GRAINS

Dr. David Jenkins, a nutritionist at the University of Toronto, Medical School, has been doing research for over 15 years with whole grains, often called cereal foods. His research has shown that whole grains are slow-release carbohydrates that allow the body to need less insulin than refined carbohydrates need for digestion. This is great news for diabetics, as his studies have shown. This slow-release of sugars also helps to regulate the rate of release for specific hormones and other nutrients. He has recommended the use of whole grains and other high fiber foods such as lentils, peas, and beans for heart, liver, colon, and kidney disease.[1] Here is one instance when medical research has shown that health can be improved by including whole grains and the other high fiber foods mentioned in the Bible into one's diet.

REFINED CARBOHYDRATES

Grains are carbohydrate foods. Around the 1400's a process was invented that stripped some grains of the fiber and B vitamins, leaving a pure white refined grain. Since this was a new process and was expensive, only those with money could afford to eat the new refined grains. Thus, they began to be equated with a higher class in society than were the peasants.

The grains most commonly "refined" were wheat, rice, and barley. The brown part that was removed proved to be the healthiest part of the grain. In wheat, for example, the bran layer contains about 86% of the niacin (B3), 73% of the pyridoxine (B6), 50% of the pantothenic acid (B5), 42% of the riboflavin (B2), 33% of the thiamin (B1), and 19% of the protein of the wheat kernel. Therefore, removing the outer layer would mean removing a high percentage of the nutrients that were in the wheat. With the removal of the B vitamins from the staple foods of the diet many B vitamin deficiencies began to be seen in society. This was also the start of problems with constipation due to the lack of fiber in the average diet. Many of the health problems associated with alcoholics, such as night blindness, confusion, and "the shakes" are often associated more with the lack of B vitamins in their diet than with the alcohol itself. Alcohol uses up or destroys B vitamins as any stress will do. If they are not replaced through eating B vitamin rich whole foods, it could be very difficult for an alcoholic to recover.

WHOLE WHEAT

Wheat, *Triticum aestivum*, is the main grain for North Americans. It grows in Canada as well as the U. S. Whole wheat, when properly grown, contains calcium, magnesium, zinc, iron, copper, chromium, and other trace minerals. It contains unsaturated fatty acids, vitamin E, and fiber. Whole wheat contains at least 16 amino acids including isoleucine, leucine, lysine, methionine, phenylalanine, threonine, tryptophane, valine, alanine, aspartic acid, cystine, glutamic acid, glycine, histidine, proline, and serine. Whole wheat contains the B vitamins, especially riboflavin or B2, pyridoxine or B6, and pantothenic acid or B5.[2] In recent years the nutrients in the soils of North America have been depleted due to chemical farming methods and many of the commercially produced grains do not contain the nutrients they should. This is why I always buy grains that have been grown with the eater's health in mind. These are usually certified "organically grown." This tells me that the food producer has my health in mind when growing and selling his products.

Many people are suffering from overweight, high blood fats, and other problems brought on by faulty fat and carbohydrate metabolism. This can be remedied by eating foods high in chromium. Naturally grown wheat is one of the few sources of chromium in the diet. Most whole grains have chromium. It is also found in brewer's yeast and some fortified cereals. Chromium has long been known to help in the regulation of blood sugar, an important factor in diabetes, weight loss, and muscle building.[3] When I worked in a nutrition clinic in Toronto, Ontario, I found that about 80% of our "hardening of the arteries" patients had very low chromium. I found that 90% of the people with blood sugar or hypoglycemia related problems had low chromium. Many people with fatigue had low chromium and were unable to stabilize their blood sugar levels to normal, even levels, thus causing an up and down syndrome (known as the yo-yo syndrome) that caused great fatigue.

CHROMIUM AND LONG LIFE

Much research is being done with chromium in the '90s for weight loss and muscle building, but the best research is being done for longevity. In 1991–92 Biochemist Gary W. Evans of Bemidji State University in Minnesota did experiments with rats. His conclusions showed that the rats fed chromium picolinate lived an average of one year longer than the control group.

This would mean that eating whole wheat bread made from organically grown natural grains could help us to have longer and happier lives. This would also mean that anyone with any kind of blood sugar problem would do well to add brewer's-type nutritional yeast to his diet to help with the sugar and prevent early aging.

Recent research also at Bemidji State University showed that chromium picolinate played a role in preventing heart disease and lowered cholesterol in 28 otherwise healthy subjects at the university.[4]

Fiber

Whole grains, peas and beans, vegetables, and fruits contain fiber. Nearly every week we read or hear that certain things we are doing in our lifestyle can have a negative affect on our health. One of the big ones now is the lack of fiber. All whole grains, vegetables, and fruits contain fiber. Legumes, peas, beans, lentils are all vegetables and still contain large amounts of fiber even though they are dried. Prunes and figs are the highest fiber fruits.

WHY EAT FIBER?

Fiber is in foods to nourish us, keep our digestion functioning, and keep sludge and poisons from remaining in our body. Man removed the fiber from wheat, sugar, rice, and barley so that it would be refined (as if the original food was made only for peasants, not refined, high-class people like us). The thinking at the time seemed to be that we must show that we are better, less crude, so we will have pure white food with no crude ingredients like fiber and B vitamins. So, even today, we eat white bread and then take laxatives, aloe vera, or even bran to make up for not having it in the food. By removing the fiber from the grains we eat we also don't have to bother to chew them, and that slows down our digestion as well. Medical experts suggest we add 30–35 grams of fiber to our diet if we eat a regular American diet of 10–15 grams of fiber a day. One level tablespoon of millers bran contains 1 gram of fiber. Two slices of whole wheat bread has 4 grams of fiber. Fiber is also found in vegetables and fruits so the entire day's worth of fiber doesn't necessarily have to come from grains. This need for fiber in our diets is part of the reason the Food Pyramid is suggesting we eat so many servings of grains, fruits, and vegetables. The World's Oldest Health Plan is a high fiber diet when properly done.

New evidence is beginning to show a link between high fiber diets and low incidences of cancer of several types including bowel, colon, and breast.

HOW TO ADD FIBER

Fiber should be added to your diet slowly. Start by adding whole grains instead of refined. Eat brown rice in place of white rice, whole grain pasta in place of white, whole wheat or whole grain bread in place of white. Add more vegetables to your diet a little at a time. Each day add more fruits and vegetables. Don't take 2 tablespoons of fiber at each meal when you start. This could produce unwanted stomach, intestinal, and flatulence problems. Start with a teaspoon at each meal or 1 teaspoon before bed and one in the morning. When you add more fiber to your diet, you generally need to take in more liquids to make the fiber work at its most efficient level. Read labels on all products that have them. When there is a choice always pick the product with the highest fiber content. You might be surprised at the difference in the fiber contents of commercial cereals. Some of the ones that you thought were high fiber by the name on them may not be as high as some others. Read! Read!

IS IT PASTE?

One friend of mine told me that she had a hard time eating anything made of flour because as a child she had made paste of white flour and didn't want to eat paste. But she also noticed then that when she ate white flour or didn't chew any flour products well that it felt like paste was in her intestines. Even children often know what is best for them.

FIBER AND HEMORRHOIDS

When there is constipation, there is often straining to produce elimination. This straining can produce hemorrhoids, which are generally uncomfortable, and often unnecessary. Adequate fiber and

B vitamins in the diet can prevent constipation, and therefore, reduce the occurrences of hemorrhoids. There is some evidence that vitamin B6 is also necessary in the diet to prevent hemorrhoids.[5] Vitamin B6 is found in whole grains, especially wheat.

HOW FIBER WORKS

Fiber works in two different ways. It makes you have to really chew it, and it acts like a broom to sweep out any foreign matter in the digestive tract. It is the fiber that holds the water in the stools allowing the intestines to work better, faster, and with ease. This is how fiber helps to prevent constipation. When the waste matter is dry it plugs up the action of the muscles in the intestines and allows the body to slow down the transit time of the waste matter. The intestines re-absorb the poisons that you were trying to get rid of in the first place. Then you have autointoxication or self poisoning which is why constipation is often associated with headaches, and other aches and pains. The fiber exercises the muscles in the intestinal walls, keeping them working smoothly and efficiently, allowing the waste to be eliminated as soon as it reaches the large intestine, without getting bogged down, dried out, and hard. This must be what the old Scottish proverb was getting at when people were told: "The whiter your bread, the sooner you're dead."

CHEWING STARTS DIGESTION

You really need to chew whole grains. The mechanical or muscular activity of digestion, which produces gastrointestinal motility, is begun by chewing. Mastication, or chewing, breaks up food into smaller particles, thus giving more surface area of food to constantly be exposed to enzyme action. Ptyalin, an enzyme specific for starches, is the first digestive enzyme secreted by the body. It is secreted from three pairs of salivary glands in the mouth during chewing. The nerve reflexes that control the peristaltic waves that begin the process of digestion allowing food to pass through the esophagus, and continue through the digestion cycle, begin through the stimulus of the presence of food in the mouth.[6] It seems logical, then, that the longer food is in the mouth and the more it is chewed, the better digestion will be.

This is why most health diets and health care practitioners recommend that each mouthful be chewed until it is well broken down. This could be 10 times, in the case of watermelon or 50 times in the case of nuts or grains. The rule I like to use is: **Never swallow**

unless it is liquid. If you want to have good digestion chew your food first, then swallow. If you want your body to be under less stress, chew your food before you swallow.

THE SECRET OF WEIGHT LOSS

The more you chew whole grains the more you will be able to digest them fully. You will also eat less if you chew each mouthful very, very well. People who are constantly on weight reduction diets often talk jokingly of the "appestat," the regulator of appetite. The end-of-hunger signals you get while eating are regulated by the amount you chew. Therefore, the more you chew each mouthful the sooner you will get the message that you have eaten enough, and you will not overeat. They say it takes 20 minutes for your brain to signal you to stop eating once your need has been satisfied. If you are eating at the rate most North Americans do, and not chewing, it means you might eat 20 minutes more food than you need. If you chew each mouthful well, the stomach gives the signal at the correct time, long before you have overeaten. So chewing functions like an "appestat." Since there is no "real" research on this theory, there is no footnote.

Chewing tells each of the organs and glands of digestion how much and how often to work. The more you chew each mouthful, the more the body will be able to get nourishment from what you do eat, and you will eat less. This is just logical. This really shouldn't be a secret. When I taught weight loss classes I found that this was the one common denominator in overweight people's lifestyle. They didn't chew each mouthful enough and they ate more than they needed; thus, the unused energy turned to FAT to be stored.

CHEWING AND ALLERGIES

Dr. David Cropland, an allergist in Montreal, Quebec, often discuses the effects of poor chewing with his patients. He feels that partially chewed grains can ferment in the gut while the body is trying to break down the grains that should have been chewed. This can set the person up for stomach, sinus, or intestinal trouble that could lead to allergies and other dis-eases related to the chemical reaction in the body. If you have allergies, please try chewing grains, starches, and fruits more. This might help reduce the strain on your body and prevent it from reacting to something irritating. It's worth a try, and it's free. You might find many other health benefits once you chew more.

HOW MUCH SHOULD WE EAT EACH DAY?

Nutritionists agree that we need at least 2 to 3 full servings of whole grains a day to keep us healthy and supply the necessary roughage, or fiber (as it is now called) that we need to be healthy. Whole wheat French toast for breakfast and a whole grain muffin for dinner would be two servings. Oatmeal for breakfast, then later, brown rice with stir fried vegetables and tofu, almonds, ginger, and a small amount of fish or chicken would be two servings of whole grains. Although it isn't as good when all the grains are eaten as sweets, you might have your two servings in the form of freshly baked whole wheat and oatmeal muffins, corn bread, or whole grain apple pie, even butter cookies just to get started. I love eating Ezekiel-type multi blend flour muffins, pancakes, or biscuits for breakfast. Since the flour contains legumes as well as whole grains it is higher in fiber and lower in starch than whole grain flours individually would be.

It is possible to eat grains at every meal. It is possible to eat grains for snacks several times a day. You might be getting the picture that the more servings of grain you eat the better off you will be.

WHY ARE GRAINS THE STAFF OF LIFE?

In the third edition of The New Combined Bible Dictionary and Concordance published by Baker House Books in Grand Rapids, Michigan "staff" is defined as a "scepter." A scepter is defined as "a rod or reed which served as a symbol of authority." Sheaves of grains and stalks of grains were often used as decorations. They were often woven or embroidered into tapestries, rugs, and clothing. This shows the important place grains held in the lives of people in Bible times.

WHOLE GRAINS OR PASTE?

If you are interested in eating the food intended for us to eat, then you might want to try some whole grain recipes. Don't ever let anybody tell you that you can't make bread out of all whole grain flours. You can, and it is wonderful. It isn't that sort of fluffy, cotton-wool, whoosh type of white bread that dissolves in your mouth before you even chew it, slithers down your throat before you even swallow it, and sticks in your intestines like paste to wallpaper before you even get to receive any nourishment from it (mainly because there isn't much). Bread made from whole grains, preferably freshly ground, is real bread. It is the same kind of bread that Jesus and Elisha ate when they walked the earth and shared meals with their friends. Do you think huge crowds of people could be sustained by white bread and fish?

WHOLE GRAIN FLOURS

The easiest way to start eating whole grains is with whole grain flour products. You can substitute whole wheat pastry flour for white in recipes like cakes, pies, muffins, pancakes, cookies, waffles, and other foods that you usually make from white flour. Hard wheat flour can be used for breads, strudel, or noodles since they have to be kneaded. Gravy can be made from whole grain flours. It is generally nuttier tasting. Many natural food, Chinese, Japanese, Korean or gourmet food stores sell noodles made of many kinds of whole grain flour such as whole wheat, buckwheat, brown rice, corn, and soy. Whole grain macaroni with cheese and vegetables is a dish that kids of all ages love. There are even whole grain alphabet noodles for putting in children's soups. There are whole grain lasagna, spaghetti, and other pastas. Experiment with these foods from other cultures and cuisines using whole grain flour products.

RECIPES USING METRIC

You may notice that some of the recipes give the ingredients by weight; some by volume measure. The metric system, to be effective, is a system of weights for dry measures and volume for liquid measures. This will make measuring and shopping very easy. If a recipe calls for 200 grams of chopped carrots, you can weigh the carrot and know that you have the exact amount. If the recipe calls for 1 cup of finely chopped carrots, packed down it might be difficult to determine if the quantity is exact. There may be variations in how finely one grates the carrots, and in the pressure applied to pack down the grated matter, and so on. Due to North Americans being used to the volume measure system, I have included some recipes in volume and some in weights. All the customary U.S. measurements are by volume. So if you have the old cups in which 1 cup is 8 ounces you will have no trouble following the recipes. I recommend that you try to accustom yourself to the weight system, since this is the standard in most British and other European cookery books, as well as the system used by most chefs.

In the case of whole grain flours the weight system gives a more accurate end product due to the variation in moisture and bulk in some whole grain flours. The grinding method and growing area can also influence the weight of the flours and cause variations in the final outcome.

SOFT OR HARD WHEAT?

When using whole wheat flour you need to remember two things: (1) hard wheat is for anything where the dough has to be beaten or treated rough, like bread and strudel; and (2) soft wheat is used where the end product should be light and flaky, usually the dough is handled very little.

Soft flour is also called pastry flour.

A breakfast of freshly baked whole wheat biscuits, rich and nutty, with a little butter, a poached egg, and a bowl of fresh berries would make an ideal start to a great day. Often I eat muffins or biscuits made of the Ezekiel-type multi blend flour to have high protein grains mixed with high protein beans and lentils. The mixture of the grains and the addition of the beans ensures that the food will be complete protein for the eater. We know that grains should be mixed or mixed with legumes for full protein value. God told Ezekiel about this more than 2,000 years before scientists even knew what proteins were.

WHOLE GRAIN FLOUR GRAVY

Gravy is very easy to make from whole wheat bread flour. There are three points to remember: (1) the flour must be toasted or at least heated first, (2) the flour should soak up all the fat and the fat should coat all the flour, and (3) cold liquid should be used as the first liquid.

The general rule is: for each tablespoon of fat use one heaping tablespoon of whole wheat bread flour (hard) and 1 cup of liquid in total. This will result in a thin gravy. Two parts each flour and fat to one cup liquid will give a thicker gravy.

Using a heavy pan heat the fat over medium/high heat. Add the flour and, using a fork, mash and stir until all the fat is soaked into all the flour. There should be no extra flour or fat that you can see. Continue cooking, mashing, stirring until the flour begins to give off a toasted nut-like aroma. The mixture should look kind of frothy. Quickly pour cold or cool liquid into this mixture so that it boils up, quickly add more liquid while stirring. This can be hot if desired. There should be no lumps at this point. If some have formed either use a whisk to break them up or whirl in the blender for a few seconds. Continue to cook and stir over a lower heat until the gravy thickens. For additional flavor, you may wish to add sea salt to taste (1/4 teaspoon for each 1 tablespoon flour), cumin, coriander, Chinese 5 spice, or salt substitute while cooking. Herbs can be added once the heat has been turned to low and simmered to impart the most flavor to the gravy.

When you cook the flour and fat together in this manner you are making "roux" which is a basic cooking technique used in sauces and gravies. More recipes for sauces and gravies appear in Chapter III—Our Daily Proteins–Legumes & Vegetables, under Chinese stir-fry cooking and in Chapter IV—Dairy In The Diet, under butter.

Whole Wheat Pie Crust

2 cups	whole wheat pastry flour
1/2–1 tsp.	sea salt
2/3 cup	unsalted butter, chilled
6 Tbsp.	cold water

Sift salt and flour together, remove any bran left in the sifter and replace it with flour if there is a lot. Cut in the butter with 2 knives or a pastry blender until the mixture resembles coarse meal. Using a fork, begin fluffing up the flour mixture and gradually pouring the cold water onto the flour. Fluff and mash the water into the flour mixture as quickly as you can without pouring the water in only one spot. When all the water is used, mash with a fork to blend, then gather with hands and roll into 2 balls.

Using the sifter lightly, dust a pastry cloth or smooth tea towel with a small amount of the flour. Roll over it with the rolling pin. Place one ball of dough in the center then turn it over so that it will be floured on both sides. Roll the pin in a little more flour if needed. Start from the edges and roll a little here and a little there all around the edges, continuing to turn and roll until you have advanced enough to be rolling the center. If you start by rolling from the center, it will cause the dough to crack, then you will have to mend it and it won't look nice when it is patched up. If you have to patch it, use cold water on the edges to seal the new piece to the old one, lightly flour it and roll it smooth.

When dough is rolled evenly check the size by inverting the pie pan over the dough, making sure that there is extra dough to allow for the sides of the pan if it is for the bottom crust. Slip one hand under the crust, cloth and all, keeping the palm up. Pick up the pie pan with the other hand and with one quick and calculated motion flip the crust into the pan. Remove the cloth from the crust. Put filling in pie then roll out the top crust. Now, carefully place the top crust over the pie. To ensure a good seal, wet the edge of the bottom crust with cold water just before adding the top crust.

Cut away extra dough, press crusts together and seal. You can crimp it or just mash it with a fork. Cut several 1/2 inch slices in the top crust for steam vents. Place the pie on a baking sheet and bake in a pre-heated 425°F oven for 10 minutes to set the crust, then lower it to 350°F and bake for an additional 40–50 minutes or until the crust is golden and the filling is thickened.

This recipe makes two 9 or 10 inch pie crusts. It can be doubled, but use less water at first.

Although I made pies like this for years, I now use a food processor. Put the flour and salt in the bowl with the steel blade and process for a few seconds to mix (this eliminates sifting, which is OK if there is very little extra bran in the flour), add chilled butter in small pieces and pulse it off and on until it looks like coarse meal. Add water slowly through the feeder tube while machine is running. It generally only takes 5 tablespoons of water for a 2 crust recipe with a food processor. When dough forms a ball remove it and shape into two balls and continue as above.

FRUIT OR SAVORY PIES

Dessert pie recipes are in Chapter V—Special Treats. Savory pie recipes are in Chapters III—Our Daily Proteins and VI—Alternative Proteins.

EZEKIEL FLOUR

Take wheat and barley, beans and lentils, millet and spelt; put them in a storage jar and use them to make bread for yourself. Ezekiel 4:9 (NIV)

Eugene Fox, an Ontario lay minister and businessman, developed and marketed a flour called Ezekiel Flour that he feels is close to the flour used by Ezekiel. It contains 14.5 grams of protein and 2.5 grams of fiber for each 100 grams of flour. The bread, cakes, cookies, pastry, and pancakes it makes are richer, sweeter, and more robust in flavor than any made with just whole wheat flour. The breads are more like European breads in texture. And, of course, they should be well chewed. Beans should always be cooked before eating, and Ezekiel-type multi-grain blend flour products should never be eaten uncooked. This flour is sold by many different flour blenders often called multi-blend flour or Ezekiel-type flour, or Ezekiel blend. Anything that can be made of regular whole wheat flour can be made of Ezekiel-type flour. It is richer tasting and has more fiber and protein than whole wheat flour. *The World's Oldest*

Health Plan Recipe Book has many recipes using whole grain flours, including the Ezekiel-type flour blends.

Easy Crackers

2 cups	Ezekiel* flour (or use all whole wheat)
1 1/2 cups	whole wheat pastry flour
1/2 cup	sesame seeds
1 1/4 tsp	salt or less
1/2 cup	oil, safflower, soy, olive, toasted sesame, etc.
1 cup+2 Tbsp.	water

Using the plastic blade of a food processor mix together the first 4 ingredients. Mix water and oil and pour over flour mixture, process until blended. Roll very thin on floured surface; prick all over with a fork and cut into shapes. Bake in a 350°F oven for 15–20 minutes or until very lightly browned around the edges. Salt or seasoning salt can be added and rolled onto the top before pricking with a fork. This double recipe makes 6 or 8 dozen crackers depending on the size of the cutters.

Keep the dough covered at all times so that it doesn't dry out. I keep it in a plastic bag when not being rolled.

To the oil I usually add 1 tablespoon toasted sesame oil that I purchase at an Oriental market or health food store. For variety, virgin olive oil can be used with Italian seasonings. Almost any dry herb can be added to the flour mixture.

Children love these crackers and can help make them. They can be baked with a small amount of tomato sauce and cheese on them for little pizzas as a snack or party appetizer.

I often make these for parties and serve them with Tofu Paté. There is never any left over.

Fruit Juice Sweetened Ezekiel* Muffins

6 oz. (1 cup pressed)	finely grated carrots
2 Tbsp.	butter, melted
1/2 cup	concentrated pineapple or orange juice
1 large	egg
2/3 cup	natural yogurt
1 8 oz. can	crushed pineapple in its own juice, drained
1/4 cup	chopped walnuts or sunflower seeds
1/2 cup	oat bran

1 1/2 cup	Ezekiel-type multi-blend flour
2 tsp.	baking powder
1/4 tsp.	ground ginger
1/2 tsp.	ground nutmeg
1 tsp.	ground coriander

Mix first 8 ingredients together in bowl or food processor. Sift together flour, baking powder, and spices. Add to other mixture, stir until mixed.

Spoon into batter muffin cups, filling almost full. Bake in a pre-heated 350°F oven for 30 minutes.

NB: When I make these muffins I grate the carrots in the food processor by weighing the carrots first. Then change to the plastic blade and continue to mix them. This takes only about 5 minutes to do once the ingredients are out, so turn the oven on first!

Honey Ezekiel* Muffins

1/2 cup	mashed banana
2 Tbsp.	cold pressed oil or melted butter
1/4 cup	honey
1 large	egg
3/4 cup	yogurt + water to make 1 cup
1/2 cup	finely chopped dried fruit like pineapple apricot, papaya OR use currants or raisins
1/4 cup	wheat bran
1/3 cup	oat bran
1 1/2 cup	Ezekiel* flour
2 tsp.	baking powder
2 tsp.	cinnamon

Mix first 8 ingredients together. Sift flour, baking powder, and cinnamon together and stir into banana mixture. Bake in buttered muffin cups in pre-heated 350°F oven for 30 minutes. Makes 12 medium.

Ezekiel* English Muffins

1 Tbsp. (pkge.)	dry yeast
2 Tbsp.	honey
2 1/4 cups	hot water
1 Tbsp.	salt
1/2 cup	non-instant milk powder, heated
2 cups	whole wheat bread flour

4 Tbsp.	oil
3 cups	Ezekiel* flour
	corn meal
	extra bread flour

Blend water and milk powder. In a warm bowl mix oil, honey, and salt. Add 1 cup of the milk, when it is very warm to the touch, and the yeast. Stir with a whisk until blended. Let stand for about 10 minutes or until frothy. Add the whole wheat flour and remaining milk and whisk for 3 minutes or use an electric mixer for 2 minutes. Using a wooden spoon stir in the Ezekiel* flour. Dump onto a bread cloth and knead to thoroughly mix dough. Once mixed knead for 10 minutes. Dough will most likely be streaky and seem dry.

Oil a large bowl. Place dough in it smooth side down, turn over to coat with oil and place in a warm place to rise. Cover with a tea towel that has been rung out with hot water. Leave for 1 to 1 1/2 hours to rise until double in bulk.

Punch down and turn out onto a cloth that has been lightly sprinkled with the corn meal. Roll to 1/2 inch thickness, cover with a hot towel and let rise again until double in bulk. Cut with a 3 inch cutter.

Heat a heavy cast iron pan or griddle over very low heat. Place muffins corn meal side down in pan. "Bake" for 15 minutes on each side. Makes about 15 muffins. (I prefer to use a fry pan so that I can cover them while baking.)

Ezekiel* Pie Crust

Make regular pie crust but use half whole wheat pastry flour and half Ezekiel-type multi-blend flour. This makes an even richer, nuttier crust. It is wonderful for fruit pies as well as savory pies.

*Ezekiel-type multi-blend flour is the type I use.

NUTRITIONAL VALUES

Whole Wheat Bread (one slice)
> 61 calories
> 2.4 g protein
> 2 g fiber
> vitamins B1, B2, B3, B6
> folic acid
> pantothenic acid
> 18 mg calcium
> 23 mg magnesium
> 0.86 mg iron[7]

Ezekiel-Type Multi-Blend Flour (2 oz.)
200 calories
8 g protein
1 g fat
0 mg sodium
7 g fiber.
Percentage of RDA: protein 15%, B1 20%, B2 4%,
B3 10%, calcium 2%, iron 10%[8]

TYPES OF BREADS

And he looked, and behold, there was at his head a cake baked on hot stones and a jar of water . . . . 1 Kings 19:6 (RSV)

There are several types of breads that were eaten. One kind referred to as "cake" was often eaten. It was made from sprouted grains that were ground and made into a round flat cake and baked in a community oven or in the sun on rocks. There was also leavened and unleavened bread.

Yeast was the most common leavening agent that was used, but it is possible that something like sourdough was also used. The custom of the time was to keep a lump of the previous batch of fermented dough to "start" a new batch of bread. This was added to the flour and water mixture and kneaded in a dough trough and allowed to ferment or "work" until the bread could be baked in an oven or over coals.

A method of leavening that we no longer seem to use was called "salt rising." This may have referred to soda bread which uses baking soda as the leavening agent. This type of bread is regaining popularity since so many people seem to be allergic or sensitive to yeast or the fermentation method of making bread.

ANCIENT BAKERY UNEARTHED

In November of 1991 in Giza Plateau, Egypt, a very large bakery was unearthed. It is believed to date from around 2575 B.C. It is such a large bakery that they estimate it was built to feed daily bread to 30,000 people a day. It is estimated that this bakery was used to bake the "daily bread" that was part of the pay given to the people building the pyramids. At the reporting of the find in December of 1991 they had found two grains: barley and emmer wheat. Records report 14 kinds of bread being made in the region at this time.

UNLEAVENED BREAD

The feast of unleavened bread you shall keep. Seven days you shall eat unleavened bread, as I commanded you, at the time appointed in the month Abib; for in the month Abib you came out from Egypt. Exodus 34:18 (RSV)

Unleavened bread was eaten when there wasn't time to wait for the bread to rise. It was used as part of a religious commemoration of the hasty departure of Egypt called the feast of unleavened bread. It was also made when unexpected guests dropped in and bread was needed for a meal. We often do the same today with crackers, hot biscuits or muffins.

During Passover Jewish people eat unleavened bread called matzos as a reminder of the flight from Egypt. Matzos or matzoth is similar to crackers, and usually contains no oil. Whole wheat matzos are excellent for people who want a whole grain, low fat snack. Unleavened bread played an important part in the feasts of Israel.

YEASTED OR LEAVENED BREADS

He told them still another parable: "The kingdom of heaven is like yeast that a woman took and mixed into a large amount of flour until it worked all through the dough." Matthew 13:33 (NIV)

Leavened or yeasted breads were eaten but were forbidden to be used as sacrifices or during special holidays. There is no health reason given for this, just the implication that leavening is not pleasing to God. We are finding many ways that yeast is causing allergic or sensitivity reactions in people since the 1960's and this is dealt with further in Chapter III—Our Daily Proteins–Legumes & Vegetables under Garlic.

OVEN AND COOKING TEMPERATURES

All oven temperatures are for pre-heated ovens unless it is specified otherwise. It is best to allow 10–15 minutes for an electric oven to heat up. Generally there will be a little light that goes out when the oven is heated. Gas stoves usually take less time for the oven to pre-heat to the temperature. I suggest that you use an oven thermometer no matter how new your oven is so that you can always be sure of the correct temperature. When a temperature for cooking something in a pot on top of the stove is given it also should be heated to the asked-for temperature before placing the pot on the heat. There are times when it will say to put the pot on the burner, then turn on the heat, as in the case of hard-boiled eggs.

YEASTED BREADS

Always use hard wheat flour for bread so that it will stand up to kneading. Have all the ingredients at room temperature. Have all the necessary tools, utensils, and working space ready before you begin to work. Read the instructions over first and calculate the time required for rising and baking to make sure that the bread will be ready to eat at the right time, or that you have enough time to finish it before you have to go somewhere or distractions occur.

KNEADING

Use a smooth, clean surface. A kneading board or cloth is easiest to use and easiest to clean. A non-terry cloth can be used if you have no pastry cloth. Make sure that the kneading surface is below your waist enough so that you have the right amount of control and pressure for kneading. If you are tall the counter top might be just right. Generally the kitchen table works best.

If you grease your hands with whatever you are using in the bread, nothing will stick to your hands while kneading.

Press the dough into a flat circle on the prepared surface. Fold a section of the dough that is farthest away from you to the middle of the circle and press the fold flat with the heels of your hands. Turn the dough slightly and repeat the fold-and-press motion using the heels of your hands to press down and away from you on the fold part and the edge that now is in the center of the circle. Keep going around the circle folding, pressing, and turning until the dough is very smooth and elastic feeling. It should feel like your ear lobe. The dough should never be stringy or lumpy when you finish kneading. Push your finger into the dough. If it springs back, it is ready for rising.

The movement should be a rocking one coming from your feet and not your wrists. Place one foot in front of the other, one slightly under the table, the other slightly behind you. Keeping the knees slightly bent, lean forward on the front foot as you press down with the heels of your hands. When you pick up the dough to rotate it, rock back onto the rear foot. In this manner the legs do most of the work and not the wrists.

Don't worry if you don't use all the flour called for or if you use more than what is called for in the recipe. Many things can determine how much flour is needed. As long as the dough feels and looks right, it is right, and only you can be the judge of that . . . not a recipe on a piece of paper.

TESTING FOR DOUBLED IN BULK

Press the dough with the tip of your finger, making a small dent. If the dent disappears, let the dough rise a little longer and test again. If the dent remains, the dough has risen enough and is ready for the next step. Do not let it rise any longer or the dough might collapse and the bread will be very porous and have a pale crust.

COOL RISE AND FREEZER METHOD

After the first rise, you can shape the loaves and put them into the prepared tins. Then leave them in the refrigerator to rise for up to 24 hours, generally overnight is enough. Or you can wrap them in freezer paper in the loaf shape that suits your pans and freeze them. To bake, allow up to 12 hours for the dough to thaw and one more hour to rise. Or you may allow 24 hours to thaw in the refrigerator and one hour to rise in the pan. If you freeze them in the pan don't forget to grease the pan first; if you freeze them without a pan don't forget to grease the pan before you put the frozen loaves in to thaw and rise. It is best to use butter or shortening to grease the pan for any bread that is or will be frozen.

PREPARING DOUGH FOR PAN

Press the dough with the palms of your hands into a uniform rectangle as wide as the bread pan is long and about 10–12 inches (25–30 cm) long. Roll dough up like a jelly roll, seal edges by pressing them to the loaf, pinch the end edges together so that the ends are smooth and do not look like a jelly roll, but like a pinch in the middle of the end of the loaf. Grease the top of the loaf after you put it in the pan. The pan should be two thirds full with the dough; it will finish filling up as it rises and during the first ten minutes or so of baking. If the dough is larger, remove it and take some off the loaf. Don't forget to grease the top again, and the pan.

TROUBLE SHOOTING

If the bread is condensed and doesn't rise, the yeast may be too old. If the outer crust is browned, but the bread doesn't seem to have risen after putting it into the oven and the inside of the bread is not done, the oven was too hot. If the bread has a big hole in it especially between the crust and the rest of the bread the oven may have been too low, or the bread not kneaded enough. If the bread falls during baking, the yeast may not be right or you may have let it rise too much before putting it into the oven.

Whole Wheat Protein Bread

1 pkg.	dry yeast
4 Tbsp. (50 mL)	honey or molasses
1 cup (250 mL)	lukewarm water
1 cup (250 mL)	milk scalded and cooled to lukewarm
2 Tbsp. (30 mL)	oil or melted butter
4 cup (630 g)	whole wheat hard flour
1 Tbsp. (15 mL)	soy flour
1 cup+2 Tbp. (125 g)	whole wheat hard flour

Mix yeast, water, milk, and honey together and stir to dissolve. Add oil or butter and then gradually add 4 cups (630 g) flour, salt, and soy flour, sifted together. Use a wooden spoon for the stirring. Flour a cloth or board with part of the remaining flour using the sifter and turn the dough out onto it. Knead following the basic directions at the front of this chapter, adding flour as needed. When all flour has been added, knead for 8–10 minutes or until dough is smooth and elastic. Oil bowl and put dough in and then turn the dough over so that the top is oiled. Cover with a cloth wrung out from hot water and put in a warm draft-free place to rise until double in bulk, about 1 1/2 hours. Punch down with fist and turn onto a floured cloth or board. Divide in two. Press each section into a rectangle and then roll up like a jelly roll. Pinch ends together and place seam side down in well greased bread pans. Cover with a cloth wrung out from hot water and set in a warm draft-free place to rise until double in bulk, about 3/4 to 1 hour.Bake in a 375°F (180°C) oven for 45 to 60 minutes, remove from oven and brush with oil or melted butter and place on side on a rack to cool. Makes two loaves.

Bread is done when it shrinks away from the side of the pan and a knock on the bottom of the loaf produces a hollow sound.

NB: Use all honey for a light loaf, 1/2 honey and 1/2 molasses for a medium loaf, or all mollasses for a heavier, darker loaf. Some of the whole wheat flour can be replaced by other grain flours like barley, oat, rye, millet, buckwheat, or triticale, but it will give a different texture, depending on the flour and amount used.

Egg Bread or Challah

2 pkgs.	dry yeast
2 1/2 cups (625 mL)	warm water
5 Tbsp. (75 mL)	honey
2 tsp. (10 mL)	salt
1/2 tsp. (2 mL)	ground cardamom
1/3 cup (60 mL)	vegetable oil
4	eggs
4 tsp. (20 mL)	soy flour (optional)
5 cups (1 kg)	whole wheat bread flour
2 3/4 cup (675 mL)	whole wheat bread flour
1	egg yolk
1 tsp. (5 mL)	water to blend with egg yolk
4 tsp. (20 mL)	sesame or poppy seeds

Warm a large mixing bowl with warm water and dry. Dissolve yeast in 1/2 cup (125 mL) of the water and 2 Tbsp. (30 mL) of the honey and let set for 10 minutes or until foamy. Add remaining honey, salt, cardamom, eggs, and oil. Beat with a whisk or electric mixer for 2 minutes. Add 5 cups (1 kg) of the flour and beat in with a wooden spoon or mixer. Continue to add the remaining flour stirring until the mixture leaves the side of the bowl. Turn mixture onto a bread board or cloth that has been floured with some of the remaining flour and knead with the heels of your hands, turning to keep it even. Add flour as needed and knead until dough is smooth and elastic and has the texture and feel of your ear lobe. (See instructions for kneading at the beginning of this section.)

Rinse the bowl with hot water and dry it and oil it well. Place the dough, smooth side down, in the bowl, then turn it over so that the oiled side is on top. Cover with a clean dry cloth and place in a warm draft-free spot to rise. A warm oven is great for this but it must never be warmer than 80°F (30°C). A pan of hot water on the bottom of the oven will keep it warm enough.

Let rise for 1 1/2 hours or until triple in bulk. Remove dough, punch down with fist. Turn onto bread board and divide into 12 equal portions. Roll each into a rope 1 inch (2.5 cm) in diameter. Braid three ropes together, turn ends under to seal. Braid remaining ropes in the same way. Place each braid in well greased bread pans or on a well greased baking sheet for a free form loaf. Cover with a cloth and let rise in a warm place until triple in bulk, or about 45 minutes. Brush tops with egg wash and sprinkle with seeds. Bake in a pre-heated 375°F (180°C) oven for 25 to 30 minutes or until golden.

Makes 4 loaves. This can also be braided into small individual loaves, or made into dinner rolls by placing small braids into muffin tins and baking.

Since egg bread does contain eggs, it is not cholesterol free. This is a very old traditional recipe from a time when no one cared about cholesterol. It is delicious toasted with butter and jam. It is great served with a dark green dinner salad. You might want to make sure that you have bitter herbs with this or just serve it on special occasions. See Chapter III—Our Daily Proteins–Legumes & Vegetables under Bitter Herbs for more information on the traditional way to counteract cholesterol. Each loaf contains 1 egg. Depending on the number of slices you cut from each you will have that percentage of cholesterol from the eggs. So say one loaf was cut into 15 slices, you would have 1/15th of a yolk in each slice. That is less than some muffins that have one egg per batch of 12 muffins.

BREAD VARIATIONS

Cinnamon Bread

1	dough for one loaf
2 Tbsp. (30 mL)	butter or oil
2 Tbsp. (30 mL)	honey or brown sugar
1 Tbsp. (30 mL)	cinnamon

Roll or press dough into a rectangle as in basic bread recipe. Mix butter and honey together and spread evenly on dough, sprinkle with cinnamon. Roll up tightly, shape, and place in prepared pan to rise. Bake as in recipe for bread.

Raisin or Fruit Bread

1	dough for one loaf
1/2 cup (75 g)	raisins, currants, or chopped dried fruit
1 tsp. (5 mL)	cardamom

Add the cardamom to the dough when mixing or sprinkle on with fruit. Roll or press into a rectangle. Sprinkle raisins, currants, or dried fruit over dough and roll up, shape, and place in prepared pan. Bake as directed in bread recipe.

Onion Bread

1	dough for one loaf
1/2 cup (75 g)	chopped onions
1 Tbsp. (15 mL)	butter

Melt butter and sauté onions until lightly golden. Roll or press dough into a rectangle and spread onions over it. Roll up, shape, and place in prepared pan. Bake as in bread recipe.

Herb Bread

Add herbs of your choice to the dough before the last addition of flour. Fresh or dried herbs can be used. Use 2 tsp. (10 mL) of strong herbs such as oregano, cumin, dill, garlic, fenugreek, mint, caraway, anise seed, celery seeds, sage, or crushed rosemary. Use 1 Tbsp. (15 mL) of mild herbs, singly or in combination, such as thyme, marjoram, savory, parsley, or basil.

Clover Leaf Dinner Rolls

	basic bread recipe
1	egg, beaten
1 Tbsp. (15 mL)	water OR milk

Instead of forming the bread into loaves, roll dough into balls the size of walnuts and place 3 in each cup of well greased medium muffin pans. Cover and raise as in basic recipe. Brush with egg wash made of egg and water for shiny tops or with milk for soft tops. Bake in oven at the temperature recommended in recipe for 20 minutes or until browned.

Don't handle the dough too much when forming balls. Work quickly with greased hands. One bread recipe should make close to 3 dozen rolls depending on the size of the rolls.

Poppy or sesame seeds can be sprinkled over after brushing with egg wash or milk.

Bread Sticks

Any basic bread recipe
coarse salt
sesame seeds
poppy seeds
caraway seeds

celery seeds

egg beaten with 1 Tbsp. (15 mL) water

Instead of shaping dough into loaves make sticks by pinching off a small amount of dough the size of a walnut and rolling it under your palms on a lightly floured surface to a stick the size of a pencil. Place on prepared baking sheet, cover with cloth and allow to raise until double in bulk. This may only take 15 to 20 minutes. Brush with egg wash and sprinkle with one of the toppings listed above or leave plain. If you would like a less shiny stick just brush with water. Bake at the temperature used for the bread recipe decreasing the time to 10–20 minutes depending on the size of the sticks. For soft centers remove after 10 minutes, just when they begin to brown. For hard sticks allow to bake longer until darker brown.

Cinnamon Rolls

	basic bread recipe
	cinnamon
	raisins
	butter or oil
	honey
	nuts and sunflower seeds
2 Tbsp. (30 mL)	honey
2 Tbsp. (30 mL)	water

Roll dough into rectangle 15 x 15 inches (38 x 38 cm), 1/2 inch (1.25 cm) thick. Spread with butter or oil. Sprinkle lightly with cinnamon. Put three strips of raisins, nuts, and honey 2 inches (5 cm) wide with spaces of 2 inches (5 cm) at each edge and between each row. Lightly dampen the strip at the far edge with water. Roll up like a jelly roll starting with the edge nearest you. Roll as tightly as you can using the dampened edge to seal the roll. Grease a 9 x 9 inch (23 x 23 cm) pan or 9 x 14 inch (23 x 35 cm) pan. With a sharp knife cut the roll into 2 inch (5 cm) pieces and place cut side down in pan. The rolls should be spaced apart so that they will touch when they have doubled in bulk. Brush tops with water, cover, and put in warm place to rise. Bake at temperature used in basic bread recipe for 20 minutes or until golden brown. Mix water and honey and brush over tops of rolls as soon as they come from the oven. A pie pan may also be used.

Sticky Buns

Make cinnamon rolls as directed. Grease pan and put in a layer of honey, nuts, and melted butter. Use 1/2 cup (125 mL) honey, 1/4 cup (50 mL) melted butter, and 3/4 cup (100 g) chopped walnuts, pecans, or sunflower seeds combined for a 9 x 9 inch (23 x 23 cm) pan and half again as much for a larger pan. Place rolls cut side down on top of sticky mixture and proceed as in cinnamon roll recipe. Place rolls upside down on rack to cool. Remove the pan as soon as possible. Loosen edges with a knife first if needed.

No Knead French Bread

1 pkg.	dry yeast (1 Tbsp. or 15 mL)
1	egg + warm water to make 2 C (500 mL)
2 Tbsp. (30 mL)	honey
1 1/2 tsp. (7 mL)	salt
2 Tbsp. (30 mL)	vegetable or seed oil
4 1/2 cups (600 g)	whole wheat flour
	corn meal
	cold water
1	egg white
2 Tbsp. (30 mL)	water
4 Tbsp. (60 mL)	sesame seeds

Dissolve yeast in part of the lukewarm water and let it sit for 10 minutes until it foams up. Add the remaining water, honey, salt, egg, oil, and beat with an electric beater or hand mixer for 1 minute. Add 3 cups (300 g) of the flour and continue to beat for one minute after all the flour is mixed in. Remove the beaters and add the remaining flour and beat by hand with a wooden spoon for 1 minute after all the flour is mixed in.

Cover with a non-terry cloth towel that has been rung out from hot water, and put in a warm, draft free place to rise for one hour. After the first 15 minutes remove the towel and stir up or beat the dough for 1 minute. Re-wring the towel with hot water and cover and return to the warm place to rise. Do this again after the second 15 minutes and the third 15 minutes, also, so that you work through the dough 3 times in the hour it is rising. After the hour is up, turn the dough onto a lightly floured cloth and divide in two. Shape each piece into a ball and cover with the cloth and let it rest for 10 minutes. Oil one baking sheet very well and sprinkle lightly with corn meal. Roll each ball on the floured cloth to a rectangle 12 x 9 inches (30 x 23 cm). Start with the long side and, using the cloth, roll the dough up like a jelly roll. Seal the edges by pressing on it with your hands. Turn the ends under to seal. Place the roll on one side of the baking sheet. Do the other ball and place it alongside the other one on the sheet so that there is room between them and also a little room at the edges too.

Make 3 or 4 diagonal slashes with a knife across the tops of the loaves. Brush with water and cover with the cloth, and put in a warm place to rise until double in bulk, about 30 minutes.

Place the loaves in a 375°F (190°C) oven and bake for 35 to 45 minutes. After the loaves have been baking for 20 minutes brush with water and sprinkle on sesame seeds, continue baking until done.

Makes two loaves. Brush with ice water as soon as they come from the oven and allow to cool in a draft to get the crust of a baguette, if desired.

NB: If using a wooden spoon for beating up the bread, it helps to keep it in a glass of water between beatings to prevent sticking.

NB: Use water without the egg for a lighter texture.

English Muffins

1 pkg.	dry yeast
2 cups (500 mL)	milk
4 Tbsp. (60 mL)	honey
1 tsp. (5 mL)	salt
5–5 1/2 cups (800-850 g)	whole wheat bread flour
	corn meal

Rinse sauce pan with cold water and do not dry. Pour in milk and bring almost to a boil over medium or medium/high heat. (This is called scalding it.) Stir often. Remove from heat and cool to lukewarm by setting pan in bowl of cool water. It must be comfortably warm to the inside of the wrist, but not burning. Soften yeast in half of the milk, stirring to dissolve. Then let it sit for 10 minutes. Add oil and honey to remaining milk. Place salt and flour in sifter. Add yeast mixture to milk and honey, followed by the sifted flour. Stir after each addition of flour with a wooden spoon, adding only enough flour to form a soft dough. Dump contents onto board or cloth floured with some of the flour from the sifter. Continue to knead and add flour until dough no longer sticks to board. Knead with heels of hands until dough is smooth and elastic and feels like your ear lobe. This should take 10–20 minutes. Place top side down in an oiled bowl and turn over so that both top and bottom are oiled. Cover with cloth and put in a warm place to rise for 1 1/2 to 2 hours or until double in bulk. Punch down. Place bottom side down on cloth or board sprinkled with corn meal. Roll dough to 1/2 inch (1.25 cm). Cut with 3 inch (8 cm) cookie cutter or English muffin cutter. Cover with cloth wrung out from hot water and allow to rise in warm place until double in bulk, about 1/2 to 3/4 hour. Bake cornmeal side down on a dry griddle or cast iron pan over low or medium/low heat. Turn after 10 minutes and bake 10 minutes more. Or bake cornmeal side down on a dry baking sheet in a 375°F (190°C) oven. Turn after 10 minutes and finish as above. Makes 15 to 20 muffins. Store in plastic bag or freeze.

The heat must be low on the griddle to be right, so check the bottom of the muffins often. Do not cover while baking.

Irish Soda Bread

2 cups (500 mL)	whole wheat pastry flour
1/2 tsp. (2 mL)	sea salt
1 tsp. (5 mL)	baking soda
1/8 tsp. (0.5 mL)	cardamom
1	egg, beaten
1 Tbsp. (15 mL)	honey
1 cup (250 mL)	yogurt or buttermilk

Stir dry ingredients together. Beat honey and yogurt together into beaten egg; gradually pour this into dry ingredients. Blend with hands to work in all flour. (Add more milk if too dry or more flour if too wet.) Knead for 5 minutes, shape into a flat, but round loaf. Place on oiled baking sheet, cut 2 parallel slashes (scores) in the dough about 1/2 inch (1.25 cm) long. This allows dough to rise during baking without cracking. Bake at 375°F (140°C) for 25 to 30 minutes or until well browned and tests done as yeast bread would. (See page 48)

NB: caraway, sesame, or poppy seeds can be added. Raisins or currants can also be added to the dough while kneading.

Carrot Tea Bread Ring

2 cups (500 mL)	whole wheat pastry flour
2 tsp. (10 mL)	cinnamon
1 Tbsp. (15 mL)	baking soda
1 cup (250 mL)	raisins or currants
1/4 cup (60 mL)	soy grits or okara*
1/2 cup (125 mL)	nuts and seeds mixed
2	eggs, beaten
1/2 cup (125 mL)	cold pressed oil or melted butter
2 tsp. (10 mL)	vanilla
2/3–1 cup (165–250mL)	honey
2 cups (500 mL)	grated or ground carrots, raw

Stir first 6 ingredients together. Blend remaining ingredients together and stir them into the first mixture with a minimum of strokes. Turn into an oiled and floured ring or large loaf pan and bake at 325°F (165°C) for about 1 hour or until tester comes out clean. This can also be baked in muffin cups for 35 minutes or until done.

Food Processor—grate carrots with fine blade. Put first 6 ingredients into sifter, put remaining ingredients in bowl with plastic blade and mix, add grated carrots. Sift dry into mixture and process just until mixed, put in prepared pan and bake.

*Okara is the pulp that is left over when making tofu and can often be purchased at tofu shops and immediately refrigerated or frozen until used, or can be saved when making tofu and frozen for use in breads, cakes, or muffins.

Biscuits

2 cups (280 g)	whole wheat pastry flour
2 tsp. (10 mL)	baking powder
1/2 tsp. (2 mL)	sea salt
5 Tbsp. (55 g)	chilled butter
1/2 cup (125 mL)	milk (or more)

Sift dry ingredients together. Cut in butter with pastry blender or 2 knives until mixture resembles coarse meal. Mixing with a fork, add enough milk to form a soft dough. Work gently with fingers and turn out on a lightly floured cloth or board. Quickly pat to 1/4 inch (0.50 cm) thickness. Fold over in 3 layers and pat again to 1/2 inch (1.25 cm) thickness. Cut out with floured cutter. Bake close together on ungreased cookie sheet at 450°F (230°C) for about 12 minutes or until evenly browned. Makes 9 to 12 biscuits depending on size of cutter.

Food Processor—Place dry ingredients in bowl with butter, use steel blade to process with quick pulses until texture of coarse meal. Add liquid and process until ball is formed. Start with less liquid than recommended and add more if needed.

Ezekiel Biscuits

Substitute Ezekiel flour for the whole wheat flour, using a little more liquid or more flour as needed to obtain right consistency.

Herb Biscuits

Add fresh or dried herbs to biscuits after adding liquid and bake. Try one or a combination of: chopped fresh parsley, basil, dill, thyme, Italian mix, cilantro, marjoram, rosemary. If using fresh herbs, add 2 Tbsp. (30 mL) finely chopped. Use less if using dried. This will make a quick addition to a meal to replace rice, bread, or potatoes. Try dilled biscuits with salmon, rosemary with lamb, and parsley and garlic any time. Parsley and basil biscuits are great with stews and soups and add a festive touch to what might be an ordinary meal, they also add homemade taste to a quick meal. When served for breakfast with a poached egg, herbed freshly made biscuits turn breakfast into a gourmet meal. They are also great for brunch or tea breaks.

Instant Biscuits

Cut biscuits and lay on cookie sheet, place in freezer. When frozen, remove and place in bag or stack up and wrap in foil. To bake, remove from freezer, unwrap, place on ungreased baking sheet and bake for 15–20 minutes at the temperature used in the biscuit recipe.

COOKIES AND CAKES

Always use soft wheat whole wheat flour for pastry. Brown rice flour can also be used, especially in shortbread type cookies. Whole wheat pastry flour substitutes equally in cakes and cookies for white flour in your old recipes. If there is a lot of bran in the flour, sift it out first before measuring. Bran in delicate cookies and pastries tends to make them dry out faster or seem harder. Save the bran to use in cereals and bran muffins.

SUGAR = HONEY?

To reduce sugar and switch to honey replace 1 cup (250 mL) sugar with 2/3 cup (170 mL) honey or less and reduce the liquid in the recipe by 1/4 cup (60 mL). Many recipes use too much sugar for our modern tastes and can be reduced by as much as half without losing the texture or body of the finished end product.

When creaming honey and butter or oil for cookies or cakes, it is better to use solid or creamed honey than liquid. This will give the same texture as sugar and butter would.

SWEET RECIPES

Recipes for cookies, cakes, pies, and other sweets are in Chapter V—Special Treats–Fruit, Nuts, Sweets, & Oils.

WHOLE GRAINS AS GRAINS

Many cuisines include whole grains as their staple food. Oriental diets use rice as the staple grain. Wheat is used in some parts of the Orient, so are buckwheat and barley. On the Indian Continent whole wheat chappatis, an unleavened flat bread, are eaten as well as rice. Corn bread is also eaten in parts of India. In Europe buckwheat is eaten along with rice, rye, and wheat. Millet is eaten in Eastern Europe and parts of Asia, so is barley. In North America we traditionally eat wheat, corn, barley, rice, rye, and buckwheat. In the British Isles oats have been the staple grain for many centuries.

There are many ways that wheat is made into other products like cous cous, bulgur (or bulgar), and pasta. Cous cous is made in Morocco and other Middle Eastern areas. A paste is made from flour and water, then it is pushed through a net or sieve to make small pieces the size of rice. This is really a form of pasta. It is light to carry and cooks quickly and easily. Bulgur, often incorrectly called cracked wheat, is eaten in Europe and the Middle East. Bulgur is wheat that has been cooked, chopped, and dried. To eat it one just needs to add boiling water and let it soak for an hour. Bulgur is part of the Middle Eastern diet often eaten in the form of tabouli (also spelled tabbouleh) salad or cooked into desserts flavored with honey, nuts, dried fruits, and rose water. Cracked wheat has been chopped, but not precooked first, so it needs to be cooked. It takes less time to cook chopped or ground grains than it does whole grains. For more cooking instructions and recipes see *The World's Oldest Health Plan Recipe Companion.*

PREPARING GRAINS FOR COOKING

Always look over the grains to be cooked and remove any that are discolored, or injured. Also remove any sticks, husks, pebbles, or other matter that is not the grain. Measure desired amount and place in large pot or bowl. Cover with cold water and rinse, stir with your hand to dissolve any mud or powder, and also to allow husks to rise to the top. Pour off water. If it is very cloudy, rinse again until the water is clean, drain. Generally any empty grains and husks will rise to the top and can be removed with a small strainer or spoon.

Shake grain to remove excess water, it is best to do this in a strainer or sieve. Proceed with one of the following methods.

BOILING METHOD

Always start with the water boiling, add salt or sea weed if desired. Add grains and stir once, allow to come to the boil again, turn heat to simmer, cover, and cook until done. Do not remove the lid or stir the grains until the time is nearly up or the grains will be sticky, and take longer to cook.

BAKING METHOD

Boiling or cold water can be used, it generally doesn't change the cooking time. Add all ingredients, cover and bake in pre-heated 350°F (180°C.) oven for the specified time.

SPECIAL METHOD

Whole grains can be dry roasted in a heavy skillet over medium or low heat until they have a pleasant "nutty" fragrance or take on a darker color, before cooking to give a richer flavor. This will also prevent them from sticking together while cooking. Sometimes this is a problem with rice and barley depending on the variety used. Whole grains can also be roasted in oil or sautéed before adding the water.

LIQUIDS TO USE

Water is the general liquid to use when cooking grains. Any liquid can be used. Milk would give added protein and calories, and is almost essential when making rice pudding. Vegetable cooking water will give a nice taste to the cooked grain. Stock made from bones, browned onions, or vegetable scraps can also make a nice liquid. Tofu packing water can be used if it is fresh, or the soaking water from beans, which will give added nutrients.

OTHER ADDITIONS TO COOKING

Various herbs can be added to the water at the simmer stage or in the beginning with the bake method, see the recipe section and the herb section for ideas. Joanne Andreski, who taught me to bake rice, used to add a package of dry onion soup mix to the rice, and it was delicious. Almost any dry soup mix can be added, as long as it doesn't have pasta in it, which would change the outcome of the cooked grain. If you are using a dry soup mix don't add salt to the grain, and try to use the soup without MSG. Dried fruit can be added such as raisins, apricots, currants, papaya, etc. Nuts and seeds can be added near the end of cooking for a change in texture and additional protein.

COOKING CHART

Grain	Amount	Water	Boil	Water	Bake
Barley	1 cup	2 1/2 cups	45 min.	2 cups	40–60 min
Buckwheat	1 cup	2 1/2 cups	15 min.	2 cups	20 min.
Cornmeal	1 cup	4–5 cups	25–30 min.	4–5 cups	25-40 min.
Millet	1 cup	3 cups	30 min.	3 cups	30 min.
Oatmeal	1 cup	2 cups	10 min.	2 cups	20 min.
Rice–brown	1 cup	2 1/4 cups	30–45 min.	2 cups	60 min.
Rye	1 cup	4 cups	60 min.	4 cups	60 min.
Oat groats & Wheat berries	1 cup	3–4 cups	60–90 min.	3–4 cups	60–90 min.

1 cup=250 mL   2 cups=500 mL   2 1/4 cups=560 mL   2 1/2 cups=500–625 mL
3 cups=750 mL   3–4 cups= 750 mL–1 L   4–5 cups=1–1250 mL

PRESSURE COOKER METHOD

The pressure cooker method can be used to cook whole grains. The cooking times will be cut in half. Use at least twice as much water as grain for most grains. Use four times as much water for wheat berries, oat and rye groats. Follow the instructions that came with the pressure cooker for exact amounts of water and cooking times.

OVERNIGHT COOKING METHOD

Whole grains are very easy to cook and there are several methods that can be used. Generally it is better to use low or medium heat and to cook them for long periods of time. Dr. Carolyn Dean, an holistic physician in Toronto, suggests to her patients that they can cook whole grains like oat groats, rye, barley, and wheat groats easily. Using a wide mouth insulated bottle, put in a small amount of washed grains and add three times as much boiling water or more, seal it up and leave overnight. Pour out in the morning for an instant hot grain breakfast. This can be served with fresh fruit, milk, tofu cream, or just eaten plain, as I often do.

The old-fashioned stoves used to have a special soup well that was a large pot recessed into the stove with a burner underneath it that could be set very low so that grains could be simmered overnight or during the day. Now we have slow cookers and special rice cookers that can be purchased in Japanese, Chinese, or natural food stores. There are special ones for cooking brown rice. All of these things are great ways to slow cook grains.

MILLET

Judah and the land of Israel were your traders. They traded for your merchandise wheat of Minnith, millet, honey, oil, and balm. Ezekiel 27:17 (NKJ)

Millet is called Pannag in some translations of the Bible. This is mainly due to the botanical name being *Panicum miliaceum. Panis* is the Latin word meaning bread, so it is possible that millet was used for bread. Generally it is felt that millet flour was mixed with other flours as it is in Ezekiel's flour recipe. *Miliaceum* refers to the one thousand seeds each stem is supposed to produce.[9]

Barley, wheat, and millet were used in making Ezekiel's flour. Most of us are familiar with wheat and, maybe even, barley, but millet is not usually used in the average North American household. Unless they happen to keep a canary or budgie, then they might have millet. Millet is often sold on sticks in pet stores to encourage birds to sing sweetly. Why shouldn't it help us to sing better? Millet is a small round pale cream colored grain that looks like a seed. It can be quite dark, almost light brown, or very light yellow in color, depending on the variety and the place that it is grown. It has a very mild taste, which makes it especially suited for children.

Millet can be cooked up as a grain much like rice can be cooked and served, or it can be cooked with three times as much water and served as porridge for breakfast. It is very easy to digest, has no gluten so it can be eaten by those who are sensitive to gluten, is low in calories and starch. It is also one of the highest in protein. I use millet to thicken stews or soups because it seems to explode when boiled up. Often I use millet meal in place of corn meal for an interesting change since it is less flavorful than corn. It is a very good substitute for "Cream of Wheat" type cereals, since they do not contain the whole grain of wheat.

In my weight loss classes we found that eating millet was a great help to those who suffered from hypoglycemic swings or low blood sugar problems. Millet helps to stabilize the production of blood sugar as well as the levels of insulin. Millet is one of the slow-release carbohydrates that we mentioned earlier.

Often I eat cooked millet for breakfast with lightly sautéed onions, garlic, mushrooms, garnished with soy sauce (tamari, really) and freshly chopped parsley.

NUTRITIONAL VALUES

Millet (100 grams cooked)
- 327 calories
- 9.9 g protein
- 2.9 g fat
- 72.9 g carbohydrate
- 3.2 g fiber
- 20 mg calcium
- 311 mg phosphorus
- 6.8 mg iron
- 430 mg potassium
- 162 mg magnesium
- 0.73 mg B1
- 0.38 mg B2
- 2.3 mg B3[10]

RICE

Rice is similar to wheat in that many cultures polish it and remove the fiber and B complex vitamins, eating mostly just starch in the same way we do with wheat. Rice requires a much different climate for growing than wheat. Whole grain rice is called brown rice because it looks light brown. The brown outer layer or rice bran has fiber and nutrients in it, the same as the outer layer of wheat. There are whole grain rices that are red, bluish, black, or very dark brown depending on the variety. North American wild rice is a grass, not a grain, but it does have nutritional value as a vegetable.

Rice is one of the grains that we usually eat in North America that is not mentioned in the Bible. Although it was eaten by the Romans and is mentioned in *Apicus, Cookery And Dining In Imperial Rome,* edited and translated by Joseph Dommers Vehling, Dover Publications, New York, 1977. Rice is used in a great many dishes in Middle Eastern cooking even today. Some of these recipes date back to the Old Testament times.

WHITE OR BROWN RICE?

When rice is polished the outer coat is removed. This outer layer contains the fiber, vitamins E and B complex, and choline, which are missing in white, unenriched rice. Brown rice contains more protein, unsaturated fatty acids, calcium, magnesium, and iron than polished rice does. The process of enriching rice puts into it some of the nutrients that were removed by the process of polishing, and, of course, there is always the possibility that the nutrients that are put back in are not the most essential ones for rice. It is also possible that there are still nutrients that are in rice that men have not discovered yet and, therefore, haven't been able to replace.

An example of the process of refining and what it removes is the vitamin E content of rice. Brown rice has, per 3 1/2 oz. (100 g), 1.2 mg of vitamin E, while white rice has 0.35 mg for the same amount.[11] Another example of this is the choline content. Brown rice has 218 mg for 1 cup (195 g) cooked rice while white rice has only 89 mg for the same amount.[12]

CHOLINE, A MATTER OF LIFE OR DEATH

The choline content of rice may not seem important to us in North America because we have other ways of obtaining it, mainly in animal source foods. To many people in the third world, the difference between life and early death can depend on choline in their rice. Drs. Emmanuel Farber and Amiya Ghoshal at the University of Toronto recently published the results of their 2 year study showing that diets deficient in choline were directly responsible for causing liver cancer in rats as well as the development of pre-cancerous lesions. The control group who were fed normal diets that contained choline had none of the same effects. Their study was unusual because it investigated the link between diet and cancer without actually giving the animals a chemical which causes cancer. Dr. Ghoshal speculates that in those areas of the third world where people eat very little, if any, meat and also eat only polished rice, like in Northern China, that the cancer rates would be correspondingly high, as they are in Northern China.[13]

A friend of mine from China once told me that Chinese people were called the yellow race years ago because so many of them had a yellowish tint because of liver problems. He didn't look yellow, nor did any of his modern relatives who lived in North America and were able to afford more than just polished rice as their diet. He said that his family had left China in the late '50s because work and food were so scarce that many days all they had was the white rice his mother could borrow from neighbors. How sad it is to think that there are people in the world today who are getting so little food that the entire race could be changing or in danger of extinction because of the nutritional deficiencies brought on by food shortages.

So it would seem that many Chinese people years ago only ate white rice which contained no choline and very little else that contained choline, and that affected their liver so that they became yellow looking. They then became known as "the yellow race." In North America I have never seen a Chinese person, even one recently arrived from China who was yellow. One would hope that this is now eradicated.

RICE, THE LONG AND SHORT OF IT

There are several types of rice in common use in North America, short grain, medium grain, and long grain. The major difference is the size and shape of the grains, not the nutritional value. Some people claim that one size is for winter and one size is for summer. For us in North America, we have the choice of being able to eat which ever kind we prefer. I prefer to eat the short grain varieties most of the time. And, of course, I always eat the biologically grown brands. (This is the same as organically grown or grown without synthetic chemicals.) There is also sweet rice or glutinous rice which is high in gluten and is used for making "sticky rice," various kinds of rice pudding, and is often made into a meat substitute-type food called mochi.

Fried Rice

1	small onion
1 clove	garlic
1–3 Tbsp. (15–45 mL)	cold pressed peanut, safflower or blended oil
1	small carrot cut in match stick pieces
2 cups (500 mL)	chilled, pre-cooked brown rice
1–2 tsp. (5–10 mL)	natural soy sauce or shoyu
1 inch	piece fresh ginger root

Have everything ready before starting to cook. Heat a heavy skillet or wok over medium/high or high heat. When the pan is hot add the oil. As soon as the oil is hot add the onions either chopped or cut into crescents, finely chopped garlic, and carrots and stir to coat with oil. Cook until the onions are transparent. Add rice and stir, then sprinkle with soy sauce and stir. Heat thoroughly. A 1 inch piece of fresh ginger can be grated or pressed and added with the soy sauce.

FRIED RICE VARIATIONS

Add other vegetables or left over meats cut in small pieces. Mushrooms can be added with the onions. Broccoli, cauliflower, sweet potatoes, squash, or zucchini can be added, cut into small pieces, with the onions. With broccoli and cauliflower add the stems with the onions and the flowers just before adding the rice. Red, green, or yellow peppers can be added, pea pods, peas, green beans, all cut into small pieces, can be added. Left over meats can be cut into slivers and added just before the rice. If adding tofu it is best to sauté it first, remove it from the pan, add more oil and proceed as above, then return it to the pan after stirring the rice. Freshly chopped parsley is a welcome addition to any style fried rice and it should be added at the very end just before serving to maintain its bright green color as well as its nutritional value.

SPICY

Mix grated fresh ginger with the soy sauce before adding it. Also cayenne pepper, chili powder, ground anise seeds, ground or whole cumin seeds, star anise, curry powder, or Chinese Five Spice can be added if desired.

ADDITIONAL IDEAS

Use this method to make a side dish for a meal using green onions, mushrooms, sweet red peppers, and parsley, with or without a topping of grated cheese. I often eat this for breakfast.

CURRY FRIED RICE

Make basic fried rice and add curry powder to the oil and cook for a few seconds just before adding rice. Start with 1/4 tsp. (1 mL) and add more to taste

NUTRITIONAL VALUES

Brown Rice (4/5 cup cooked)
> 178 calories
> 0.9 g fat
> 0.1 g polyunsaturated fatty acids
> 0 cholesterol

3.8 g protein
38.2 g carbohydrate
0.4 g fiber
0.14 mg B1
0.03 mg B2
2.1 mg B3
18 mg calcium
45 mg magnesium
105 mg potassium
110 mg phosphorus
0.80 mg iron

White Rice (4/5 cup cooked)
164 calories
0.2 g fat
0.1 g polyunsaturated fatty acids
3 g protein
36.8 carbohydrate
0.2 g fiber
0.03 B1
0.01 mg B2
0.6 mg B3
15 mg calcium
12 mg magnesium
42 mg potassium
42 mg phosphorus
0.300 mg iron[14]

BARLEY

. . . and they came to Bethlehem at the beginning of barley harvest.
Ruth 1:22b (RSV)

Barley, *Hordeum distichon,* is most often eaten in soup and less often in certain crackers, but the main way that most people have any contact with barley is in beer or whiskey. Barley is roasted or malted before it is included in foods. It was used in the old soda fountain "malted milk," malted milk drink powders, and for making beer and various other fermented drinks as well as malt vinegar. Many people who find sugar intolerable are using barley malt syrup to replace the sweetener in baking. It is a thick, sweet syrup that is also used as a sweetening agent in many Japanese and natural food candies. Because it has recently been introduced for baking there are not many nutrient breakdowns available to tell us if there is any nutritional reason for using barley malt syrup to replace sugar. It is still a sweet and not to be regarded as anything else just because it comes from barley.

There are records as far back as the 19th century B.C. that show that bakeries made barley bread to be consumed as breads as well as to be used as the starting agent for a kind of beer that was drunk by wealthy Greeks and Romans. See Chapter VII—Drinks for more details on this.

BARLEY FLOUR

Barley flour is often used to thicken prepared products and to make crackers and teething biscuits. Many doctors recommend barley cereal as one of the first whole grain products babies can eat, along with rice and oat cereals. These grains seem to be more easily tolerated than wheat. Oriental children often eat a baby cereal made of roasted rice that is ground up and then cooked with water to resemble pudding or soft porridge. This can easily be made from rice, barley, millet, oats, or buckwheat and is called "cream" of rice, etc.

BARLEY LOAVES

There is a lad here who has five barley loaves and two fish; but what are they among so many? John 6:9 (RSV)

In the feeding of the five thousand noted in John, Chapter 6, Andrew points out that there was a young man present who had five barley loaves and two fish, which Jesus used to distribute to the crowd, leaving 12 baskets with fragments from the five barley loaves. This is considered a miracle, feeding a huge crowd of people with only five loaves. I'm tempted to mention here that if barley loaves were worthy of a miracle they certainly might be worthy for us to eat as well. Elisha also multiplied barley loaves to feed a crowd making twenty loaves feed one hundred men.[15]

Barley flour has less of a strong taste than whole wheat flour so it makes a milder end product. Barley flour can be added to other whole grain flours when making bread. It is not the same consistency as wheat flour, but it is high in gluten so it rises well. Barley flour is great to use when making crackers.

Barley Flour Crackers

1 cup	barley flour
1/2 tsp.	sea salt
1/2 tsp.	baking soda
1 cup	buttermilk

Sift flour, salt, and soda together. Stir in buttermilk. Press into an oiled jelly roll pan or cookie sheet with a lip all around it. 12 x 18 inch is the best size for this. Use two sheets for very thin crackers. Bake in preheated 300°F oven until very brown all over. After they have been baking about 10 minutes, score the dough into squares or rectangles so they will break apart when done. I also like to prick all over with a fork to give the look of saltines. Bake for a total of about 20–25 minutes. Coarsely ground sea salt or herbs can be added to the tops before baking. Always press toppings lightly into the dough.

POT OR PEARL BARLEY

Pot barley is scoured three times during the refining process, while pearl barley is scoured six times making it more refined. Only some of the outer layer of pearl barley has been removed, unlike refined rice and wheat where all the outer layers are removed. Of course some of the pearl barley may have had more surface removed than others; this can be seen with the naked eye. If it looks very pale it is refined, if it has a brownish tinge, it is less refined. Sometimes pot barley is called "scotch barley" because of its use in "scotch broth" soup. Many Japanese grocery stores carry pot barley for use in soup type dishes or baby food. Just be sure to look at the color of it to see if it has been pearlized or not before you buy it.

BARLEY AND RICE AS MEDICINE

Many people use barley for medicinal purposes. In Great Britain "Barley Water" or "Lemon Barley Water" is sold for use in children's and adult's stomach complaints such as diarrhea, stomachache, or gripe. This medicinal formula dates back to Biblical times. The barley and lemon is cooked in a large quantity of water and then strained and the resulting water is then drunk. Of course it has to be the whole barley. Barley contains calcium, magnesium, and potassium[16] which are useful in stopping vomiting and stomach pain. And, in addition, it is a good way to get some nutrients into a sick person in a readily acceptable and easily tolerated manner. Rice is used in the same way in the Orient, and is excellent in stopping diarrhea. The same kinds of nutritional values can be obtained from drinking rice water that has been slowly prepared as eating rice, except that there is no fiber. Barley and rice waters are also very good to give to older people who are having trouble eating. This should never, however, be continued on a long term basis without consulting a doctor. There is always a possibility of a medical problem both in the case of diarrhea and stomach complaints and in the case of older adults who don't eat for whatever reason.

Mushroom and Barley Soup

1/2 lb.	fresh mushrooms
3 Tbsp.	butter or butter and oil mixed
1/3 cup	pot barley
6 cups or more	boiling water or stock
1	stalk celery
3	generous sprigs parsley
1 tsp.	sea salt

Remove stems from mushrooms and chop. Slice the caps. Heat butter in soup pot over medium heat. Sauté caps only for 2 minutes or until they change color, remove from pan and set aside. Add the barley to the butter, stir and sauté until it turns golden brown, add the chopped stems, stir, and sauté for 2 minutes more. Add remaining ingredients except the caps and boil hard for 3 minutes. Turn heat down, cover and simmer for 20 to 30 minutes or more until barley is soft and cooked through. Remove celery and parsley, add the caps and simmer for 3 or 4 minutes to heat caps. Serves 4.

Sprinkle freshly chopped parsley in the center of each bowl as a garnish just before serving.

Barley Salad

Toss cooked barley with chopped vegetables and dress with oil and lemon. Almost any veggie can be used but you may want to try one or more of the following. Green onion, grated carrot, cooked peas, red, green, or yellow bell peppers, cooked green beans, cooked zucchini, broccoli, cauliflower, celery, jicama, radish, sprouts of any kind, sun dried tomatoes packed in oil, olives. Chopped fresh herbs can also be added such as basil, marjoram, thyme, oregano, savory, or dill. Olive oil is a stronger oil and mixes well with lemon juice, but other oils can be used as well as flavored vinegars in place of the lemon juice.

NUTRITIONAL VALUES

Pot Barley (1 cup uncooked)
- 696 calories
- 19.2 g protein
- 2.2 g fat
- 154.4 g carbohydrate
- 68 mg calcium
- 580 mg phosphorus
- 5.4 mg iron
- 592 mg potassium
- 0.42 mg B1
- 0.14 mg B2
- 7.4 mg B3[17]

RIE, RYE, OR SPELT?

There are many varieties of each grain, some are ancient, some are modern, some are the same strains as the ancient ones still in use. There are also problems with translations and meanings of many of the words which refer to the foods and plants in the Bible. Rye is one of those confusions. The Authorized Version, commonly known as the King James Version, refers to the use of "rie" in the several passages where the reference exists.[18] This is generally thought to be *Tritium Spelta* which did grow in Egypt and still does today.[19] Secale cereale is the variety that Europeans know as rye. This grain is now being grown in Egypt.[20]

In more modern translations the word is translated as "spelt," or "kind of spelt," which refers to a type of wheat known as "German Wheat" or Dinkel in Europe. German wheat could well be the same basic type of grain having a smooth ear rather than a hairy one as most true wheat does.[21] In Italy spelt grain is known as faro. Many farmers are now growing spelt from which pasta is being made that is sold in health food stores. The flour is not the same as the wheat flour we are used to, it is very full-bodied and nutty tasting. Although there is little research on whether spelt is a true wheat, more is being done to show whether those allergic to wheat or gluten can tolerate spelt. Many people have reported to me that they cannot take wheat without getting stomach distress, but do not have the same reaction with spelt.

ADDING IN SPELT

Experiment with spelt by adding some to your regular recipes. Start by substituting 1/2 the whole wheat flour or 1/4 of the white flour in your favorite recipes. I have made bread with all spelt and it took a little more kneading, about 3 minutes, but it was great tasting and worked the same as the whole wheat flour I normally use.

RYE

Rye has been used in Europe for centuries for making bread. It has less gluten than wheat flour so it makes a softer, free formed loaf. Whole grain rye, and dark rye flour contain the highest amount of vitamin E of all the whole grains.[22] There are many crackers on the market now, made in North America or Europe, that are made of whole rye grains. Generally they are low in calories since they have no sugar or fat added. These crisp breads are very popular for parties and are often eaten with cheese or dips. This is a great way to introduce whole grains to a reluctant family. Even though this is not the rie of the King James Version of the Bible it is still a wholesome grain worthy of eating for health.

In North America rye is generally eaten in the form of flour in bread and crackers. Some people do eat the grains whole, cooked up as a cereal or in soups, stews, or in place of rice or potatoes, but this is not commonly done. Rye and barley are often roasted, fermented, or distilled to make alcoholic drinks in North America, Europe, and Asia. There is evidence that I have found that shows that these grains were used for the same purposes in Biblical times. There are many references to these alcoholic brews called strong drink in the Old Testament, see Chapter VII—Drinks for more information.

NUTRITIONAL VALUES

Dark Rye Flour (1 cup unsifted)
    419 calories
    20.0 g protein
    3.3 g fat
    87.2 g carbohydrate
    69 mg calcium
    686 mg phosphorus
    5.8 mg iron
    1 mg sodium

    1,101 mg potassium
    0.78 mg B1
    0.28 mg B2
    3.5 mg B3[23]

Spelt (100 grams)
    382 calories
    14.26 g protein
    2.94 g fat
    74.51 g carbohydrate
    9.3 g fiber
    38 mg calcium
    4.17 mg iron
    1.72 mg sodium
    385 mg potassium
    2.90 mg manganese
    0.62 mg copper
    3.40 mg zinc
    41 I.U. vitamin A
    0.649 mg B1
    0.227 mg B2
    8.46 mg B3 (furnished by Purity Foods Okemos, MI)

OATS

Oats, *Avena sativa*, are not mentioned in the Bible, the climate is not suitable for growing oats. There is mention of straw, but it is thought to be referring to barley or wheat straw. In North America we use oat straw as well as barley straw in animal husbandry. Oats have been eaten in the British Isles as a staple grain for centuries. Oats are eaten as whole grains, in cakes, crackers, puddings, and stews and the flour is also used for thickening gravies and stews and in crackers, breads, and muffins. Oats are eaten in North America as rolled oats or steel cut oats, mostly in porridge. There are some newer cereals that have become popular made from oat flour and shaped into rings. Rolled flakes are toasted and made into a cereal called granola. Oat flakes are often used in snack foods such as candy bars and granola bars to give more texture or fiber, higher protein, and more nutritive value.

Porridge is made of either the flakes, the steel cut, or the whole groats that are cooked in water and eaten hot. Oatmeal is more finely ground oats. Oat flakes are also used in short bread, biscuits, tea biscuits, and some bar cookies or squares. Oats are often mixed with fruit in desserts such as matrimonial bars, often called date squares, and apple or other fruit crisps. Oat bran is now being marketed in many stores, it is the bran from the whole grain removed during refining.

Rolled oats come in many different ways. For the highest nutritional value to your body, I recommend that you eat them as close to the natural state as possible. This means without much sugar, salt, or fat. Many researchers report that fruit sugar or fructose is more easily handled by the body than the simple sugar of sucrose, our table sugar. Often when trying to cut down on refined sugar, many people add dried fruit like currants, raisins, or apricots to oatmeal when it is cooking to impart sweetness in a more complete way than using sugar. This is a good way to replace sugar on cooked cereal, but it is still a sweetness that, when added in large amounts, can cause a blood sugar rise in some people. Some people find that mixing fruit and grains is difficult to digest, especially if they also add milk as well. See Chapter V—Special Treats for more information.

Often I recommend to people that they replace the cow's milk and sugar with a mixture of banana, tofu, lemon juice, and water that looks and tastes like a rich dairy cream, with less fat and calories. (See the recipe for "Tofu Cream")

OATS , CHOLESTEROL, CANCER, AND DIABETES

Oats have long been known to "be good for you," the trouble was we never knew how or why they were supposed to be good for us. Dr. James Anderson, professor of medicine at the University of Kentucky in Lexington, can now tell us how and why. He is often called "the father of oat bran" because of his research. His original research was with diabetics, and the findings showed that oat bran added to the diet could reduce and sometimes eliminate insulin requirements for diabetics. (This is not something a diabetic should try on his or her own without guidance from a physician who is a specialist in diabetes and nutrition.) Other fiber foods can also be helpful to diabetics, as we saw with Dr. Jenkins' work earlier.

Barley and oats contain cholesterol inhibitors which reduce the LDL or low-density lipo-proteins, often called the "bad" cholesterol, and help to increase the HDL or high-density lipo-proteins, often called the "good" cholesterol. The water soluble fibers in oat bran help to smooth out blood sugar levels and keep diabetics from getting their blood sugar levels elevated. During a recent study at the

University of Wisconsin it was shown that 100 g of oat bran daily added to the diet of diabetics not only lowered cholesterol levels but also enabled them to function normally without a daily insulin shot.[24]

Dr. Kenneth Storch at the Massachusetts Institute of Technology was able to show that when oat bran was added to the diet, cholesterol levels dropped by about 5 per cent. This means that such a drop in cholesterol levels can produce a 10 per cent drop in the chances of the person having a heart attack. To do this he used MIT students. To one group they gave four wheat bran muffins a day, the other members were fed four oat bran muffins. Each muffin contained 13 grams of the respective fiber. The students who ate the oat bran muffins had a consistent decrease in cholesterol immediately and a total reduction of 5 per cent within two weeks. The serum cholesterol level was reduced by 20% and sustained for 2 years while on the oat bran diet. Those eating the wheat bran muffins had no change in their cholesterol levels.[25]

BETA GLUCAN

Oats have a special sticky substance or gummy material that makes the oat porridge sticky when cooked. This is beta glucan, a polymer of glucose, which is indigestible. As it passes through the bowel, it carries with it bile acids. When the beta glucan increases the excretion of bile acids, the body is stimulated to convert more ingested fat into bile acids rather than into circulating fatty acids. It also has been shown to reduce the amount of cholesterol manufactured by the liver.[26]

Oat Bran Muffins

2 cups (225 g)	oat bran
1/3 cup (75 mL)	whole wheat flour
1/4 cup (50 mL)	sunflower and pumpkin seeds, mixed
1/4 cup (50 mL)	currants
1 Tbsp. (15 mL)	baking powder
1/2 tsp. (2 mL)	salt
1/4 tsp. (1 mL)	cinnamon
1 cup (250 mL)	milk
2	eggs, beaten
1/3 cup (75 mL)	honey
2 Tbsp. (30 mL)	vegetable oil

Blend together wet ingredients. Mix together dry ingredients. Then mix together both sets of ingredients with as few strokes as needed. Line muffin tins with paper liners, fill 3/4 full and bake at 425°F (220°C) for 17–20 minutes or until golden.

Food Processor—follow instructions above using plastic blade to mix wet ingredients, add dry and mix.

NB: Each of these muffins contains over 18 grams of oat bran. The research muffins contained just over 13 grams each and four were eaten a day so these muffins could be used to help lower cholesterol, triglycerides, and blood sugar levels with your doctor's guidance following a full diet program.

NUTRITIONAL VALUES

Rolled Oats (1/3 cup dry or 3/4 cup cooked)

> 108 calories
> 4.5 g protein
> 0.3 g fiber
> 0.7 g polyunsaturated fatty acids
> 29 I.U. vitamin A
> B complex vitamins
> 1 mg sodium (unless salt is added during cooking, then the sodium becomes 280 mg if following directions on the package of regular oats)
> 15 mg calcium
> 42 mg magnesium
> 0.86 mg zinc
> 1.02 mg manganese
> 99 mg potassium
> 1.19 mg iron
> 0.096 mg copper[27]
> (If milk is added the nutritional values increase accordingly.)

OVERNIGHT COOKING METHOD

Whole grains are very easy to cook and there are several methods that can be used. Generally it is better to use low or medium heat and to cook them for long periods of time. Dr. Carolyn Dean, an holistic physician in Toronto, suggests to her patients that they can cook whole grains like oat groats, rye, barley, and wheat groats easily. Using a wide mouth insulated bottle, put in a small amount of washed grains and add three times as much boiling water or more, seal it up and leave overnight. Pour out in the morning for an instant hot grain breakfast. This can be served with fresh fruit, milk, tofu cream, or just eaten plain, as I often do.

The old-fashioned stoves used to have a special soup well that was a large pot recessed into the stove with a burner underneath it that could be set on very low so that grains could be simmered overnight or during the day. Now we have slow cookers and special rice cookers that can be purchased in Japanese, Chinese, or natural food stores. There are special ones for cooking brown rice.

CORN OR PARCHED GRAINS

And it came to pass on the second sabbath after the first, that he went through the corn fields; and his disciples plucked the ears of corn, and did eat, rubbing them in their hands. Luke 6:1 (KJV)

The corn referred to in this passage and others in the Bible that use the word "corn" is meant to be "grain." The New King James Version translates the word *sporimos* that is used in this passage to mean "grain." Although *sitos* and *sition* are also used in the Bible to mean grain or corn, it is not the maize known in Europe nor the corn found in America by the early settlers, to which it refers. Corn meant grain, but it also meant wheat or seed, so it is difficult to know which meaning was intended. The newer translations take into account that we in North America have another meaning for the word "corn," and that the use of the word corn to mean grains, ear of grains, etc. is falling out of use.

The corn grown in North America is known by the botanical name *Zea mays*. Corn is eaten more frequently and in more ways in the Southern states than in the North. Corn bread, corn meal mush, and hominy grits are staples of the Southern diet. In the Southwest, Mexican cuisine has influenced eating habits and there are more corn products eaten like tortillas, corn chips, posole, and tacos. Here also is the seat of the fast becoming popular blue corn, also known as Indian corn. Corn has been recorded as far back as the1600's in Ontario, Canada, having been introduced to the Native Indians through Mexico and the Spanish trading influence.

CORN ON THE COB

Corn on the cob is probably one of the most favorite grain/vegetable foods for children of all ages. It is especially wonderful to pick it fresh and rush it to a pot of boiling water to flash cook it and eat it immediately. It is probably one of the fading memories of most adults since so few people have the time or place to grow their own corn any more. It is also wonderful roasted in the husk over an open fire at the cottage or in the oven at home. Roasting it in the husk imparts a wonderful sweetness and richness that can't be described.

If using an open fire soak the corn, husks and all, in water for up to an hour. Gently and carefully remove the silks and close up the ear. Place the cobs on a rack over hot coals and turn every 3 minutes until roasted, this should take about 15 minutes. If roasting in the oven, pre-heat oven to 375°F (190°C) and place soaked cobs on rack and bake for 15 minutes or until steamed. Often I have frozen corn in the husks and baked them in the oven while frozen and found them to have the taste of fresh picked corn. Corn in the husks does not have to be blanched, but you must be very sure that there is no blight or insect infestation before you freeze it.

Corn Bread

1 cup (150 g)	yellow or blue corn meal
1 cup (130 g)	whole wheat pastry flour
1/2 tsp. (2 mL)	sea salt
4 tsp. (20 mL)	baking powder
1/4 cup (35 g)	milk powder (non-instant)
1	egg
1/4 cup (50 mL)	honey
1 cup (250 mL)	milk or water
1/4 cup (50 mL)	oil or melted butter

Sift dry ingredients together. Whisk together eggs, honey, milk, and oil until honey dissolves. Pour over dry ingredients and stir vigorously until smooth. Bake in a greased 8 or 9 inch (20 or 23 cm) square pan for 20 to 30 minutes in a pre-heated 400°F (200°C) oven or until nicely browned.

Ezekiel Flour Corn Bread

Substitute Ezekiel-type multi-blend flour for the whole wheat pastry flour and add 1/4 cup more water or milk in the basic Corn Bread recipe above.

Corn Bread Coffee Cake

Make corn bread recipe and add the following topping:

2 tsp. (10 mL)	cinnamon

1/4 cup (50 mL)	honey
1/4 cup (50 mL)	oil or melted butter
1/2 cup (70 g)	sunflower seeds and chopped nuts mixed
1/2 cup (50 g)	wheat germ
1/4 cup (25 g)	oat or wheat bran

Draw a knife through topping and into the batter to swirl topping into some of the cake. Bake as above.

Spicy Bean Roll
(Filling)

3/4 cup	cooked beans, black, pinto, navy, etc.
2 Tbsp. each:	oil and butter
1	cooking onion
1 clove	garlic, or more to taste
1/2 tsp.	ground black pepper
1/4 tsp.	red pepper sauce
1 tsp.	tamari, shoyu, or other natural soy sauce
1/2 cup	tomato paste
2 tsp. each	basil and oregano
1/4 tsp.	ground cumin
1/8 tsp.	chili powder, optional

Filling—Finely chop onion and garlic. Melt butter and oil together and sauté onion and garlic until transparent. Mash beans a little so some are fully mashed and some are still in pieces. Add all ingredients together and set aside to cool.

(Crust)

1 1/2 cup	whole wheat pastry flour
1/2 cup	yellow corn meal
1 tsp.	sea salt
1 tsp.	baking powder
1/2 cup	butter
1/2 cup + 2 Tbsp.	milk

Crust—Sift dry ingredients together. Cut in butter as for a pie crust. When it has the texture of coarse meal add milk and knead lightly with your hands. Turn out onto a lightly floured pastry cloth or smooth tea towel. Roll with rolling pin into a rectangle about 12 inches by 15 inches.

Spread pastry with filling leaving a strip along one side about 1 inch. Using the cloth, roll up starting with the side opposite the empty strip.

Place seam side down on ungreased baking sheet. Bake in 425°F oven for 15 to 25 minutes until lightly browned.

Cut into slices and serve. This should serve 4 as a main dish. Always try to have a green salad with this.

Variations—Use tofu that has been frozen for at least 3 days, thawed, squeezed and finely chopped or crumbled in place of the beans. This will have a meaty texture that the beans don't. Browned tempeh can also be used.

This is a basic recipe that can be made into several smaller rolls and served warm as an appetizer. This crust can be pressed into a 9 inch x 13 inch pan and spread with the filling and covered with grated cheese for a pizza type meal.

More Variations—finely chopped green and/or sweet red peppers can be added to the onions when sautéing. Sliced green or black olives can be added.

This recipe is an emergency standby when you have kids or whenever unexpected company comes because it is made from all the staple ingredients that you would find in a well-equipped pantry.

NUTRITIONAL VALUES

Yellow Corn or Sweet Corn (1/2 cup [120 ml] frozen)
> 88 calories
> 3.1 g protein
> 0 cholesterol
> 0.6 g fiber
> 238 I.U. vitamin A
> 6 mg vitamin C
> small amounts of the B complex vitamins
> 4 mg sodium
> 196 mg potassium
> 5 mg calcium
> 21 mg magnesium
> 0.07 mg manganese
> 0.43 mg zinc
> 0.46 mg iron
> 0.04 mg copper

Corn Meal, White or Yellow (cooked, (1 cup [225 ml])
> 120 calories
> 2.6 g protein
> 0 cholesterol

0.2 g fiber
144 I.U. vitamin A
0 sodium (if cooked without salt)
38 mg potassium
2 mg calcium
20 mg magnesium
1 mg iron[28]

CORN PRODUCTS

Corn flour is used in various baked products like pancakes, waffles, and many varieties of breads and specialty breads. Corn starch is also used as a thickening agent in many puddings, desserts, and pies. Corn starch is added to baking powder as a filler, and is often found in breading on chicken, fish, and sea food. It is frequently an ingredient in many processed and prepared foods, which reading the label can verify.

CORN CHIPS, ETC.

Corn chips are generally fried and may contain high fat content. One ounce of corn chips, which isn't very much, contains 8.8 g of fat. Another brand contains 9.7 g per ounce and has 155 calories. If you want to eat corn chips try to get the baked, not fried kind.

POP CORN

The most universally accepted form of corn in North America has become popped corn. People of all ethnic backgrounds eat it. Recently in larger cities gourmet pop corn stores have sprung up that sell pop corn natural, buttered, and coated with dozens of different flavor coatings. Beware of the sweet coatings. One cup (225 ml) of popped corn "au natural" contains: 54 calories, 1.8 g protein, 0 cholesterol, 0.3 g fiber, vitamins B1, B2, B3, 24 mg magnesium, 28 mg potassium, and 2 mg calcium. The same amount of popped corn with a sugar coating has 134 calories, one tablespoon of butter would add 123 more calories.[29]

THE PERFECT SNACK

I often eat popped corn as a snack. Some times I add butter, fresh garlic and parsley, and cayenne pepper. Many times I just shake the freshly popped corn in a bag with curry powder or seasoned herbal mixtures without adding salt or butter. It is easy to fix, easy to serve, quick, and relatively low in calories compared to some of the snack foods on the market. It is also a source of fiber. I much prefer to eat popped corn to ice cream as a snack. My uncle Glenn told me that during the depression they grew popping corn in the garden, popped it and ate it for breakfast with milk on it as a cereal. (People were eating popped corn for breakfast long before there were corn flakes on the market the way we have now.) I remember thinking how weird he was when I was a child and he told me this. Now I am recommending the same thing as a low cost, homemade snack any time of the day. Of course popped corn is another food that requires a lot of chewing, don't forget to remind yourself and your family to chew it well, especially if you are eating it in the evening.

BUCKWHEAT

Buckwheat is a very useful grain. It has the strongest taste of any of the grains. It can be used to extend or replace meat in cabbage rolls, stuffed peppers, kishka, casseroles, and many other dishes. We usually see it in flour form in pancakes. Buckwheat takes the least amount of time to cook of any of the grains so it can be ready as a hot cereal in as little as 5 minutes.

It is found in bulk food and natural food stores as well as in European delicatessens. Some grocery stores carry it in the ethnic food or European food section under the name Kasha. Buckwheat is sold plain and roasted. It is a multi-cornered grain, light beige and green in color, it is not the same shape as wheat, rice, or oats. When it is roasted it is a rich brown color and has a nutty smell. This is the form that is used to replace or extend ground meat. Toasted buckwheat is also the traditional way it is used in European cooking. The buckwheat flour found in the supermarkets for pancakes or used in pancake mixes is ground with the hulls on so it is a dark grayish/brown color with black flecks in it. This gives it additional fiber and taste.

BUCKWHEAT AND STRENGTH

When the Soviet hockey team came to Canada for a playoff, it was reported that they inquired if buckwheat was available. It has long been known to build strength and stamina. Folklore has it that buckwheat lowers blood pressure, but scientific evidence is in short supply. Buckwheat is a cold climate plant, it grows in colder climates than rice. This is why it is more popular in Middle European, Russian, and Northern Japanese cooking. This also means that it is a good food to eat during the cold winter months. Buckwheat is not actually a grain, it is really the seed of a plant in the rhubarb family.[30]

CREPES

When crepes were popular and there were crepe restaurants in most cities, the French crepe called crepe de sarrasin was always on the menu. This is better known as buckwheat crepes. They were stuffed with sweet or savory fillings, and were very popular.

BUCKWHEAT PASTA

Soba noodles made from buckwheat flour is my favorite buckwheat product. They are flat Japanese noodles that cook in 5 minutes and are usually made from all or partially buckwheat flour. I often eat them for breakfast when I don't have much time to prepare a meal. This is a traditional food, but is often referred to as "health or natural" food by modern Japanese people. Buckwheat noodles are not eaten with tomato sauce, but are served in a bowl with a broth and some vegetables or sea food with them. Buckwheat noodles, sweet potato, onion, garlic, broccoli, kombu (also called deep sea kelp), and a dash of soy sauce may not be a traditional dish, but it is the most popular western interpretation of a traditional Japanese Soba dish, and my favorite breakfast.

Buckwheat Delight

Cook buckwheat according to the basic directions. Serve with maple syrup and pecans. This can be eaten for breakfast or as an accompaniment to a main dish.

Kasha and Bows

Cook 1 cup buckwheat according to the basic directions. Sauté half a diced onion, 4 chopped mushrooms, and 1 clove garlic in 2 tablespoons butter. Cook 2 servings of bow pasta, drain. Toss all ingredients together and serve. This is excellent served topped with mushroom gravy and freshly chopped parsley or green coriander. Any kind of pasta can be used, but bows or bowties are traditional.

Buckwheat and Egg

When cooking buckwheat grains a beaten egg can be added. The egg white coats the grain in such a way as to keep it whole and not mushy at the end.

NUTRITIONAL VALUES
Dark Buckwheat Flour (1ounce)
  92 calories
  3.3 g protein
  0 cholesterol
  0.4 g fiber
  vitamins B1, B2, B3
  9 mg calcium
  184 mg potassium
  0.78 mg iron.

Raw Buckwheat (100 grams)
  335 calories
  11.7 g protein
  2.4 g fat
  72.9 g carbohydrate
  9.9 g fiber
  114 mg calcium
  282 mg phosphorus
  3.1 mg iron
  0 sodium
  448 mg potassium
  229 mg magnesium
  0.60 mg B1
  0.16 mg B2
  4.4 mg B3[31]

THE OTHER GRAINS
There are many other grains/grasses that are eaten around the world that are now becoming popular like triticale, sorghum, quinoa, and amaranth, but they are not as readily available so I will reserve these for future books.

PROTEIN IN GRAINS
Protein is a general term. Amino Acids are the specifics of protein, they are the building blocks for the cells of all living animals. All proteins are composed of amino acids. There are eight amino acids that must be eaten in food. They are called the essential amino acids. They are: tryptophan, leucine, isoleucine, lysine, valine, threonine, phenylalanine, and methionine.

The other 13 or more amino acids can be manufactured by the body from food in general and, therefore, are called non-essential.[32]

Protein is found in beans, legumes, vegetables, dairy products, grains, eggs, nuts and seeds, animal flesh, and in very small limited amounts in fruits.

Some of the vegetable sources of protein were made to be eaten together to allow for obtaining all the essential amino acids. Most traditional diets mix the foods in the right combinations to give complete protein, that is all eight essential amino acids in one meal. Animal proteins, generally, contain the essential amino acids, along with high amounts of saturated fats, and calories. In Chapter III there will be more detail regarding complete and incomplete proteins, and mixing proteins in the diet to obtain complete protein.

REFERENCES

1. Jenkins, Dr. David, "Metabolic Effects of Slow-release Carbohydrates," Clinical Value of Dietary Fiber, Yale University School of Medicine, 1982, p. 19.

2. Pennington, Jean A. & Helen Nichols Church, *Food Values of Portions Commonly Used*, Harper and Row, New York, 1985.

3. Margen, Sheldon, MD & the Editors of the University of California at Berkeley Wellness Letter, *The Wellness Encyclopedia of Food and Nutrition*, Health Letter Associates, 1992, p. 35.

4. Evans, Gary, Western Journal of Medicine, Jan. 1990.

5. Airola, Paavo, *How To Get Well*, Health Plus Publishers, Phoenix, 1978, p. 107.

6. Williams, Sue Rodwell, *Nutrition and Diet Therapy*, The C.V. Mosby Company., St. Louis, 1973, pp. 188–194.

7. Pennington & Church.

8. Package for Multi-Blend Flour, Arrowhead Mills, Box 2059, Hereford, Texas.

9. Walker, Winnifred, *All The Plants Of The Bible* , Lutterworth Press, London, 1958.

10. Phillips, Ph.D., ND., BE., David A. *Guidebook to Nutritional Factors in Foods*, Woodbridge Press Publishing Company, Santa Barbara, 1979, p. 36.

11. Pennington & Church.

12. Pennington & Church.

13. Goshal, Amiya K. & Emmanuel Farber, "The Induction of Liver Cancer by Dietary Deficiency of Choline and Methionine Without Added Carcinogens," Carcinogenesis, Vol. 5 no. 10, 1985, pp. 1367–1370; and personal interview by author.

14. Pennington & Church.

15. II Kings 4:42–44.

16. Pennington & Church.

17. *Nutritive Value of American Foods, Agriculture Handbook No. 456,* Agricultural Research Service, US. Dept. of Agriculture, Nov. 1975.

18. Exodus 9:32–33 and Isaiah 28:25.

19. Walker.

20. Shewell-Cooper, W.E., (intro. by Billy Graham), *Plants, Flowers, and Herbs of the Bible,* Keats Publishing, Inc., New Canaan, 1977.

21. Shewell-Cooper.

22. Pennington & Church.

23. USDA Handbook 456.

24. Food Engineering, Vol. 57, no. 8, Sept. 18, 1985.

25. Anderson, J. and K. Storch, "Oat Bran Muffins Lower Serum Cholesterol of Healthy Young Men," American Journal of Nutrition, 41 (4) 846, 1985.

26. Anderson, J. and K. Storch, "Oat Bran Muffins Lower Serum Cholesterol," Clinical Research,33 (2) A711, see also: *Diabetes: A Practical New Guide To Healthy Living,* K. Storch.

27. Pennington & Church.

28. Pennington & Church.

29. Pennington & Church.

30. Albright, Nancy, *Rodale's Naturally Great Foods Cookbook,* Rodale Press, Emmaus, 1977.

31. Phillips, p. 32.

32. Wade, Carlson, *Carlson Wade's Amino Acids Book* , Keats Publishing, Inc., New Canaan, 1985.

Then God said, "I give you every seed-bearing plant on the face of the whole earth and every tree that has fruit with seed in it. They will be yours for food." Genesis 1:29 (NIV)

Our Daily Proteins:
Legumes & Vegetables

Legumes

LENTILS

Then Jacob gave Esau bread and some lentil stew. He ate and drank, and then got up and left. Genesis 25:34 (NIV)

The first vegetable mentioned in the Bible is lentil. It comes from the Latin word *lens*, referring to the actual shape of the legume itself, that of a convex lens. A magnifying glass such as we might use for magnifying small print is also a convex lens. Apparently, this legume is one of the oldest vegetables or plants known to man as it has been recorded as existing as early as the Bronze Age.[1]

In Genesis Jacob gave Essau a meal of red pottage, or red lentil stew or soup.[2] There are at least two kinds of lentils that we still use today: the small red ones and the larger greenish-brown ones. Lentils don't need to be soaked like other beans, they can just be cooked. Lentils were also a farm crop as mentioned in 2 Samuel 23:11. Lentils were brought as a gift to David and his people, as we see in 2 Samuel 17:27–29, along with whole grains and other beans. Lentils grow all over the Middle East. They are particularly suited to growing in waste places, thus it is easy to see why they were such a well-known and staple food, and continue to be so today. The lentil is a close relative of the vetch which also is being used to grow in waste places as a ground cover such as along the sides of major highways in Canada and the U.S., to reduce the necessity of cutting the grass there and to save money on road maintainance. The vetch is also fed to cattle because it is high in protein, just the same way that we are given to understand that the lentil plants were fed to cattle in Bible times after the seeds had been harvested for human food.

There is much talk today of needing crops that are high in nutrition, especially carbohydrates and protein, that can be grown in any terrain for use as human food in areas where there is little rain and much poverty and suffering. Lentils (along with amaranth) are one of the foods that should be considered for aid to drought stricken areas of the world. They do not take much cultivation or know-how to grow, they will also help to keep the top soil in place to rebuild the land that may have been affected by drought and high winds or parching sun. It seems that God had this in mind when he created lentils for use in the Middle East.

We have become so caught up with the more inefficient forms of protein like beef, that we have left behind the simple wisdom of using the plants of the Bible to meet all the needs of all people. If you want to read some statistics about this please read: *Earth Keeping, Christian Stewardship Of Natural Resources,* by the Fellows of the Calvin Center for Christian Scholarship, Calvin College, William B. Eerdmans Publishing Co., Grand Rapids, Michigan as well as; *Food First, Beyond The Myth Of Scaricity,* by Frances Moore Lappe and Joseph Collins, Ballantine Books, New York. I am putting the titles to these books here instead of in the notes because I feel that it is very important for all of us to be part of the cleaning up of hunger and food scarcity, since we are all part of creating it. These books will help us to see that it is not impossible and that each of us can do something toward making sure that all people everywhere have food to eat. This is something that Jesus felt very strongly about, and so do I. In Matthew's Gospel he talks of this in Chapter 25:34–46.

"... for I was hungry and you gave me no food ..." Then they also will answer, "Lord, when did we see thee hungry ... and did not minister unto thee?" Then he will answer them, "Truly, I say to you, as you did it not to one of the least of these, you did it not to me." Matthew 25:42a, 44a, c, 45 (RSV)

PROTEIN

Two tablespoons (30 mL) of dried lentils contain 7.1 grams of protein, the exact amount in two tablespoons (30 mL) of cheddar cheese. Protein is made up of smaller units called amino acids.

Amino acids are the building blocks for all cells in our body. It is not a coincidence that lentils are eaten often in the Bible. Daniel conducts a test with his three companions; they eat vegetables and pulses (another name for dried beans, lentils, & vegetables) and water for 10 days after which they are seen to be better in appearance than the youths who ate the King's diet of rich food and wine. (Daniel 1:8–21)

Pulses, legumes, or just plain old beans, were eaten in Bible times as the main source of protein. They are easy to grow, light to carry around, and easy to prepare, as well as being nourishing. They also need no refrigeration until they have been soaked or cooked, so it was obvious that in a hot climate, before electricity, refrigerators, or even ice boxes, they would keep very well. Meat and dairy products, on the other hand, did not keep very well and were not used as often.

BEAN FIBER AND HEALTH

We know that bean fiber, as well as grain fiber, is able to break up or lower triglycerides in the body thanks to the work of Dr. David Jenkins at the University of Toronto.[3] In Israel research done by Dr. Yoram Kanter at Rambam Hospital in Haifa showed that diabetics could reduce their daily insulin requirements by 25% if they ingested a supplemental protein and fiber product made of soybeans. Soy helps to lower blood sugar after meals, thereby requiring less insulin. Dr. Juan Munoz, a US diabetes specialist found the same to be true as early as the 1970's in studies he conducted for the US. Department of Agriculture. It is, therefore, very important for people with any type of diabetes or any prediabetic condition to eat soy bean products often. Later in this chapter we will look at some of the more popular ways of eating soy products.

Research done at the Gerontology Research Center in Baltimore, Maryland has shown that with each gram of fiber added to one's usual diet on a regular basis a decreased risk factor was evidenced for systolic and diastolic blood pressure, glucose problems, cholesterol and triglyceride problems.[4] This means that a higher fiber diet than we generally eat in North America, such as *The World's Oldest Health Plan* promotes, will be the healthiest one for people as they begin to age. That means all people over 25 years of age!

Actually, aging starts way before then, but I would like to give you time to adjust to the idea of building up your body. Anyone over

25 should be very concerned with his diet and health, your life and family depend on it. You will reduce the time and money you spend on health care and medicine if you begin to change your lifestyle before or at age 25. But don't worry if you are older, as I am. Anytime is a good time to change your habits. And you will always notice results. It might take a few weeks, months, or days, but you will notice a change.

CHICK PEAS AND SESAME SEEDS

Beans are usually eaten with whole grains or seeds or both in most traditional diets. Two of the most popular foods of Israel today are made of beans and sesame seeds: humus and tahini, and falafel. Humus (also spelled hummus or hommos) is made of puréed, cooked chick peas, sesame seed tahini, lemon juice, olive oil, garlic, and spices, usually cumin and hot peppers. It is often eaten as an appetizer with whole grain pita bread used to scoop it up or as a dip for vegetables.

Falafel is a patty made of uncooked chick peas ground up and mixed with onions, garlic, cumin, and other spices and deep fried or baked in the oven. It is served in whole wheat pita bread as a pocket sandwich with lettuce, tomatoes, mint, and a dressing of yogurt, tahini, olive oil, and lemon juice. These are very popular foods even now because of their high nutritional value, low cost, and exotic taste. They also contain less calories than a traditional hamburger and no cholesterol. Because they are made from vegetable protein, they are high in fiber and low in fat. Tahini also is called sesame butter or paste, and is made of unroasted or roasted sesame seeds and oil, ground until a fine paste is obtained. Sometimes salt is added. It is quite similar to peanut and almond butters, but blander in taste.

There are falafel mixes that are made of dried beans and spices that one only needs to add water to and let it sit or add tofu to for even more texture and protein. This can be formed into a falafel patty and baked or lightly browned in a fry pan, as well as the more traditional method of deep frying. Kids love these sandwiches. They also give the mouth a feel of regular burgers so that fussy eaters don't feel deprived of a hamburger and bun.

Falafel

1 cup	chick peas (Garbanzo beans) soaked overnight in
2 1/2 cups	water
2 cloves	garlic
2 Tbsp.	chopped fresh or dried parsley
1/4 tsp.	ground cumin
1 tsp.	sea salt
1	egg (optional)
1/2 cup	finely ground dry whole grain bread crumbs
1 Tbsp.	virgin olive oil

Drain chick peas and reserve liquid. Grind in blender or food processor with a small amount of the reserved liquid. Try to use as little liquid as possible, but grind until fine. Add remaining ingredients by hand or use plastic blade in food processor. Form into 1 1/2 inch balls or patties. Place on ungreased baking sheet and bake in pre-heated 350° F oven for 15 minutes covered with foil, and another 10 minutes without.

To Deep Fry—Omit the bread crumbs from the patties. You can use the crumbs to coat them. Heat oil to 370°F and deep fry until golden on each side.

Tahini Sauce

1/2 cup	tahini
1/4 cup	yogurt
1/4 cup	fresh lemon juice
1/4 tsp.	sea salt
1/4 tsp.	ground cumin or more to taste
1/8 tsp.	ground cayenne or other hot pepper(optional)
3 Tbsp.	virgin olive oil
	Water to give pouring consistency

Blend first 7 ingredients together, add water as needed to make pouring consistency. It should be just diluted enough to pour slowly, like pancake batter.

Heat pita bread for 5 minutes to open pocket. Cut in half or cut end off, form pocket with hands. Stuff 1/4 full with shredded lettuce, sliced or diced tomatoes, green onion, cucumber. Add two or more cooked falafel patties, lettuce, and cover with sauce. Serve immediately. Chopped fresh mint can be added to the lettuce.

Pita Bread

Using a recipe for wholewheat bread that calls for 7 to 8 cups of flour, make the bread omiting most or all of the oil. After punching down, divide dough into balls the size of golf balls or a little larger. Roll into circles 1/4 inch thick and about 5 inches across. Bake on ungreased baking sheets for 8 minutes in a pre-heated 475° F oven.

START SMALL

Chickpeas, beans, lentils blend easily with ground meats. Just cook them and mash them and add them to your favorite ground meat recipe. They can be used in meat loaf, burgers, stuffed cabbage or peppers, lasagna, spaghetti, tacos, burritos, enchiladas, the list is endless. This will give the taste of ground meat and less calories and fat and more fiber than only meat would. Remember to add more seasoning when "enriching" ground meats with beans. *The World's Oldest Health Plan Recipe Companion* has many recipes for using part or all beans in your usual family recipes plus many new exciting recipes.

NUTRITIONAL VALUES

Canned Cooked Chick Peas or Garbanzo Beans (100 grams or 3 1/2 oz.)
  179 calories
  2.4 g fat
  10.2 g protein
  75 mg calcium
  54 mg magnesium
  3 mg iron.

Medium Fat Hamburger (100 grams or 3 1/2 oz.)
  224 calories
  14.5 g fat
  21.8 g protein
  6 mg calcium
  18 mg magnesium
  22 mg iron[5]

BEANS

. . . brought beds, basins, and earthen vessels, wheat, barley, meal, parched grain, beans and lentils, honey and curds and sheep and cheese

*from the herd, for David and the people with him to eat . . . .*2 Samuel 17:28–29 a (RSV)

Beans are mentioned in the Bible, mainly because they were considered a necessary foodstuff, and were part of the daily food. Ezekiel used them in his flour as God commanded him to do. They were grown as a crop to be used as vegetables, dried and used in the winter time or ground and mixed with grain flour for bread.

It is the Hebrew *Pol* that was grown. This translates most closely as the Broad Bean, *Faba vulgaris*.[6] Some botanists prefer to translate *Pol*, from the Hebrew as *Vicia fabia*[7], which is more like our green bean. It is the seed of the green or other beans that are allowed to stay on the plant and mature, and then dry that is mostly used. Beans were fed to the horses as well as to people, and the stalks were fed to camels. Kidney beans are the main beans used in the Middle East today, although there are also Chick Peas, black beans, turtle beans, lentils, soy beans, and many other varieties in general use.

CLEANING BEANS

Before soaking beans they should be well cleaned. Remove all sticks, dirt, and rocks before rinsing them. This is usually done by pouring the beans into an open hand a handful at a time and looking for dirt, rocks, and sticks. Or spread them on a baking sheet and go over them. Then rinse the beans with clear, cool water. Cover the beans with water and stir them with a wooden spoon or your hand to dissolve any dirt and rinse off any other matter. Cover them with water and pour it out until the water runs clear, this may take one time or many times.

NO SOAK BEANS

Red and green lentils, mung and aduki beans do not need to be soaked before cooking. They will expand to two or three times their size so enough water must be added when cooking to account for this. These beans can be cooked in 20 minutes to an hour.

SOAKED BEANS

Most other beans should be soaked before cooking if using the traditional method of cooking. These include kidney, pinto, garbanzo or chick peas, peas, lima, black-eyed peas, navy, black, turtle, and soy beans, etc. Cover the beans with water two to three times the volume of the beans, etc. One cup (250 mL) of beans should be soaked in 2 to 3 cups (500 to 750 mL) water.

Put them in a large vessel. This can be a pottery or glass bowl, stainless steel pot, plastic bowl or storage container, or enamel pot or bowl. Do not use aluminum or copper for this. Cover the beans with at least twice as much water as beans. The large beans will take three times as much water. If you add too much water while soaking it is never a problem; too little water will be. The soaking water is great for watering plants. Soy beans can ferment easily in hot weather so they should be soaked in a cool place.

Soak the beans for 6 to 8 hours or overnight. It is best for the nutritional value if the beans are cooked as soon as they are fully re-hydrated. Do not allow the beans to give off bubbles as this could mean that they are beginning to ferment and give off gas, a product of the breakdown of the sugars and starches. When soaking soy beans for making tofu, over soaked beans will yield less tofu and lower protein quality.

SOAKING OVERNIGHT

Cover the legumes with 2 to 3 times more cool fresh water than volume of beans. Allow to soak in cool place. For soy beans and lima beans soak in the refrigerator if it is very hot inside to prevent fermentation. Soak for up to 6 hours, or until rehydrated.

SOAKING ADDITIONS

Garlic, bay leaf, pepper corns, onions, cloves, chives can be added while soaking. Never add salt, lemon, or tomatoes!

COOKING

Pour off soaking water and add fresh water, at least 2 to 3 times the volume of the beans. The same things can be added while cooking as while soaking. NEVER add salt while cooking.

QUICK SOAK METHOD

Boil 3 times the amount of water as beans. Slowly add beans so that the water continues to boil. Cover and boil hard for 2 or 3 minutes depending on the size of the bean. Turn off heat and leave covered for up to 2 hours. Cook as usual. Do not add salt!

REGULAR COOKING METHOD

Soak overnight in double or triple the amount of water. Change to fresh water double or triple the volume of beans; this is only necessary if beans give you gas, the sugars change during soaking and can cause gas if left in the water. Use soaking water if desired.

Bring to a boil over medium heat, immediately reduce heat to simmer or fast simmer once it has reached the boiling point. Covering is optional, but suggested if you are leaving the house or sleeping, this will allow the water to evaporate less. Using a hard boil may cause the beans to split apart, the skins to come off, or the beans to get mushy; this is acceptable for soup or refried beans, but not for bean salad or other recipes where the beans will be eaten whole. **Never, Never** add salt!

PRESSURE COOKER METHOD

Soak beans overnight or don't soak. Wash beans and pick over, place in pressure cooker, cover with water and at least 2.5 cm (1 in) more water than called for usually. If soaked add 2 to 3 times the water, if unsoaked add 3 to 4 times the water since you must add the water to rehydrate the beans and be absorbed during cooking as well. Add bay leaf, pepper corns, garlic, cloves, onion, or browned onions and garlic, carrot, celery, lemon peel or slices, fresh tomatoes, and a piece of kombu. Kombu is a type of deep sea kelp that can prevent the beans from giving you gas once they are cooked. It can be found in many Japanese, Korean, or natural food stores. Oil the seal of the pressure cooker according to the directions. Cover and place over high heat (for aluminum) or medium/high heat (for stainless). Bring to pressure, when rocker starts, begin timing and lower heat. Or follow directions in cooker booklet. When time is up remove from heat and set in bowl or sink of cold water to cool the pot and allow the top to come off, you may try running cold water over the lid and sides of the pot, but not over the valves. As long as the lid stays on the cooking will continue until the pot cools completely. If beans are not fully cooked return to heat and continue cooking for 10 more minutes and then check again. Do not use pressure cooker for small peas, lentils, or dal since they may foam up and clog the air vent and cause an explosion. Do not add salt.

SALT AND BEANS

Adding salt to beans while cooking can make them stay firm and never fully cook. Once the beans have become soft salt may be added. Even the salt in prepared tomato juice can be enough to prevent them from softening. If you are using chicken, beef, fish, or vegetable stock for cooking the beans make sure that it is unsalted.

COOKING TIMES

Type of Bean	Regular Cooker	Pressure Cooker
	(soaked)	(unsoaked)
black	1 1/2–2 hrs	30–35 min
black-eyed peas	1 1/2–2 hrs	20–25 min
chick peas (garbanzo)	2 1/2–4 hrs	20–45 min
great northern (white)	1 1/2–2 hrs	25 min
kidney (red or white)	1 1/2–2 hrs	25–30 min
lentils	up to 1 hr	No!
lima (large)	1 1/2–2 hrs	25 min
lima (small)	1 hr	20 min
pea beans (white, navy)	1 1/2–2 hrs	25 min
pinto	1 1/2–2 hrs	25–30 min
soy (yellow, black)	2–3 hrs	25 min
split peas	45–60 min	No!

COOKING HINTS

Oil the upper edge of the inside of the pot to prevent the beans from foaming over. Stir beans while cooking to prevent sticking and promote even cooking, this is not necessary in a pressure cooker. Use the size of element that is the same size as the pot for most efficient cooking.

Bean Salad

Lightly steamed green and yellow beans cut in 1 inch pieces, kidney or black beans, chick peas, sliced green onions, slivered red or green peppers. Dressing: mix together juice of one lemon, add two to three times as much olive oil, small pinch of cumin powder or to taste, twice as much ground thyme as cumin, shoyu or soy sauce to taste (optional). Toss with bean mixture and chill before serving.

Use the proportions depending on the number of people served. Left-overs can be frozen in serving sized portions. Frozen salad is great to take on a picnic, it should be thawed yet still cool by lunch time.

Baked Beans

2 cups	beans, navy, pinto, or baby lima
	water to cook
1	onion
1 clove	garlic
2 tsp.	oil or butter
1/2 cup	tomato paste or puree
1 cup	molasses

Cook beans in water following one of the methods given above. Chop onions and garlic and sauté until brown in the oil or butter. Mix remaining ingredients with beans and onions and bake in covered casserole or bean pot in a 375° F oven for up to one hour. Or cook all day in a slow cooker.

Variations—Sauté 1/2 chopped green pepper with the onions and garlic, 1 tablespoon of dried herbs such as thyme, savory, or marjoram, or 1 teaspoon of dry mustard powder can be added when baking.

Other vegetables can be sautéed with the onions such as chopped celery, grated carrots, chopped mushrooms, or hot peppers such as red or green chile or jalapeño.

Bean Dip

2 cups	cooked beans, reserve the water
1	small white onion, chopped
1 clove	garlic, pressed
1/4 cup	virgin olive oil
2 tsp.	tarragon vinegar or apple cider vinegar
1/4 tsp.	tarragon
1/2 to 1 cup	mayonnaise or tofu mayonnaise

Sauté onions and garlic in small amount of oil until soft if desired or use raw for a stronger taste. Blend beans, onions, garlic, oil, vinegar, tarragon, and 1/2 cup mayonnaise. Add more water or mayonnaise to obtain desired texture. Serve with corn or tortilla chips.

Frijoles Refritos

	Cooked beans, pinto or black, reserve the water
2 tsp.	butter or oil
2	green onions OR 1/4 cooking onion

1 clove	garlic
1/8	green chile pepper (optional)
1/4 tsp. each:	cumin and chili powder
	grated jack or farmers cheese.

Sauté onions, garlic, pepper until soft. Mash beans with seasonings using some of the reserved water to obtain desired texture. I always leave some of the beans partially mashed for texture. Stir to heat thoroughly, then add grated cheese after last stirring. Serve when cheese melts.

This can also be rolled in a tortilla and smothered in salsa or chile sauce. Bean burritos are great for breakfast.

Lentil Burgers or Balls

1 cup	green lentils soaked overnight in 2 cups water
1/2 cup	water
1 large	bay leaf
2 tsp.	butter
1 tsp.	oil
1 small	cooking onion
1–2 cloves	garlic
1 tsp. each:	dry celery leaves, thyme, sage
1/2 tsp.	sea salt (optional)
1/2 tsp.	dry mustard
1 tsp.	soy sauce
1/4 cup	chopped sunflower or sesame seeds
2 tsp.	corn or arrowroot starch
3/4 cup	finely ground dry whole grain bread crumbs

Cook lentils, water, and bay leaf by bringing to boil then turning down heat to simmer. Simmer covered for 7 to 10 minutes or until just tender.

Sauté onions and garlic until brown in butter and oil. When cool enough to handle mix lentils, onions, and remaining ingredients. Oil or butter hands and form into patties or balls. Sauté in a mixture of oil and butter until cooked through. Or bake in 375°F oven for about 15 minutes.

Burgers can be served in whole grain buns garnished with lettuce and mayonnaise or your choice of garnish. These taste remarkably like most other burgers. When I was teaching vegetarian cooking classes one of my students served these to her family and her six year old son refused to eat them because he was a vegetarian. He thought his mother had flipped her lid and started serving him meat.

Lentil Balls can be served as a main dish or party dish with mushroom gravy over them. They go well with brown rice or whole grain noodles and a green salad.

Humus or Homos

1 cup	chick peas, soaked overnight and cooked
2	green onions, white parts only
2 Tbsp.	lemon juice
1 Tbsp.	virgin olive oil
1/4 tsp.	ground cumin
1/4–1/8 tsp.	cayenne pepper
1–2 cloves	garlic, finely chopped or pressed

Drain chick peas and reserve water. Place all ingredients in blender or food processor and blend until smooth or the consistency of peanut butter. Use the reserved water to give the exact consistency. I like it with a few lumps. Serve with Tahini Sauce and hot sauce.

Tahini Sauce

1/4–1/3 cup	tahini
juice of half lemon	
water to thin	

Combine in blender until the consistency of pancake batter.

Hot Sauce

1 Tbsp.	hot pepper finely chopped
4	green onions finely chopped
4 Tbsp.	fresh parsley finely chopped
2 Tbsp.	virgin olive oil
2 tsp.	ground cumin

Mix together and serve with Humus and Tahini.

Method of Serving—On a plate spoon on Humus and smooth it flat. Pour the Tahini sauce from a cup or pitcher in a spiral starting at the middle and going out. Place a scoop of the hot sauce in the center. This can be served on individual salad plates or one large plate as a party appetizer.

Method of Eating—Humus and Tahini is eaten with whole wheat pita bread. A piece of the bread is torn off and used as a scoop to scoop up a small amount of Humus, Tahini, and hot sauce for each bite.

Vegetable sticks can also be used as the scoops. Celery, carrot, turnip, jicama, green onion, green or red pepper sticks, etc.

Tabouli (Salad)

1 cup (250 mL)	bulgar wheat
2 cups (500 mL)	boiling water
1 bunch	parsley, finely chopped
4 Tbp. (60 mL)	dried mint leaves*
1/2	Spanish onion
2	tomatoes, finely chopped OR
1 small	sweet red pepper, cut in slivers
1/2 –1	lemon, juiced
	olive oil

Pour boiling water over bulgar and mint and cover and leave for up to 1 hour. Toss with remaining vegetables. Measure lemon juice and add twice as much olive oil as you use lemon juice, mix together and pour over salad, toss and chill. Traditionally this is made with more parsley in some areas and more bulgar in other areas, so the amounts are up to the eater.

*Fresh mint leaves can be used and chopped with the parsley, not added with the hot water, that is only if using dried mint.

Eating the bulgar and chick peas with the tahini gives complete protein and also a complete meal. Often tabouli is a good dish for pot luck suppers since it is healthful and colorful, and will not go off like mayonnaise salads might. Often cooked chick peas are added to tabouli when it is not served with humus.

SOY BEANS

Soy beans or soya beans are the most widely used and most versatile beans in the world today. They have been used for human and animal food for centuries. Although they grow all over the world, the Orient has made them well known. In China soy beans were traditionally called the "cow that has no bone" because they were used to make milk, cheese, meat substitutes, and fiber, as well as forming the basis of condiments such as soy sauce and miso paste.

Soy beans have the wonderful property of being able to take on the taste of whatever is mixed with them.

HENRY FORD AND SOY BEANS

Once when I was visiting at the Henry Ford Museum/Greenfield Village in Dearborn, Michigan, I met a man who was involved in the media during the early 30's. He told me of a banquet that was given by Henry Ford where all the courses were made of soy beans. Apparently Mr. Ford was very involved in promoting soy beans and believed that they were the food of the future and the most economical and practical food around. He was so interested in soy beans that he even had them spun into fibers to try to make seat covers of them for the first Ford cars. Many foods are now "engineered" from soy beans, but I prefer to eat them in the more simple ways.

TOFU AND SOY BEANS

Tofu is the most commonly known soy bean food. Tofu is often called Chinese bean curd or bean curd. Tofu is made from soy milk that has been curded with minerals in much the same way that milk is curded with acid to make cheese. Tofu is not fermented, it is curded, pressed, and stored in cold water, and eaten while still fresh. Soy milk is fully cooked before it is made into tofu, it is not made from raw beans. Soy beans contain complete protein for human needs, they are the only beans that do. Most other beans need to be combined with seeds, grains, or nuts to form complete protein. This was shown by Nevin Scrimshaw and Vernon Young of M.I.T. (Massachusetts Institute of Technology) in their work published in 1979, now considered the basis for the new method of determining utilization of all proteins by humans.[8]

TOFU IN THE BIBLE

. . . she brought him curds in a lordly bowl. Judges 5:25b (RSV)

Tofu is not mentioned in the Bible as such. Beans are mentioned and curds are mentioned (sometimes "curds" are translated as "butter"). It is generally thought that the curds refer to animal milk, but we really do not know for sure. This is another time when the real translation is dependent on the knowledge of the translator. Soy beans have been known for over 3,000 years in the Orient. According to William Shurtleff founder of the Soyfoods Center in Lafayette, California there is a record of soy bean use written about in the *Book of Odes* dated 1100 B.C. in China. A mural was uncovered in a cave in China dating to A.D. 24 to A.D. 220 that depicts the manufacture of tofu, also called bean curd. We know that trade routes went to the Orient in Old Testament times . . . it is certainly possible that tofu was known to fashionable Greeks, Romans, and Jews.

NUTRITIONAL VALUES

Soy Beans (1 cup [180 g] cooked)
>234 calories
>19.8 g protein
>10.3 g fat
>19.4 g carbohydrate
>3.2 g fiber
>131 mg calcium
>322 mg phosphorus
>4.9 mg iron
>4 mg sodium
>972 mg potassium
>50 I.U. vitamin A
>0.38 mg B1
>0.16 mg B2
>1.1 mg B3

Tofu (3 1/2 oz. [100 g])
>72 calories
>7.8 g protein
>0.1 g fiber
>128 mg calcium
>111 mg magnesium
>126 mg potassium
>1.9 mg iron[9]

Tofu is a low calorie protein source food, it also contains no cholesterol, or saturated fatty acids, since it is made entirely from vegetable protein.

TOFU THE WONDER FOOD

Tofu can be made to taste like almost any thing you want it to taste like, whether it's meat, cheese, cream, eggs, cream cheese, or pudding. It takes on the taste of whatever you mix with it. If you replace half of the meat in a meat loaf with mashed tofu and add more seasoning, you will have a meat loaf that is moister and richer with less calories and less cholesterol, with all the taste of meat loaf.

I call it "wonder food" because when I bring food to friends' homes they always say, "I wonder if it is tofu or something else?" Usually they can't tell if it is or isn't tofu.

The tofu hot dogs were one of the manufactured products that nobody realized were tofu. I put them on the grill next to the expensive Gourmet hot dogs at a friend's barbeque and kept a close eye on them. When the hot dogs were served everybody thought they had the Gourmet hot dogs, I was the only one who knew which were which, and nobody believed me. They thought I ate all the tofu hot dogs. There were 6 of them and I certainly didn't eat all of them, but they couldn't think that they hadn't been able to tell them from regular, let alone Gourmet, hot dogs.

KINDS OF TOFU

There are several kinds of tofu sold and eaten in North America. They are named after certain characteristics that distinguish the texture or the curding agent. The traditional Chinese type is found in most grocery stores, Chinese markets, and most places where Chinese vegetables are sold. It is a soft curd made with the mineral calcium sulfate and generally contains 6 to 7% protein. It is used in stir fry, scrambled tofu, blended into puddings, mixed with grated cheese as an extender, and made into cream sauces and desserts. Silken tofu is a very soft Japanese type of tofu that is the equivalent of curds and whey in one smooth silky block. It is most often sold in a small non-refrigerated carton on the shelf of supermarkets and Japanese markets. It is formed in the packing box and does not have the whey removed so it has less percentage of protein per weight. It is easy to store since it doesn't need to be kept cold. It can be used in Japanese recipes calling for Silken tofu or blended into shakes and made into sauces. It is very custard-like and is not used for stir fry. Some silken tofu may be curded with GDL or glucona delta-lactone.

A firmer tofu, sometimes called Japanese style tofu, that is curded with magnesium chloride (or nigari) is sold in most health food stores and some groceries as firm tofu and is best for slicing or cubing and frying. It is great in stir fry, or it can be marinated and broiled. Grated and/or crumbled it can be mixed with grated cheese or ground meats as an extender or meat substitute. It has 7 to 8% protein depending on the beans. Another type of tofu gaining prominence is made from a combination of the two minerals and is even more firm, having up to 14% protein. The firm tofu can be vacuum packed for longer shelf life and easier shipping and storage. Because it does not have to be packed in water it is easier to handle in the store and at home.

A LOW-FAT PARTY

A low-fat party would include tofu dips and vegetables, whole grain crackers and tofu pate, and corn chips with bean dip. Canapes could be made of bean sandwiches cut out with little cookie cutters. Humus and tahini served with whole grain pita bread wedges surrounding it would add variety and an international flavor. Tofu spread made with chives and garlic could be arranged with melba toast or bagel chips. A dip made with tofu and fruit could be the hub for a wheel of fruit spokes. Use strawberries, cantaloupe, green grapes, pineapple, kiwi, watermelon, apple slices dipped in diluted lemon juice to preserve the color, etc. Decorate the table with flowers, fruit, or a seasonal or theme centerpiece.

FAT REPLACEMENT

Using tofu to replace high fat items like cream cheese, whipping cream, custards, mayonnaise, and dips is a smart way to reduce animal fat in your diet. Because it is not processed with chemicals and preservatives which might be harmful to your health like processed foods are it will be healthful in 2 ways: reducing animal fat and reducing chemicals and preservatives. For recipes using tofu to replace the fat and puréed fruit to replace the fat and sugar see *The World's Oldest Health Plan Recipe Companion.*

We who are the stewards of the foods and meals in our houses have the responsibility to bring healthier foods and lifestyles to our family. Using soy bean products is a good way to start. Just by adding more vegetables of all kinds and reducing animal fats you will be on your way to better health.

FROZEN TOFU

Tofu can be frozen, thawed, and squeezed, then crumbled and cooked like hamburger for casseroles, chili, soups, and many Mexican dishes. If it is browned in a small amount of oil along with chopped onion and garlic, and perhaps grated carrots, it will have the same texture, color, and taste as browned beef.

Eggless Salad

8 oz.	tofu
1 Tbsp.	finely chopped fresh parsley
4	finely chopped green onions
3/4 tsp.	turmeric powder
3/4 tsp.	ground celery seeds
2 tsp.	dijon mustard OR
1/4 tsp.	dry mustard
1 tsp.	salt, or to taste
	Tofu mayo to taste

Wrap tofu in several layers of toweling and press water out with a weight. Cube tofu. Combine all ingredients and add mayo to taste. Let set for 10 minutes for flavors to meld. Serves 4–5 as a salad with lettuce, cukes, and tomatoes or as a sandwich with whole grain bread and lettuce.

Keeps for several days covered in the refrigerator. Drain off water that separates before using.

This salad can be made with 1 piece of tofu and 2 eggs or 1 piece of tofu and 1 can of drained tuna fish or salmon. The tofu will pick up the flavor of the other ingredients and the entire salad will taste like egg, tuna, or salmon, whichever is used.

NB: Start with less celery seeds and turmeric the first time, to adjust to their strong flavors.

Mayonnaise

8 oz. (225 G)	tofu
1/4 cup (60 mL)	cooking or olive oil or a mixture of the two
1/4 tsp. (1 mL)	salt
1/4 tsp. (1 mL)	paprika
1/2 tsp. (2 mL)	dijon mustard OR
1/4 tsp. (1 mL)	dry mustard
1 Tbsp. (15 mL)	each–lemon juice and apple cider vinegar

Wrap tofu in several layers of toweling to drain. Place all ingredients except tofu in blender or food processor. Blend on medium speed or process until well mixed. Remove cap and add tofu pieces until desired consistency is obtained. Makes 1 cup (250 mL). Keeps in the refrigerator for 2 weeks if covered. Pour out water that may separate out during storage.

This is a no-cholesterol, low-calorie mayonnaise. It can be used in any instance where mayonnaise would be used. If the water is not fully drained off of the tofu it may soak into the bread of a sandwich. I generally keep the bread separate and then add the mayo filling just before eating.

This mayonnaise can be added to yogurt to make low calorie dips.

One tablespoon regular mayonnaise has 57 calories, 4.9 g fat, and 4 g cholesterol. One tablespoon tofu mayonnaise has 41 calories, 2 g fat, and 0 cholesterol.

Vegetables With Cream Sauce

8–10 oz.	tofu
4 Tbsp.	lemon juice
2 tsp.	grated or zested lemon peel
1/4 tsp.	ground nutmeg

Wrap tofu in several layers of toweling to drain off all excess water. Blend or process all ingredients except nutmeg. It should have the consistency of pancake batter or thick cream. Serve over steamed vegetables with a grating of nutmeg over it. Serves 4–5.

Use cauliflower, broccoli, asparagus, green beans, Brussels Sprouts, zuccini, summer squash, or spaghetti squash. Lightly steam the vegetables until they are crisp tender, immediately pour over the sauce and serve. This could also be used as the base of a veggie and cream sauce to be served over pasta.

Tofu Bean Paté

2 cups (500 mL)	tofu
1 cup (250 mL)	cooked beans like kidney, aduki, or black
1 Tbsp. (15 mL)	soy sauce or tamari*
1 Tbsp. (15 mL)	dried whole leaf thyme
1	large cooking onion
1 clove	garlic, or more to taste
1 Tbsp. (15 mL)	cooking oil
	grinding of black pepper to taste

Wrap tofu in several layers of toweling to drain. Finely chop the onion and garlic and sauté in the oil until deep brown. Stir often. Mash, blend, or process part of the beans and tofu together until very smooth. Mash in the remaining ingredients.

Oil a 6x10 inch (16x25 cm) pan lightly. Spoon paté into pan and bake in a preheated 350°F (180°C) oven for 1 hour or until lightly browned.

*The original recipe used 1–2 tablespoons of dark miso paste in place of the soy sauce. It is richer if you use this, but it is not as readily available as soy sauce. Most health food, gourmet, or Oriental stores carry miso paste, just make sure that there is no MSG in it.

Cool and serve with hot or dijon mustard on whole grain crackers.

A cup of finely chopped or grated carrots and celery can also be added with the onions and garlic for a sweeter pate. Mushrooms can also be chopped and added to the onions and garlic while sautéing.

This is a great no-cholesterol way to have paté for a party or just use it for your dinner along with some freshly baked whole grain bread and a very green salad. Serve it on a plate with thinly sliced cucumbers, a sprig of parsley or watercress, some steamed asparagus or green beans, and carrot flowers.

This also makes a great lunch on dark bread with hot mustard and dill pickles. Remember to keep it cool.

A fancier version of this paté was served in Santa Fe at the opening reception of a well known artist. Rich and I knew it wasn't liver, but nobody else did. You should have heard the comments around the table as grown men elbowed each other to keep a place in front of the serving area so they could eat this paté. They were saying things like: "This must have taken $40 worth of liver to make this," "Have you ever seen so much paté at a party?" "I haven't had such good homemade paté in years." Rich tried to tell one of them that it was tofu and they laughed at him. There was one man who heaved a great sigh and began to eat the paté with the same gusto as the others. He was a vegetarian and was eager to eat it.

Bean Sandwich

          whole grain bread
          lima or other cooked beans
          green onions
          slivered red peppers
          tofu mayonnaise to moisten.

Lightly mash the beans add chopped green onions, peppers, and enough mayonnaise to moisten. Serve open faced on a plate garnished with fresh parsley. Grated carrots or cucumbers can be added. This is a gourmet treat for special dinners or a leisurely brunch.

Crudités (Vegetables and Dips)

Arrange veggies on a plate in a pleasing and eye catching manner. Try to alternate the colors in some way. Often a wheel and spoke arrangement is nice with the dip at the center and the veggies forming the spokes. Put only one kind of veggie in each spoke alternating the colors. Green, red, green, orange, white, green, brown, etc. would give the right feel. Try to include as many types of vegetables as possible like: mushrooms (nice with a curry dip), carrot straws or circles, cucumbers, red and green peppers, broccoli, cauliflower, celery, squash or turnip sticks, green onions, green or yellow beans, zucchini, jicama, sweet potato, watercress, beets, parsley, etc.

The dips can be different combinations of ingredients. Tofu dip with dill and garlic, tofu mayonnaise and yogurt with cumin and basil, sour cream and tofu dip with curry, yogurt dip with chopped cucumbers and onions with cumin seeds, blue cheese and tofu mayonnaise dip. Try to be creative and invent your own combinations.

Tofu Dip

3/4–1 cup	soft or Chinese style tofu
2–3 Tbsp.	lemon juice
1/4–1/2 tsp.	garlic powder OR
2 small cloves	fresh, minced
2 tsp.	dried dill weed OR
1/2 bunch	fresh, chopped
1/2 tsp.	salt or soy sauce, optional

Wrap tofu in several layers of toweling to drain off excess water, leave for 10 minutes. Blend all ingredients together on medium speed. Serves 4–6.

To use for vegetables or bread sticks, the dip should be thinner than for using with potato or corn chips.

A richer dip can be made by adding 2–3 Tbsp. olive or other pure vegetable oil during blending. This will be like a sour cream dip with less calories, no cholesterol, and less fat. Substitute chives for the herbs and serve this on a baked potato.

Variations—Try other herbs such as sweet basil, tarragon, thyme, or oregano. 1/4 tsp. curry power could be used instead of herbs. Curried dip goes well with mushrooms and cauliflower.

Tofu Herbal Spread

1 cup (250 mL)	regular or firm tofu
2 Tbsp.(30 mL)	lemon juice
1/8 cup (25 mL)	fresh dill, basil, or mint
OR 1 Tbsp.(15 mL)	dried herbs
1 tsp. (5 mL)	dijon mustard
	salt to taste
1/4 cup (50 mL)	olive oil, optional

Wrap tofu in several layers of toweling to drain for 15 minutes. A weight should be placed on regular tofu to extract more water. Generally a wooden bread board can be used. I often put the tofu in a colander with a plate resting on the tofu and a sealed jar of water on top to act as the weight.

Blend or process all ingredients except for the lemon juice. Add juice to obtain the desired consistency for spreading on a cracker or bread.

If the optional oil is used this can taste just like cream cheese, and also have the same consistency and mouth feel. It will, however, have less than 1/5 the calories. This is excellent for people who are on a low fat, non-dairy, or low or no cholesterol diet.

Scrambled Tofu

1	cooking onion or 3 green onions
4	fresh mushrooms
1 clove	garlic or more to taste
1 piece	fresh broccoli
1/2	fresh sweet red pepper
1 lb.(454 g)	tofu
1/2 tsp.(2 mL)	soy sauce or to taste
	oil for cooking

Wrap tofu in several layers of toweling to drain off excess water. Slice onions into crescents lengthwise, slice mushrooms, chop or press garlic, sliver the broccoli stems, cut flowers into flowerettes, sliver the red pepper.

Heat enough oil to cover the bottom of a wok or heavy frying pan. Sauté onions, mushrooms, garlic, and broccoli stems until onions are transparent. Add broccoli flowerettes and red peppers, stir and cook for 2 more minutes. Mash drained tofu and soy sauce together. Reduce heat and add tofu, stir and heat until tofu is heated through. Serves 3–4 as a main dish.

This tastes like scrambled eggs. It also has the mouth feel of scrambled eggs. There is no cholesterol in tofu since it is made from only soy beans and is excellent for people on a no or low cholesterol diet. This can be eaten for breakfast, lunch, dinner, or brunch. It can also be served as a side dish vegetable with any meal.

One egg has 5.6 g fat, 274 mg cholesterol, and 79 calories. 3 1/2 oz. tofu has 4.2 g fat, 0 cholesterol, and 72 calories.[9] 31/2 oz. tofu served this way would be enough for one person when eaten for breakfast with a slice of whole grain bread.

Try several different combinations of vegetables such as: cauliflower, mushroom, onions, curry powder; red and green peppers, onions, tomatoes, mushrooms, oregano; cabbage, onions, mushrooms, poppy seeds; zucchini, onions, mushrooms.

Tofu Tomato Surprise*

1/4 cup	cooking oil
2 cloves	fresh garlic
32 oz.	fresh tofu
16 oz.	spaghetti sauce
1/4 tsp.	pepper sauce (like Tabasco Sauce) or to taste
1/4 tsp.	salt or soy sauce or to taste
	grinding of black pepper
1	bunch green onions
3–4 springs	fresh parsley, coriander, or dill

Wrap tofu in several layers of toweling to drain off water, leave for 15 minutes while you prepare onions and herbs.

Clean onions and cut into 1 1/2 inch pieces, including the tops. Keep the white separate from the green. Cut pieces lengthwise into slivers making 2 or 3 cuts in each piece. Coarsely chop the fresh herbs.

Heat oil in wok or heavy frying pan and sauté the garlic cloves until transparent, remove them to prevent burning, discard.

Cut drained tofu into 1/2 inch cubes and sauté in hot oil, gently turning each piece after it has browned, about 7–12 minutes. Continue sautéing until all are golden brown. Drain off excess oil. Add spaghetti sauce and carefully stir to coat all the tofu pieces. Add all the whites of the onions and 1/3 of the green pieces, lower heat, stir and simmer over low heat for 3 minutes or longer. The longer you simmer it the more the tofu will absorb the sauce. Add 1/3 of the greens and 1/2 of the herbs, stir, and cook for an additional 5 minutes. Serve garnished with the remaining onion tops and herbs. Serves 4. This is good served as a main dish protein or served with pasta.

*This recipe was designed by Stephen Yu who used to run the largest tofu shop in Toronto. I can't take credit for it.

Tofu Dinner Loaf

2 Tbsp.	cooking oil (optional, see note)
2	onions
2	carrots
2 stalks	celery
2 cloves	garlic
1 1/2 cup	cooked whole grains such as rice, buckwheat, millet (the grains are optional)
3/4 cup	dry bread crumbs
1 lb	tofu
1–2 Tbp.	miso paste
5 sprigs	fresh dill OR
2–3 Tbsp.	dried herbs such as thyme, marjoram, tarragon, basil

Grate or finely chop first 4 vegetables. Heat oil over medium heat and sauté the vegetables, stirring constantly, until deep brown, but not burnt.

Drain tofu in colander. Using a potato masher, mash tofu and all ingredients together. Or blend half the tofu until smooth and mash in remaining ingredients. Or using the plastic blade in a food processor, process tofu and add remaining ingredients until mixed. Spoon into oiled loaf pan and bake at 350° F for one hour or until lightly browned. Serves 4–6 as a main protein serving.

NOTE: You can eliminate the oil by braising the chopped veggies in water with 2 Tbsp. low sodium soy sauce added. Eliminate the miso paste.

The sautéing of the vegetables gives body to the loaf. The vegetables can be varied depending on how much body you want. This is one of those recipes that can be changed according to your mood or stock of food in the house.

Variations—Substitute rolled oats for the grains and dried bread crumbs. Use a small can of tomato paste, and substitute 2 tsp. basil and 1 tsp. oregano for the dill. This is just like the meat loaf that mother used to make except that it isn't meat. You could also add chopped green peppers.

My favorite is made from tofu, tarragon, onions, garlic, carrots, celery, cashew or hazelnut pieces lightly dry toasted, and miso paste. I serve it with fresh mushroom gravy over it and a baked potato with tofu sour cream and a green salad.

1/2 and 1/2: you might want to make this with half tofu and half lean ground beef and make a more traditional meat loaf. Just remember when you are using tofu in a meat loaf as a fat and cholesterol reducer to add a little more seasoning, since tofu tends to absorb some of the flavors.

Stir Fry

2 Tbsp.	cooking oil
1	onion
2 stalks	broccoli
6–8	mushrooms
1/2	sweet red pepper
1–2 cloves	garlic
1 inch slice	fresh ginger, grated
2 tsp.	tamari, shoyu, or other soy sauce
1 heaping Tbsp.	corn or arrowroot starch
3/4 cup	water
more	water

Keep all veggies separate. Cut onions in crescents, slice broccoli stems or cut in matchsticks, separate the flowers into bite-sized pieces. Slice or cube the mushrooms into bite-sized pieces. Cut peppers in matchstick pieces. Mix soy sauce, ginger, finely chopped garlic, corn starch, and 3/4 cup water together and stir.

Heat wok or heavy frying pan with high sides, when hot add oil. Begin to add the veggies one at a time and stir after each addition. Add the broccoli stems and onions, stir and cook until the stems just start to turn darker green. Add mushrooms, stir, and cook until they begin to change color. Working quickly add the flowers and red peppers, stir. Stir the sauce and add it immediately and keep stirring until it begins to thicken. Add more water about a 1/4 cup at a time as needed to keep the sauce from getting too thick. When sauce is thickened serve veggies over brown rice or whole grain noodles.

Any combination of veggies can be used. Snow peas, carrot circles, green peppers, zucchini, squash, sweet potato, green and yellow beans, mushrooms, tomatoes, just mix and match according to what is in season or in your kitchen.

This can be Italian style stir fry vegetables if you substitute tomato juice for the water, and 2 tsp. oregano or Italian seasonings for the ginger.

Tofu can be added to this during the cooking. Or tofu can be very well drained, cubed, and browned in the oil and removed before starting the veggies. Add the tofu with the mushrooms.

NOTE: Start with veggies that take the longest to cook first and keep adding and stirring. Add a new veggie when the previous one begins to change color. Greens and sprouts go in last.

Almond Vegetables

Toast 1/2 to 1 cup blanched almonds in a dry pan over low heat until brown.

Stir fry according to the above recipe. Use a combination of onions, carrot wheels, green peppers, celery, mushrooms, and water chestnuts if available.

Use the same sauce. Add almonds just after sauce starts to thicken or place on top after the veggies are served.

TEMPEH

Tempeh is made from soy beans that are cooked and then inoculated with the spores of *Rhizopus oligosporus* and allowed to culture or ferment. Other beans and many grains can be used to make tempeh, as well as combinations of grains and beans. This is one of the vegetable foods that does allow the body to make vitamin B12, so it is one of the essential foods for strict vegetarians. It tastes almost exactly like meat because it is fermented. When it is breaded and coated with the proper spices and deep fried it can taste just like fried chicken. Of course the texture is not the same, but that is a small difference. Tempeh can be crumbled and cooked in the same way that ground meat can be and often can be used in the same recipes as ground meats. When it is browned with onions and garlic it is full bodied in taste and has the same tooth feel as meats and can be used in casseroles, loaves, tacos, burgers, "meat" pies, chili, soups, stews, moussaka, and many of the ways that ground meats are generally used.

Pot Pie

8 oz. (227 g)	tempeh
1 cup	dry red wine
2 tsp.	red wine vinegar
2 cloves	garlic
3 Tbsp.	virgin olive oil
2 tsp.	ground cumin
1 tsp.	prepared dijon mustard
1 Tbsp.	finely chopped fresh herbs such as savory, basil, or marjoram OR 2 tsp. dried

Cut tempeh into small cubes about 1/2 inch or so. Mix the remaining ingredients and marinate for 5 to 6 hours.

Prepare the crust for a two crust pie using milk or buttermilk in place of water. Use either all whole wheat or a combination of grains.

Drain the tempeh mixture for about 15–20 minutes reserve the liquid.

Filling

2 Tbsp. each	olive oil and butter
1 small	cooking onion, chopped
1 clove	garlic, chopped
1/2 cup	chopped or diced mushrooms
2 cups	chopped or diced assorted vegetables (celery, carrot, potato, turnip, peas, corn, cauliflower, broccoli, etc.)
3 Tbsp.	whole wheat bread flour
3/4 cup	water
1 tsp.	tamari, shoyu, or other soy sauce

Melt butter and oil together and sauté tempeh, onion, garlic, and mushrooms. Add flour and stir to toast. When lightly browned add marinade, remaining water, and tamari. Cook and stir until thickened. Add vegetables. Cool. Place in 10 inch pie crust, cover with top crust. Bake for 10 minutes in a 425°F oven, reduce heat to 375°F and continue baking for 40 minutes or until browned. Serves 4 as a main dish. Serve with a green salad dressed with olive oil and lemon.

Tempeh Loaf

2 Tbsp. each	butter and cold pressed oil
4 large cloves	garlic
1	cooking onion
1/2 lb.	mushrooms
1 lb. (454 g)	tempeh
2 stalks	celery including leaves
4 pieces	dry bread, crumbed
2 Tbsp.	red or brown miso
3	eggs or 1 cup tofu, blended
2 Tbsp.	dried thyme
	grinding of black pepper

Chop onions and garlic very fine. Melt butter and sauté onions and garlic until transparent. Chop mushrooms fine and add to onions and continue to sauté. Chop celery and add to vegetable mixture and sauté. Cut tempeh in 1 inch pieces and steam for 10 minutes. Finely chop tempeh and mix with other vegetables and bread crumbs. Blend eggs (or tofu), miso, thyme, and black pepper and mix with vegetable and crumb mixture. Butter a loaf pan and line with buttered waxed paper. (I use the butter wrappers that I have saved to line the loaf pan.) Press tempeh mixture into pan and bake at 375°F for 45–50 minutes or until brown.

Remove from oven and let sit for 10 minutes. Turn onto plate, slice and serve with mushroom gravy. It's great cold in a whole grain sandwich with dijon mustard, lettuce, and dill pickles. It should be kept refrigerated.

This same loaf can be made from different herbs for a change of taste. 1/2 cup tomato paste, basil, and oregano can also be used in place of the miso and thyme for a different taste. Be creative with the herbs and seasonings.

BEANS AND CHOLESTEROL

Beans have less calories, less fat, and more fiber than most animal products. They also have no cholesterol and are a good way to get protein in the daily diet, especially if one wants to lose weight. Men who have high cholesterol have been able to reduce it by 13% when eating 8 ounces of cooked beans a day for 21 days.[10] The triglyceride levels were reduced by 12% over the same period. This puts the good old bean in the miracle food catagory as far as most doctors are concerned. Now if a person were to eat beans instead of most meat they might not even get high cholesterol levels, and the levels that they did have would gradually lower to an acceptable level. Generally adding beans to a diet and reducing animal fats will allow weight loss. They generally suggest at least 1 cup of cooked beans at each meal.

THE LOWLY BEAN

I often eat beans for breakfast. So you can imagine my surprise when I was working as a volunteer in a food room helping to distribute food to the needy, and I found that nobody wanted to eat beans. I couldn't even give them away to people who had no food. The person I offered the can of beans to had no job, no money, no job skills, and a temporary place to live, but he wouldn't be caught dead eating beans, "poor peoples' food." How did beans get such bad press? Who told us that beans were poor peoples' food? Did this come about when times were hard and this was all people had? Or did some enterprising meat packer, or even a Government agency, tell us that eating meat was a status symbol, thereby implying that anything less was lowly?

But this is not new. The Greeks and Romans wouldn't eat beans because they caused flatulence and were thought to increase the sex drive. Even then there was predjudice against the foods of average people. The Hebrews did eat beans and simple foods and they are still a thriving culture, the same as they were in those days. The Greeks and Romans ate rich foods and they didn't eat beans and their cultures are gone. Could there be any relationship? Let me say that today the Italians (Romans) eat beans in many dishes and the French (Gauls) eat beans often in with fatty meats in stews, and the Greeks (Macedonians), etc. all eat beans.

Beans are part of almost every culture's daily diet, except in North America. (Many Native Americans and Spanish descendants do eat beans daily, but, unfortunately, use additional lard, bacon, and cheese.) North Americans have high fat, high cholesterol levels, heart attacks, blocked arteries, high triglycerides and they still won't eat beans!

Some trendy restaurants in Toronto, where I was living, are serving spicey baked beans as a side dish or on toast as a main dish just like they used to in the '30s. Now the side dish costs $1.25 and the main dish on whole wheat toast sells for $4.50, not 30 cents like it did in the depression.

When I teach vegetarian and natural foods cooking classes I do an entire night on beans. You should hear the groans when they first see the recipes: "beans, ugh!" When the night is over and we have feasted on refried beans, black bean dip and corn chips, lima bean open faced sandwiches, and other gourmet treats, the tune changes, but it takes some effort to make these changes.

BEANS ARE CHEAP

Yes, it is true, beans cost less per serving than most animal products. That is what is so wonderful about them. God gave us a food that has lasted through the ages, it is easy to eat, easy to grow, easy to prepare, extremely versatile, and has health giving properties that are just now being discovered. Beans still are low priced. Once again we can see how God takes care of us in good times and in hard times. No matter what we have done to our bodies with a "modern" diet, God has provided the answer for us to overcome the health problems we have created for ourselves. That's why beans are cheap. When God told Ezekiel to eat beans, wheat, millet, lentils, and barley, he knew Ezekiel needed to eat those things, can you imagine how much we need them thousands of years later? Please, do yourself a favor, eat beans!

PROTEINS AND AMINO ACIDS

Proteins are composed of smaller units called amino acids, just as a house is composed of bricks. Amino acids are often called "the building blocks" of our body and our health. All foods contain amino acids. Of the 28 or so commonly occuring in the food we eat, eight are called "essential" because they are essential for life and because they only can be acquired from foods that contain them. The remaining amino acids can be made in our body from the food we eat so they are called nonessential. The foods that contain the essential amino acids together are usually animal products like meat, milk, fish, and eggs. Eggs have been generally used as the standard for judging protein quality. This gave people the idea that animal proteins were the standard for good health. Now other methods are being used to determine protein quality, thanks to Scrimshaw and Young. They devised a method of measuring the way the human body utilizes protein of all kinds to determine if a protein is "acceptable" for human use. Soy beans won a top place!

VEGETABLE PROTEINS

All vegetables contain protein, but not all vegetables contain the essential amino acids together. Nuts, seeds, beans, and grains contain more protein than the other vegetables. Scientists have shown through research that the protein level of vegetables is only as good as the lowest rating of amino acids. This could render the protein in vegetables, when eaten alone, less bioavailable to humans. Because of this early research, it has been thought for the last 4 or 5 decades that only animal protein was useful for human growth.

COMPLEMENTARY PROTEINS

In 1971 Frances Moore Lappé published a book that dispelled this myth. She found that the protein levels of vegetables could be brought up to the level of animal proteins if foods containing low amounts of one amino acid were mixed together with foods containing high amounts of the same amino acid. This is called mixing complementary proteins. Wheat, for example, is low in the amino acid lysine, while beans are high in lysine. If they were to be eaten together one would have complete protein.[11]

Most of the cuisines from areas where meat is not traditionally eaten daily contain foods eaten together that form complete protein. Beans and rice, beans and wheat, beans and corn, grains and small amounts of dairy products, several grains mixed together, all can be complete protein. Ezekiel-type blended flour contains complete and complementary protein. Since God created the foods, He also knew how we should eat them, this is why He has given us these eating instructions through the Bible.

Beans are native to South and North America, northern Africa, the Middle East, India, and the Far East. They were found growing in warm climates, but now can be grown in almost all climates where a garden can be planted. In the more northern regions, they must be started inside and set out when the ground has warmed up similar to tomatoes and peppers. I generally grow yellow beans in my garden. During the growing season I eat them fresh in salads, stir fry, or casseroles. Then I let them stay on the plant until they are dried out. Voila, I have dried black beans for the winter. The beans that are inside the yellow casing are black when they are mature. Often I save some for planting the next season. So from a few pennies worth of seeds a few years ago, I have had food for many summers and many winters by recycling the seeds as well as eating them. The stems and leaves are composted with other vegetable matter from the kitchen to act as the fertilizer. This is how life works.

RAW BEANS

Do not eat raw beans, especially soy and kidney. Sprouted mung and aduki are acceptable to eat raw, but soy bean sprouts should always be heated before eating. Raw beans can cause gastric distress and terrible flatulence. Raw soy beans contain a trypsin inhibitor that is responsible for this problem.[12] It is not really life threatening but could be uncomfortable trying to digest beans without trypsin.

NUTRITIONAL VALUES

Soy Beans (1/2 cup [120 mL] cooked)
> 130 calories
> 5.7 g fat
> 0 cholesterol
> 11 g protein
> 10.8 g carbohydrate
> 1.6 g fiber
> 30 I.U. vitamin A
> 0.21 mg B1
> 0.09 mg B2,
> 5.6 mg B3
> 2 mg sodium
> 73 mg calcium
> 540 mg potassium
> 2.70 mg iron

Soy beans have the highest nutritional values of all the beans, since they contain complete protein.

Kidney Beans (2/3 cup [150 mL] cooked)
> 118 calories
> 0.5 g fat
> 0 cholesterol
> 7.8 g protein
> 21.4 g carbohydrate
> 1.5 g fiber
> small amounts of the B complex vitamins
> 3 mg sodium
> 38 mg calcium

340 mg potassium
2.40 mg iron

It's plain to see that beans are very nutritious and low in calories.

BEANS ARE EXCITING

There is much more variety in the diet if beans are the main protein eaten than if meat is the main protein eaten. In general we eat beef, veal, pork, lamb, chicken, turkey, and some variety of fish or sea food. Within these catagories there might be several ways of eating the meats like roasts, chops, steaks, and bacon. But the taste is much the same. There are more than 24 different kinds of beans, peas, and lentils that are eaten regularly. Each has its own distinct taste. They can be eaten in soups, stews, casseroles, burgers, roasts, and with a variety of grains. When tofu and tempeh are included the variety of tastes and textures becomes almost infinite. It is possible to eat beans in ways that could seem as if one were eating meat, cheese, cream, eggs, cream cheese, fish, seafood, or beans. The only thing we haven't been able to make beans look and taste like is rare roast beef. I have tasted roast beef and chicken analogs that were almost exactly the same as the meat they were imitating.

Gravy made from cooked, puréed black beans has a taste that is so wonderful, you might never want to have roast beef gravy again. Because the beans have no cholesterol, it is a great way to reduce cholesterol in the diet. Because they could replace the meat and meat fat it is possible to use bean gravy for a low fat vegetarian dish with the mouth feel and taste appeal of meat gravy.

INSTANT BEANS

Beans can be cooked, spread out to drain and then frozen to keep on hand for an emergency meal. Often I add a handful to soups, stews, or casseroles, or eat them in with breakfast foods. Many times I add them to salads right from the freezer, by the time we eat they are thawed. Sometimes I make a quick dip of beans, tofu, and spices and serve it as a snack with corn chips or vegetables. This is more Mexican than Middle Eastern. Often I make a refried bean dish or a bean sandwich, all made of frozen beans that are ready to use. I try not to eat canned beans because of the salt, sugar, or other additives that might be in them. But if you can get beans that are in tins or jars that do not have additives, you would find it handy to have them in the kitchen supply cupboard.

GROW YOUR OWN BEANS

All kinds of beans can be grown at home in the garden and stored over the winter. This is how our ancestors kept healthy in the winter, eating stored beans and other vegetables. Everyone who had a garden could grow enough protein to feed the family and the beans were the seeds so that if a few were saved there would be more for the following year's growing season. Yellow or wax beans, if allowed to grow to full maturity will produce a large black bean similar in size and shape to kidney beans that can be used in soups, stews, and dips.

Lima beans, especially home grown, have always been my favorite vegetable, both fresh and dried. I like them for breakfast with steamed new potatoes and fresh corn, with a little unsalted butter, and a garnish of arame, garlic, and chopped parsley. Actually, I can eat this any time of the day or night. It is also good when cheese or tofu is added as well as sweet red peppers.

WEIGHT LOSS MADE EASY

If a person wanted to lose weight, the best way is to cut back on animal protein and therefore fat and calories, and replace the protein with vegetable protein, mainly beans, tofu, and tempeh. The high fiber will help to upgrade the functioning of the intestines and remove old waste matter as well as help to speed up the process of removing the toxins from the system.

Many people who are overweight are also toxic due to the poisons lodging in the fatty tissues. Often this is directly related to the length of time that it takes for food to be eaten and then pass out as waste matter. This is known as the "transit time." The longer the waste matter stays in the intestines, the greater are the chances that more of the poisons are reabsorbed into the system. In other words, if a person is constipated, he or she is also poisoning themselves with the toxic waste that should have been expelled. It should take several hours, not several days, for the body to use the nutrients from the food eaten, release the old waste matter from the cells, and expel it in the waste. Ideally, every time one eats, one should also pass some waste matter to make room for the new food. This, however, almost never happens in adults.

The more fiber and liquid one eats, the more waste keeps moving and is removed from the body. The vegetable foods that contain fiber, also contain minerals and water which help the body to function at its optimum level.

This is why it is so important to eat raw vegetables, cooked beans, and fresh fruit to be healthy. All these foods contain fiber as well as liquid, vitamins, and minerals. So do whole grains, as we saw in Chapter II—Our Daily Bread.

Animal foods do not contain the kind of fiber called dietary fiber, or cellulose. Cellulose forms the supporting framework of plants. The main sources are the stems and leaves of vegetables, seed and grain coverings, skins, and hulls.[13] Animal foods are much harder to digest because of this lack of fiber and therefore can slow down the entire process of digestion. This is why whole grains, or high fiber vegetables like lettuce or carrots should always be eaten with meats or cheeses. If potatoes are eaten instead of another vegetable (which I hope never happens), then they should be eaten with the skins intact. Eating the skins of the potato can add fiber at any time. I never eat potatoes without the skins, even mashed.

Legumes vs Vegetables

The New Webster Encyclopedic Dictionary Of The English Language, Avenel Books, N. Y., 1980, gives the definition of legume as a seed vessel of two valves, like the pod of a pea, in which the seeds are fixed to the ventral suture only. According to the *Collins-Robert French-English Dictionary,* Collins, Don Mills, Ontario, 1982, legume is the French word for vegetable. This is part of the confusion of the meaning of the word "legume." Generally, in North America, we use the word legume to mean those vegetables that have nitrogenous nodules on the roots, as well as the seed pods described above. This group of vegetables includes beans, alfalfa, vetch, and many other foods that we eat often. Even buckwheat is considered by some to be a legume because it has nitrogen nodules on the roots.

GARLIC AND ONIONS

We remember the fish we ate in Egypt for nothing, the cucumbers, the melons, the leeks, the onions, and the garlic. Numbers 11:5 (RSV)

Onions and garlic were used extensively by the Children of Israel in cooking both for taste and for their health-giving properties. There are many people today, especially my father, who eat raw onions or garlic if they feel a cold coming on and find that this will allay it. Garlic and onions are reputed to have antibiotic properties, and in Europe and the old Soviet Union garlic is known to help lower high blood pressure. We are experimenting in North America with garlic to help overcome Candida albicans, the dreaded Yeast Connection. Garlic is reputed to kill or repel most insects and fungus. This is why it was often used for children and animals with worms.

Once my 5 month old puppy went to a birthday party for another dog. When I went to pick her up, everybody started laughing. Finally, after much prodding, they told me why they were laughing. They had noticed that she was just like me: short stubby legs and smelled like garlic. Of course she didn't have worms, nor did she have to be wormed with any expensive medication, and neither did I. Garlic also helps to keep down the garden and household pests as well. Often I put garlic powder or crushed garlic, cayenne pepper, and a little soapy water on my garden to keep away most pests, especially on the broccoli and cabbages. Sometimes I just put dried garlic and cayenne pepper in a shaker and shake it on the plants before the dew lifts. You can actually see the bugs being repelled.

MORE GARLIC LORE

Many health food books talk about putting a clove of garlic in a child's shoe to keep worms away and help to dispel them from their system,[14] but I don't think we can get away with this today, we are so cleanly scrubbed that we would notice the smell right away.

GARLIC AND ONION

Garlic and onions are near relatives of the lily family. In France the onion is called "the lily of the kitchen." Garlic and onions have similar Latin or botanical names. Garlic, *Allium sativum*, onion, *Allium cepa*, chives, *Allium schoenoprasum*, green onion, *Allium fistulosum*, leek, *Allium porrum*, and shallot, *Allium ascalonicum*, all show their common ancestral link. Garlic, onion, shallot, and leek were used extensively in the Bible for cooking as well as medicine.[15]

HEALTH USES FOR GARLIC

Over the years garlic has been used for lowering blood pressure, colds, coughs, asthma, dysentery, gastrointestinal disorders, TB, diabetes, anemia, cancer, pneumonia, arthritis, and to fight pollution and parasites. Garlic was used for hundreds of years in cases of impotence. Scientists are now showing that it can increase spermatogenesis, making men more potent. This is useful since lead poisoning can make men less potent, even impotent, and garlic helps to remove lead from the body.

GARLIC AND POLLUTION

Garlic contains at least 33 sulphur-containing compounds (allicin is one of them). Sulphur containing foods are used to break down and remove or chelate out harmful pollutants in the body such as lead, mercury, LDL, calcium deposits, liver and intestinal parasites, and many kinds of molds and fungi.

GARLIC, CHOLESTEROL, AND HEART DISEASE

Dr. Benjamin Lau at Loma Linda University in California has successfully used garlic extract to significantly reduce blood cholesterol and triglycerides. He also found that garlic extract converts Low Density Lipoproteins (the "bad" cholesterol, so called) to High Density Lipoproteins (the "good" cholesterol, also so called).[16]

Discordies, chief doctor to the Roman army, wrote 3,500 years ago: "Garlic doth cleareth the arteries." We are just now getting around to testing garlic for this use. Folk medicine has been using it for thousands of years. It must also have been known for its health-giving properties during Old Testament times to the Hebrews.

GARLIC, YEAST, FUNGUS, MOLD, AND CANDIDA ALBICANS

The Lord will strike you with wasting disease, with fever and inflammation, with scorching heat and drought, with blight and mildew, which will plague you until you perish. Deuteronomy 28:22 (Curses for disobedience) (NIV)

During the forty years that I led you through the desert, your clothes did not wear out, nor did the sandals on your feet. You ate no bread and drank no wine or other fermented drink. I did this so that you might know that I am the Lord your God. Deuteronomy 29:5-6 (Renewal of the Covenant) (NIV)

When I first read these passages, I recognized the current "plague" of the 20th century. Perhaps the Bible is talking about the crops being affected with blight and mildew. Now it is our bodies that suffer from it. The cure is to eat no fermented foods such as bread or wine and strong drink and to eat certain foods that prevent the mildew, mold, yeast, from living or actually repel them. These foods are garlic, yogurt, butter, specific essential fatty acids like linseed oil or flax oil, and certain herbs. These foods were eaten during Bible times by the Hebrews.

There is a very distinct mind/body connection in many illnesses. Dr. William Crook talks about the things that could make a person weakened enough to become ill. These things include pollution of air, food, water, lack of certain nutrients, food allergies, improper diet, and emotional things like lack of touching, job frustration, not enough love, being put down, and more.[17] This can set the body up for weakening in ways we are just now learning about.

If you eat nutritionless foods and your body becomes weakened, you might react to strong smells like cleaning liquids, cigarette smoke, chlorine bleach, or new carpeting. This will also weaken you and you may even become allergic to something entirely different like wheat or the molds in foods or in the air. This will weaken you to the extent that you might have some different symptoms like chronic headache, backache, sugar cravings, pain or tightness in your chest, fluid in your ears (or even be losing your hearing like my husband was), digestive disturbances, terrible gas, nasal congestion, runny nose, recurrent sore throats, or just feel lousy all over most of the time.

DISOBEDIENCE OR LACK OF LOVE?

There are many things that are considered disobedience to God. The main one is not obeying the Ten Commandments. This could mean not honoring your parents like it says in Exodus 20:12, *Honor your father and your mother, so that you may live long in the land the Lord your God is giving you.* (NIV) Many times I have heard people who suffer from a health problem related to Candida albicans say things like "My mother was rotten to me as a kid and I hate her," or "My dad was an alcoholic and he ruined my life because of the way he acted to me," or "I'll never forgive my parents for what they have done to me." This is definitely not honoring your parents. It is essential for your health that you honor your parents **No Matter What They Did**. Obeying the Ten Commandments can be the key to good health. This will be discussed more fully in Chapter VIII— The Secrets of Good Health.

Many people that I have counselled on health and diet who have yeast-related problems talk about the feelings they had as children that they were not loved. Many even say that their parents said they loved them, but they had a nagging feeling that they really didn't. Why? They had a brother or sister near to them in age, or a sibling who was ill as a child and got all the attention, or their parents worked and they felt abandoned, and other similar things. As a child your feelings run you. If you are the center of attention as a child and then something happens that takes this away or lessens it, you feel not loved. As a child you don't say to yourself, "I know mommy really loves me just as much as before even though she has a new baby now. She just has to spend more time with him, just as she did with me when I was a baby." No, you think something like, "Why doesn't she come when I cry? Oh, right, the baby gets everything now, not me, I guess she doesn't love me." It might not be so obvious in a child's mind, it might be more the feeling of being abandoned, fear of being alone, or fear of being left alone. It sounds silly to adults, but children do not have the same thinking capacity as adults.

Many children say that they feel it was their fault that their parents got divorced, they think it had something to do with them or the way they acted, and if they could only be good or better, their parents would get back together. To adults, this sounds strange, but to a child it sounds real. They are very centered on themselves.

This real or imagined lack of love can supress immune function in such a way that health problems begin to develop. Runny nose, colds, ear infections, bronchitis, diarrhea, constipation, asthma, allergies, stomachaches, all sorts of things can happen. Many times parents think this is just "looking for attention" or "a nervous reaction he'll grow out of." It could be the beginning of a lifetime of serious illnesses or chronic illness or fatigue. This is especially true if the child is given antibiotics on a regular basis for this.

Taking frequent antibiotics can depress the immune system and leave you weakened. This is not to say that they are bad, they have certainly saved many lives and continue to do so. They must not be given for just any old thing. If you follow a good diet, and have a healthy lifestyle as shown in Chapter VIII—The Secrets of Good Health, you will not need them as often.

According to Dr. Crook, "When you take a diet high in refined carbohydrates, yeast germs proliferate. And increased numbers of yeast germs put out toxins which depress your immune system and increase your susceptibility to food and chemical allergies, infections, and other illnesses."[18]

The best ways to stop this, besides the dietary changes necessary, are to eat garlic, yogurt, linseed oil, and a diet high in beta carotene and vitamin C. This is basically the World's Oldest Health

Plan. This is the health-giving diet that the Children of Israel longed for when they were in the desert. Almost every food that is fermented (like wine), contains yeast (like bread), or is moldy can contribute to yeast growth in some way. They didn't need the garlic in the desert because they weren't allowed to have bread or wine, the main culprits contributing to the yeast problem in those days.

Now we have even more things that contribute to this, beer, pizza, cheese, especially moldy-type cheeses, sweet drinks, sweet foods, sugar in almost everything that is processed, even in the breakfast cereals. Often babies are given sugar water in the hospital to start the process in the very first hours after birth. Add to this the amount of pollution, chemicals in the environment, chemicals in the food and water supply, stress of all kinds, the ways that people are turning away from God, and the economic outlook for people young and old and you have even more reasons for Candida albicans, the Yeast Connection as Dr. Crook calls it, to be our own special plague.

Garlic on a regular basis can help prevent this round of physical and emotional health problems. Please add garlic to your diet every day. Eat it raw in salads, sprinkle it on your food, cook with it, or take odorless garlic capsules if you have any of the things mentioned above. Garlic is your best defense against so many illnesses it is almost like suicide to not eat it.

If you recognized your own health problems in this section you may want to study any of the many books out on yeast problems. If your own physician tells you it is not an issue for you, find a doctor that will test you in some way for it and be able to treat it and work with you if you do have it. Many doctors are slow to learn about this problem that is crippling many people everyday.

HOW I LEARNED ABOUT IT

I always had bronchitis as a child. I generally had it at home and not as much as school. At home we had a forced air coal furnace, at school they had radiators in the classrooms. I knew as a child that something in our house was making me sick, nobody believed me, talk about lack of love! We also had a kind of dingy basement. Sometimes in the dampness of the climate where I lived there was mold and mildew inside and out. My mother cleaned with strong solutions and chlorine bleach to get things spotless. So every winter, when the furnace was turned on I got bronchitis and every spring when the furnace was turned off I was better. When the house was shut up tight in the winter and my mother did laundry in the basement and hung it there smelling of chlorine, I had earaches, sore throats, sinus conditions, and bronchitis. I took lots of antibiotics. In those days the doctor even came to the house to give me injections of antibiotics. (You can probably guess my age by that statement.) My mother often made pickles that gave off yeasts as they fermented in the basement. We often had bread fresh out of the oven, even though we weren't allowed to eat it that fresh. Once I ate an entire loaf of bread that didn't rise and had very bad stomach and intestinal reactions to the yeast. My dad had a quick temper and often yelled at us. My older brother beat me up, emotionally and physically abused me, and teased me a lot. I had a sister a year and a half younger, and my mother had lost a baby a year before I was born. This was a real setup for yeast related illness.

When I moved into Detroit to go to university, I had escalating health problems. The pollution was so bad then that I would often come home from shopping further downtown with pieces of soot on my face. I also drank beer with the kids at school. Then my lungs started to collapse on overcast days. I found out later that the sulphur in the pollution had triggered a low grade form of asthma that stressed my lungs. Years later I began having severe abdominal pains from contact with sulphur and other people's cigarette smoke.

Finally, I heard about the yeast diet. I put myself on it, ate garlic and the other necessary foods, found a doctor who would prescribe the necessary anti-fungal medicine, and lived to tell about it.

Now let me say that the first collapsed lung led me to study herbs, nutrition, and health. I exercised a lot, ate right, and used forgiveness techniques. It wasn't until I accepted Jesus as my Savior in my heart and started to clean up my life as well as my diet that I actually got over the health problems. Most people who knew me thought I was a perfect specimen of health. I was always cheerful and bubbly. Little did they know that I had to drag myself out of bed every day that it was polluted. Or that I often ached all over, or that my lungs hurt every day, or that I was so stiff I had to exercise and stretch just to get through the day.

I eat garlic as often as I can, but not every single day, anymore. I eat it in food. There was a time I carried cloves of garlic with me to relieve the symptoms that often came from mold, like old leaves in the street in the rain, fungus, like mushrooms in the rain, smelly things like oil slickers and plastic wrap, chemicals like strong aftershave or floor cleaning things, or even cigarette smoke. Many of these things made me sleepy, drowsy, faint, gave me blurred vision, headaches, instant rashes or even welts. One time I got an instant sore throat from eating some packaged fish. It felt like a layer had been ripped off my throat. Garlic fixed it. Once I was shopping with a friend in a farmers' market. He was buying some cheese. When the clerk unwrapped the cheese all I could smell was the plastic wrap—it was so strong to me. My head started to spin. I stepped away and munched on a piece of raw garlic I always carried. It fixed it. I visited a food manufacturing plant where the equipment was steam cleaned but the high ceilings were not. You could see the mold and mildew on the walls and ceiling. I got a headache after a few minutes. Garlic fixed it in 4 minutes. Perhaps you might think this sounds crazy. Well, many times I felt crazy with these things happening. At least I did not suffer from depression like so many do when they are affected by yeast. Or get drunk off regular foods because it fed the yeast in my system and the yeast toxins were alcohol. If you find that you can't drink beer or wine without getting a headache or a very bad hangover from very little, you probably are affected by the yeast syndrome. This is why it is best to not drink alcohol.

ARE YOU CRAZY?

If you have the symptoms listed, any of them, and the doctor or your friends tell you that you are crazy, that it's all in your head, that you are doing it for attention, run to the kitchen and get some fresh garlic. You are not crazy! You are infected by yeast, perhaps have allergies, and you need real help. Call every doctor you can until you find one who is sympathetic and can treat you for this. Do not go to a mental hospital until you have completed the yeast treatment. Then, if you still need it, go, yeast isn't all that is wrong.

How many times have you heard people describe a drunk as acting like a crazy person? Alcohol will do this, but you can make your own alcohol by eating the foods that yeast thrives on and eliminating garlic from your diet. Your body will become a still, you will be dangerous behind the wheel of a car or on a bike, you will be dangerous operating heavy equipment or driving a train or plane.

Eating garlic, yogurt, dark green leafy vegetables, bitter herbs, yellow vegetables, and only whole grains can help you feel better fast. Avoiding fermented foods like wine, beer, cheese, soy sauce, miso paste, vinegar, and foods made with them is a good start. Avoiding foods with yeast in them like breads, pizza, rolls, crackers, and even prepared foods—read the labels—will help you strengthen your body and resist the invasion of yeast problems.

It is possible with prayer, the right foods, the right supplements, and self control to overcome even this plague.

This yeast problem is nothing new! It has just turned into a modern plague that most people don't recognize. Get back to the basics of living and eating. Follow the lead of Daniel and his friends avoid rich food and fancy drinks and gain health and strength.

COOKING WITH GARLIC

A soup made of sautéed garlic and onions with lentils and carrots will make a healthful meal that will give energy, rebuild muscle and nerve tissue, protect the body against germs or fungus, and fill you up without the added calories of fat or any of the health destroying properties of fat and meat. I'm not saying that meat is bad; but I am saying that meat or animal flesh was not eaten every day by the people in the Bible, nor was it recommended to be eaten every day, nor is it being recommended now.

ONION SOUP

Traditional French Onion Soup is made by roasting a beef shoulder bone in the oven with a low heat for several hours until it is very brown. This is then added to the onions and water and boiled, herbs are added later. This is a way of having the flavor of meat but not the fat and calories. I often make a French Style Onion Soup by browning the onions in a mixture of butter and olive oil until they are really brown, but not burnt, then add more onions to cook until they are just golden. Then add the water, bay leaf, black pepper corns, as well as a piece of kombu and bring to a boil. Turn to a simmer and cook for another ten minutes or so. Add thyme and simmer for another few minutes. Don't allow it to boil if dried herbs are used as this will remove all the herb flavor from the soup.

Slice up whole grain french bread and brush with olive oil on both sides. Toast on a baking sheet in a low oven until golden brown. Float the toast, croûtes as it is called in French, on the soup, add grated mozzerella or ementhal cheese and pop under the broiler to melt the cheese and brown it. This would make a full meal if served with a nice green salad. You could also add pre-cooked romano beans to the soup, when simmering, for added body and protein. With the whole grain bread and cheese you really don't need any more protein to make it a full meal.

NUTRITIONAL BREAKDOWNS

Compared to other vegetables, garlic is not a good source of the vitamins A, B, and C, although it does contain them, since it is eaten in small amounts. It is known to contain a special type of B1 called allithiamine, which is useful in preventing and curing beriberi, a relatively rare illness these days. Garlic does contain manganese, copper, iron, zinc, sulphur, calcium, aluminum, chlorine, germanium, and selenium.[19]

Selenium is thought to be an anti-aging mineral, which is felt to be part of the reason for the longevity of peoples regularly eating garlic in their diet. Selenium helps to normalize blood pressure, prevents against infections, and is reported to prevent platelet adhesions and clot formation, thus giving it anti-atherosclerotic properties.[20]

NUTRITIONAL VALUES

Raw Onion (one tablespoon chopped)
> 4 calories
> 0.2 g protein
> 0.1 g fiber
> 1 mg Vitamin C
> trace amounts of B1, B2, B3
> 3 mg calcium
> 1 mg magnesium
> 16 mg potassium
> 0.10 mg iron[21]

Raw Garlic—3 1/2 oz (100 g) contains 24.9 mcg of selenium while the same amount of onion has 1.5 mcg.[22]

GARLIC AND ONION SMELL

The smell of garlic and onions is set by heat, it is removed by cold. Therefore, it is best to wash your hands, knife, board, etc. with very cold water as soon as you are finished touching garlic or onions. To help my cooking school students remember this I used to sing: "I'm gonna wash that garlic right offa my hands, I'm gonna wash that garlic right offa my hands, and do it with cold water." This was to the tune of "I'm gonna wash that man right outa my hair" from South Pacific. We always have fun in cooking classes.

Garlic and onion smell can also be removed with a lemon juice and corn meal scrub, so I understand. I have never tried this since the cold water works so well.

Parsley, and other high chlorophyll vegetables, also works as a deodorizer, this is explained later in this chapter.

VEGETABLES IN THE BIBLE

Better a meal of vegetables where there is love than a fattened calf with hatred. Proverbs 15:17 (NIV)

This quote plainly shows how the Hebrews felt about vegetables and about love, some go so far as to mention that this explains their feelings against killing, especially killing animals for eating. Vegetables were very important in the diet and were not always easy to obtain when the Children of Israel were wandering. There are some records in the Bible of gardens and orchards, as we saw in the previous chapter on grains and in this chapter on lentils.

And God said, "Let the earth put forth vegetation, plants yielding seed, and fruit trees bearing fruit in which is their seed, each according to its kind, upon the earth." And it was so. The earth brought forth vegetation, plants yielding seed according to their own kinds, and trees bearing fruit in which is their seed, each according to its kind. (Genesis 1:11,12) And God said, "Behold, I have given you every plant yielding seed which is upon the face of all the earth, and every tree with seed in its fruit; and you shall have them for food." Genesis 1:29 (RSV)

The Bible teaches that God planted the first garden in Eden, so gardening is part of our heritage, so is eating vegetables. There are those who say that meat was not allowed to be eaten until after the flood, but I have not found any reference to this. Meat seems to be eaten all through the Old Testament and in the New Testament. We will see more about this in Chapter VI—Alternative Proteins.

COOKING RULES FOR VEGETABLES

Vegetables should always be cooked starting with the highest heat possible. This means always to place vegetables into live steam, rapidly boiling water, or a high oven to start cooking. This is very important and will help to retain the highest nutritional value. The high heat sears the outside of the vegetable, holds in the heat and cooks it better because the juices are left inside and heat up faster on the higher heat after the searing.

POTATOES IN WATER

Never, never cook potatoes by peeling them and placing them in cold water to bring to a boil. This will kill all the nutritional value. The water should always be boiling before unpeeled potatoes are added. It is better to steam them so that the water never touches the potatoes, just the steam does. If you must peel them do so after cooking.

COOKING VEGETABLES

All vegetables can be cooked with a minimum of water touching them. This can be done with live steam being the cooking agent. It can also be done by boiling water in small amounts in the bottom of a pot, adding the vegetables, then covering the pot so that very little steam escapes. This should only take a few minutes, not an hour. Vegetables are best to eat when cooked to the crisp stage, eaten while they are still slightly crunchy. Orange or yellow vegetables can be of higher nutritional value if they are cooked to the soft stage. Never add salt while cooking vegetables. Do add such things as lemon peel, garlic, onions, cloves, limes, or fresh ginger root. Dried or fresh herbs can be added very near the end of cooking as the high heat will cause them to lose their flavor into the air and leave very little left in the final veggies.

SUGGESTED COMBINATIONS

- peas, pearl onions, marjoram; carrots, ginger, honey
- new potatoes, mint; green beans, lemon, toasted almonds
- asparagus, lemon peel, arame
- sweet potato, cinnamon, pineapple
- onions, garlic, coriander seeds, cumin, okra or green beans or spinach
- broccoli, red pepper, mushrooms, ginger; lima beans, corn, red pepper, celery; basil, broccoli, tomatoes
- tomatoes, red and green peppers, oregano
- onions, cinnamon
- turnip, lemon, honey, cinnamon
- zucchini, tomatoes, basil, oregano, garlic

VEGETABLES AND GRAINS

Many vegetables are mixed with cooked grains and herbs for interesting side dishes. Wholewheat or buckwheat noodles, bulgar, brown rice, cous cous, millet, and buckwheat, all lend well to mixing with chopped cooked vegetables. Fried rice is one way to serve these combinations. (See Chapter II—Our Daily Bread for recipes.) The same method of cooking used in fried rice can be used with many other cooked grains. Wild and brown rice fixed in the same ways used for stuffing roasts can make an interesting meal accompaniment. If cooked beans or pulses, cubes of sautéed tofu or tempeh, or even left over cooked meats are added, the dish can become a whole meal.

Cold salads can be made of cold grains, chopped vegetables, herbs, and a dressing of mayonnaise, oil and lemon, or vinegrette. Rice salad made with brown rice, slivers of red and green pepper, and dressed with green goddess dressing (See page 143) is always a favorite at pot-luck suppers.

A whole meal can be made from half a stuffed avocado, filled with a combination of cooked rice, celery, parsley, pecans, and shrimp, dressed with a simple lemon dressing that includes a zest of the peel. Carrot and beet salad with green onions, parsley and a dressing of lemon, olive oil, and cumin is a taste treat.

Basic Soup

1	cooking onion, sliced thin
3 Tbsp.	oil or butter
2 cups	chopped mixed vegetables (no leaves or flowers)
2	very ripe tomatoes OR half a lemon
4 cups	cold water
2 tsp.	dried summer savory
2 tsp	dried parsley OR
3 sprigs	chopped fresh parsley
1 clove	garlic (optional)

Heat butter or oil in soup pot over medium heat. Add onions (and garlic if used) and sauté until just golden. Then add the remainder of the vegetables beginning with the firmest first, stirring after each addition to coat them with the oil or butter. Carrots, turnip, broccoli or cauliflower stems, potatoes, are firm. Sauté until each additional vegetable begins to turn color, then add the next group. Mushrooms, sweet potato, green onion, green beans, and peppers are softer and should be added next. (Leaves should be added at the very end.) Then add tomatoes, if used, and the water. This is where the lemon would be added if it is being used instead of the tomatoes. Bring to a boil. Lower heat and add the chopped leaves, parsley and savory, and cover. Simmer for 6 to 15 minutes depending on the veggies used and the size of the pieces.

There is no salt in this recipe. If you wish to add some use sea salt, soy sauce, or cook sea vegetables in with the soup. Kombu, arame, hijiki, or other type can be added with the water and cooked with the soup. Do not add sea weed or sea vegetable extract unless you read the label and make sure that there is no MSG in it. Many of the Japanese seasonings that contain sea vegetables also have added MSG. Most of the American made sea vegetable products or sea salt and vegetable seasonings do not.

Pre-cooked vegetables, grains, or beans can also be added during the simmering stage. If you add sliced okra during the simmering stage this soup will look quite like a popular canned vegetable soup. If you also add pre-cooked elbow macaroni and chick peas, and 1 teaspoon of oregano, and top with a little grated cheese when serving it will become minestrone.

GREENS IN THE BIBLE

Many of the vegetables mentioned in the Bible are what we call greens. The translators have translated several Hebrew words as "herbs" when they really have more defined meanings. *Eseb* is used to mean plants as a whole; *chatsir* really means grass; *botane* means herbage or shining; *deshe* is green; *yaraq* is green; *lachanon* is garden, medicinal, or culinary herbs. In the King James Version *orah* is in Isaiah 26:19 and means an herb covered with dew, or the shining herb, which we know as a type of cabbage.[23] And yet all these are generally translated as "herb."

GREENS AND HIGH BLOOD PRESSURE

Dr. Arlene Caggiula, Ph.D., R.D., associate professor of nutrition and epidemiology at the University of Pittsburg School of Public Health has often recommended her long-term non-drug eating plan for reducing high blood pressure. This comprehensive eating program incorporates all dietary aspects of blood pressure control, and includes reduction of salt and animal fats in the diet as well as the inclusion of calcium and potassium rich vegetables. (This is why the Nutritional Values sections list calcium, sodium, and potassium, when available.) These help to control important functions of the vascular system. Adequate amounts may help keep the blood pressure down.[24] Sounds like a pretty good reason to eat green vegetables, doesn't it?

NUTRIENT RECOMMENDATIONS

The Recommended Daily Dietary Allowances, Revised 1980, established by the Food and Nutrition Board, National Academy of Sciences, National Research Council, in the United States suggests for adults: 800 I.U. vitamin A for women and 1,000 I.U. for men, 60 mg vitamin C, 800–1200 mg calcium, 300–400 mg magnesium, and 10–18 mg iron, daily, all to be obtained from food sources if possible.[25] The same body recommends that a safe and adequate daily dietary intake of potassium for an adult is 1875–5625 mg. Look at the nutritional values section for each of the vegetables mentioned and you will see that eating dark green leafy vegetables daily will help to fulfill your daily requirement of these nutrients. This is why we need servings of dark orange and green vegetables, whole grains, and fresh fruit daily along with the vegetable source proteins mentioned under beans.

GREENS AND CALCIUM

Calcium is high in many dark green leafy vegetables, although dairy products often are considered to be the main source of calcium in the diet. The vegetables have no saturated fats, are low in calories, contain fiber for aiding digestion, and also contain B vitamins, iron, and lots of potassium. Green veggies also have to be chewed to be eaten and there is some evidence that this helps absorption of calcium. There are many places in the world where people do not eat dairy products and still have adequate or better than average calcium levels. Legumes, nuts and seeds, and whole grains are other sources of calcium in the diet. Look at the Nutritional Values sections to see the amount of calcium in your favorite green vegetables.

WHY WE NEED CALCIUM

Calcium is necessary in the diet to help with the contraction and relaxation of muscles. It is necessary for blood clot formation, and it is the major ingredient in teeth and bones. It is necessary for nerve conduction, endocrine and exocrine functions, cell division, membrane permeability, cytoskeleton assembly, and enzyme activity.[26] Calcium is helped in its absorption by the addition of vitamin D (generally obtained from minor exposure to sun light), boron, vitamin K, and magnesium and phosphorous balance.

EXERCISE AND CALCIUM

Research now shows that calcium is laid down in the bones when there is weight bearing exercise. Yes, exercise is very important in preventing osteoporosis, or thinning of the bones. Walking, tennis, bike riding, dancing, and any other activities that put weight on the bones is helpful. Jogging is not recommended as an exercise that is healthful on a regular basis due to the amount of jarring that the knees, heels, ankles, hips, and neck take.

Running, if done properly, is acceptable for those who are in condition for it. Running should always be done with the knees slightly bent, and the heels should touch the ground first then the foot should rock onto the balls of the feet, and then onto the toes. This is something that can be learned under the supervision of a qualified fitness instructor. Running shoes, properly fitted, are required. Never undertake running without instruction and without the consent of your family doctor. Walking, on the other hand, can be done at any time and anywhere. It is good to walk every day, try walking the few blocks to the store, or taking the stairs instead of the elevator, use every opportunity to walk your way to health.

CALCIUM ROBBERS

There are many things that can rob calcium from the body. Most notable are high protein diets and high intake of caffeine. There are many theories of things that rob calcium like nicotine, caffeine, sugar, high milk intake with its high phosphorus content, overrun of yeasts, especially Candida albicans, allergies, and more theories that are too far out for me to mention and still sleep well at night.

GREENS AND FOLIC ACID

Folic acid, a minor B vitamin, is now being recommended for all women of childbearing age who are able to conceive. On September 14, 1992 the Centers For Disease Control Director Dr. William L. Roper announced that 400 micrograms (mcg.) or 0.4 milligrams should be taken daily. Infants born to folic acid deficient women run the risk of having neural tube defects such as spina bifida and anencephaly. Good sources of folic acid in the diet are dark, green leafy vegetables, citrus fruits and juices, yeast, beans, chicken and turkey liver, and folic acid fortified breakfast cereals.

FOLIC ACID CONTENT OF FOODS

Frozen asparagus, 3/5 cup	191 mcg
1 medium avocado	113-162 mcg
sliced beets, 3/5 cup	29 mcg
black eyed peas frozen, 2/3 cup	130 mcg
chopped broccoli, 1/2 cup	130 mcg
brussels sprouts, 3/5 cup	150 mcg
butter beans, 1/2 cup	97 mcg
collard greens, 3/5 cup	59 mcg
green beans, 2/3 cup	36 mcg
baby lima beans, 3/5 cup	90 mcg
okra, cut up, 1/2 cup	25 mcg
spinach, chopped, 1/2 cup	153 mcg
turnip greens, chopped, 3/5 cup	60 mcg
butter	trace
chicken heart, 3 1/2 oz	80 mcg
chicken liver, 3 1/2 oz	770 mcg
turkey liver, 3 1/2 oz	666 mcg
skim milk yogurt, 1 cup	28 mcg
orange juice from concentrate, 8 fl oz	109 mcg
whole wheat bread, 1 slice	12 mcg
1 medium raw tangerine	17 mcg
raw strawberries, 1 cup	26 mcg
raw pineapple, 1 cup of pieces	16 mcg
medium raw pear	12 mcg
medium orange	47 mcg
raw pink or red grapefruit, 1/2	15 mcg
large egg, soft boiled or poached	24 mcg
Total cereal, 1 cup	400 mcg
Wheat Chex, 2/3 cup	100 mcg
Special K, 1 1/3 cups	100 mcg
Rice Crispies, 1 cup	100 mcg
most raisin brans, 3/4 cup	100 mcg
Product 19, 3/4 cup	400 mcg

Most of the commercial cereals are fortified with folic acid. If you eat one serving with 400 mcg folic acid you will not have to be as concerned about eating the other high folic acid foods. Chicken or turkey liver simmered, not fried, would be a good idea once a week, but I wouldn't eat it on the same day as one of the cereals fortified with 400 mcg of folic acid. If you take a supplement under your doctor's care, ask about the additional amounts you can get in foods if you are planning to become pregnant, especially if there is any family history of needing it.

BITTER HERBS

That same night they are to eat the meat roasted over the fire, along with bitter herbs, and bread made without yeast. Exodus 12:8 (NIV)

Bitter herbs are required to be eaten at the grand feast of the Passover. The bitter herbs mentioned in the Bible include: dandelion, watercress, horseradish, parsley, mint, sorrel, mustard greens, endive, chicory, lettuce, and wormwood.[27] Numbers 9:9–12 also outlines the words of Moses in giving the instructions to eat bitter herbs with the unleavened bread and roasted meat.

Bitter herbs are most often eaten when high fat meals are eaten, especially animal fats. It is thought that bitter herbs help to break up and digest the fat. Since many Bible scholars feel that the Israelites ate very little meat, except ritually, it is obvious that bitter herbs were meant to be eaten with meat, especially during the feasts.

DANDELION

Dandelion is often taken as a spring toner, the fresh, young leaves are eaten before the flowers form. It is best to gather the leaves from areas not near a road so that the pollution from the exhaust doesn't linger on the leaves. Always wash the leaves well before eating, and try to eat them raw. Most reference books cite *Taraxacum officinale* to be the bitter herbs mentioned in Numbers and this is really the dandelion that we know and love.[28]

NUTRITIONAL VALUES

Dandelion Greens (100 g [3 1/2 oz])

    45 calories
    0 cholesterol
    2.7 g protein
    1.6 g fiber
    14,000 I.U. vitamin A
    35 mg vitamin C
    0.19 mg B1
    0.26 mg B2
    187 mg calcium
    36 mg magnesium
    397 mg potassium
    3.10 mg iron[29]

It is the high content of vitamin A that gives dandelions their liver toning properties.

DANDELIONS FOR HEALTH

Dandelion leaves are eaten raw to eliminate itchy and scaly rashes and eczema. They also stimulate the liver and gall bladder and are used for chronic inflammation of the liver. The stems have been used to remove gall stones painlessly. Dandelions are used to purify the blood and are therefore useful for gout, rheumatism, and glandular swellings. The leaves also are used for jaundice and disorders of the spleen, this is generally thought to be effective due to the high vitamin A content. They also stimulate digestion,[30] hence the use at Passover feasts.

WATERCRESS

One of the most popular and "trendy" salad greens now is watercress. It grows wild along cool streams in Canada and the United States. It is served with walnuts and walnut oil and lemon dressing, this might even be an original recipe from Bible times since all these ingredients were commonly used then. It is known by the botanical name *Nasturtium officinale*, both today and in the Bible.

NUTRITIONAL VALUES

Watercress (100 g [3 1/2 oz])
>   19 calories
>   2.2 g protein
>   0.7 g fiber
>   4,900 I.U. vitamin A
>   79 mg vitamin C
>   0.08 mg B1
>   0.16 mg B2
>   0.9 mg B3
>   151 mg calcium
>   20 mg magnesium
>   282 mg potassium
>   1.7 mg iron[31]

It is good to add watercress to every salad in the spring, and throughout the year if available.

HORSERADISH

Horseradish is traditionally eaten with meat, especially roast beef and lamb. Sometimes it is combined with grated beets as well.

Beets and horseradish are known for their properties of aiding digestion of fats, toning up the liver, and cleansing the liver of fats and other toxins. Such small quantities of horseradish are eaten at a time that it is not a meaningful source of nutrients. Horseradish does contain protein, calcium, phosphorus, iron, potassium, B1, and vitamin C.[32] The vapors of crushed or grated horseradish were often used, medically, because of their inhibitory effect on microorganisms. It is also used as a stimulant to the digestion.[33]

PARSLEY

Parsley is one of my favorite vegetables. I try to eat it as often as possible. I have even used it to stop blemishes from appearing on my face, by crushing it with the back of a spoon and applying it to the area where I feel one starting and leaving it for 20 minutes or so. Mind you, I haven't used this for 20 years since I haven't needed to do so due to eating a diet that included raw dark green veggies, yellow and orange veggies, and eliminating most animal and hydrogenated fats. Folklore holds that parsley tea can dissolve kidney stones, but I have never seen it happen. Parsley is known by the name *Petroselinum sativum*. It is used today in many Middle Eastern dishes in great amounts, especially "tabouli," a salad made of parsley, mint, olive oil, lemon juice, garlic, and bulgar wheat.

NUTRITIONAL VALUES

Parsley (1 Tbsp. [15 mL] raw, chopped)
> 4 calories
> 0.4 g protein
> 850 I.U. vitamin A
> 17 mg vitamin C
> B1
> B2
> B3
> 20 mg calcium
> 4 mg magnesium
> 73 mg potassium
> 0.60 mg iron[34]

The above amount of parsley contains the recommended daily allowance of vitamin A for adult women, and almost the amount for men. This could be added to salad, soup, or any foods as a garnish and would furnish good quality vitamin A in the diet. Because the vitamin A in vegetables is in the form of beta-carotene it is water soluble and does not build up in the liver, there is no chance of getting too much or getting an overdose from it. Almost all diseases like cancer, viruses, bronchitis, coughs, colds, and most illnesses affecting the mucus membranes can benefit from the addition of this form of vitamin A in the diet. Keep a bowl of freshly chopped parsley on the table at every meal so that everyone can help him- or herself to healthful eating and eye pleasing touches, to give a gourmet or festive look to the meal.

DEODORANT & BREATH FRESHENER

Parsley also contains chlorophyll, which has been touted to be a deodorant or breath freshener. In the 50's it was so popular that even dog food had chlorophyll pellets in it. Parsley is added as a garnish on the plates of all "trendy" and French Service restaurants. This was done so that it could be chewed after the fatty, heavily seasoned main course, before the lighter courses and dessert were served. This was "to cleanse the palate" from garlic especially. Many garlic oil capsules include parsley oil in the hopes that it will help keep the odor of garlic to a minimum.

THE ONLY REAL FOOD

Sometimes when I travel, I find that the places one is forced to stay have no green vegetables, no green salads, at least not the dark green kind I like, so I order some fresh sprigs of parsley to be brought. Many places have jumped on the fast food, pre-prepared food bandwagon and parsley is the only real food in the place. Many times I order oatmeal cereal plain and chopped parsley rather than eat foods that contain M.S.G., salt, breading, bacon and other highly preserved meats, rich cream sauces, and white bread. Sometimes I also ask for chopped garlic, but many places usually use garlic salt or powder so that is harder to get.

Once on a car trip a group of us stopped at a roadside eatery in Illinois and found that they had plastic parsley on the plate as a garnish. We laughed for much of the trip about this, and still do 15 years later, wondering if they throw it out or put it through the dish-washer and reuse it. We considered what might have happened if one of us had eaten it: would there be any digestion of it, would it hurt us, on an X-Ray would it show up lodged somewhere in the body? Would a lawyer like a case like this?

Green Goddess Dressing

2	green onions
1 bunch	fresh parsley, cilantro, or dill
1 clove	garlic
1/2 cup	olive or canola oil
1–2 tsp.	lemon juice

Chop parsley and onion in a blender. Add remaining ingredients and blend until smooth. Add more oil or lemon as needed for consistency. Pour over salads. Avocado can be used to replace some of the oil if desired.

MINT

Mint was considered to be one of the lesser herbs. The Jews served mint with their meat dishes, especially at the spring Feast of the Paschal Lamb. Even today the custom of serving mint with lamb is still kept in Great Britain, Canada, Australia, New Zealand, and the U.S. Mint tea is one of the most popular of all herbal teas. It is served in the Middle East and Europe as well as in North America. There are many kinds of mint growing wild and being cultivated. Garden mint, peppermint, and pennyroyal are the three that were in popular use as cooking and medicinal herbs. There are records of mint recipes in cook books as far back as A.D. 37. It was known to the ancient Hebrews, Greeks, and Romans.[35] The mints believed to have been known in the Old World are: *Mentha longifolia* and *Mentha spicata*.[36] Peppermint *Mentha piperita* is used for stomach complaints such as poor digestion, overeating, flatulence, nausea, heartburn, colic, and often is given to children as a relaxing tea along with catnip.[37]

WORMWOOD

He has filled me with bitterness, he has sated me with wormwood . . . . Remember my affliction and my bitterness, the wormwood and the gall!
Lamentations 3:15, 19 (RSV)

Of all the herbs mentioned in the Bible this is the one that gets the most recognition. It is also the one that people know the least about. Here it is mentioned in connection with gall, and this is the reference that most people remember. Wormwood is a very, very, bitter herb. Most of the scriptural references are using wormwood to connote bitterness. Wormwood is mentioned in many herbal books with a warning that it should never be taken as an extract full strength. It should always be sipped very slowly a sip at a time over the course of an half hour. It would, however, take a large amount of wormwood, about 56,000 cups, to have any poisonous effect. This would be almost impossible for any one to drink in a lifetime, let alone in one sitting.

Artemisia absinthium or wormwood is one ingredient in many preparations, such as absinthe, used for aiding digestion. It is known as a stomachic and sedative. The oil of wormwood is so powerful that it has been known to be a central nervous system depressant and in one case was thought to cause stupor followed by convulsions. It is speculated that as little as 15 mL of the concentrated oil has been known to cause coma and convulsions in adults[38] although it is very difficult to get this much or ingest this much, and I, of course, do not recommend it.

Traditionally tonics using wormwood were given diluted to increase appetite or improve digestion. These are generally called stomach bitters, and could become habit forming from the wormwood not to mention the alcohol that was in it. It is generally considered habit forming if one takes anything to stimulate bodily functions on a regular basis, especially if the condition is not remedied and the product is taken frequently. Digestive bitters that are generally taken when overeating could be a very bad habit. If the body cannot digest a large amount all at once, one should eat less and chew more so that the body's digestive functions will work properly. Taking digestive bitters for general health tonic purposes or for internal cleaning or toning is acceptable. Using bitters occasionally, when needed, is also acceptable.

Very small amounts of wormwood are still used in digestive tonics with the approval of the government. Some of these are sold in delicatessens and health food stores, and many contain no alcohol. It is the preparations with alcohol that many alcoholics drink when they want alcohol. Because bitter herbs work on the liver and digestion in general, it is strange that this tonic is taken by the very people who need liver toners. Alcohol damages the liver and bitters help it to work better.

SEE YOUR DOCTOR

It is never a good idea to take any kind of medication for long periods without consulting a doctor for the underlying problem. Any digestion problems could be due to lack of chewing, and therefore a lack of digestive enzymes, or a lack of production of enzymes. There are many kinds of infections and illnesses that might bring on poor digestion. There are also the underlying emotional situations that could be bringing on fear, which will automatically slow down digestion. Problems with blood sugar could also throw off digestion. As you can see it is never a good idea to self-medicate for something as serious as digestive disturbances on an ongoing basis. The odd time that one does overeat and wants help with heartburn, gas, or digestion, stomach bitters are a great help.

"STRONG" DRINK

Many people who find they are obligated to order a "strong" drink when in social or business situations find that bitters and soda is an acceptable substitute. It will have very little alcohol in it and yet it is a "bar" type drink that often will keep well-meaning friends quiet where drinking soda or mineral water will bring on ridicule. It is so wonderful that people are becoming more health conscious and are drinking bottled mineral waters in social settings so that it is no longer an occasion for ridicule when soda or mineral water is drunk.

WORMWOOD IN THE NEW TESTAMENT

A third of the waters became wormwood, and many men died of the water, because it was made bitter. Revelation 8:11b (RSV)

The use of wormwood in the New Testament is to signify "undrinkable" not so much "bitterness," as is seen in Revelation 8:11. This is owing to the difference in the original words used. In the Old Testament the word translated as wormwood is *Laanah* which means "bitterness," while the New Testament word is the Greek word *Apsinthos* and is usually translated as "undrinkable." [39] According to George M. Lamsa, an Aramaic scholar, the phrase "A root that beareth gall and wormwood" was an idiom used in the time of the writing of the Old Testament to mean: A corrupt person with evil deeds. [40] In Jeremiah 9:15 he translates wormwood as bitterness and water of gall as bitterness and distress.

Wormwood is one of the herbs mentioned in the Bible that would be considered a medicinal herb only, and not one to be eaten with any regularity.

SORREL

This is another green plant that is enjoying a revival in "trendy" eating places. It is used for salads and is very high in potassium. There are several kinds. The sheep sorrel has long arrow-shaped leaves and is used as an antiscorbutic, or aid to preventing scurvy. It is often called sourgrass. The common kind that I know grows in lawns and looks like pale lime green clover leaves with a yellow flower, this is also called sourgrass. It has about the same properties as the sheep sorrel or *Rumex acetosella*. As kids, my sister and I used to eat the sorrel from the lawn in the spring and through-out the summer just because we liked the sour explosion in our mouth when a few of the delicate leaves were chewed, we didn't know we were helping to prevent scurvy.

THE OTHER GREENS

The other greens that are mentioned as bitter herbs are chicory *Cichorium endiva*, lettuce *Lactuca sativa*, and endive which is almost the same as chicory. Depending on the variety and where it was grown, all these greens can be bitter. As we saw it is a good thing to eat bitter herbs when consuming a high meat or high fat diet, just for the sake of digestion, as well as for the addition of fiber, which also helps with digestion. French and Italian tradition dictates that the salad should be eaten after the meal and should consist of dark leafy greens, virgin olive oil, and lemon juice, perhaps that is a tradition carried over for thousands of years to help digestion.

Paavo Airola found during his health cruises that eating the salad first at a meal was not as helpful for proper digestion as eating carbohydrate or protein first. His theory is that whatever the first few mouthfuls contain is the regulator for how much digestive enzyme the body should produce. It takes less for salads than protein or carbohydrates. This is why bread or rolls (carbohydrate) are often served first. Not to fill you up, but to start your digestive juices going so that you will digest the heavier meal which will come later.

HERBS AND SPICES

There are many mentions of herbs and spices used for cooking as well as for medicine in the Bible. Most of them are still in use today. Anise, coriander, cummin or cumin, dill, marjoram, thyme, and rosemary (these last three are often mentioned as hyssop), mustard, "spice" which is translated to mean cinnamon or cassia, and bay leaf.[41]

WHY EAT GREENS?

Why were greens, herbs, and bitter herbs mentioned so often in the Bible? They were the recipe for healthy living that was needed then just as it is needed now. Some of the most common dietary errors I see in nutrition counseling are eating too little green vegetables, eating no raw vegetables, and eating pale "greens" thinking they are giving nutritional value. Just remember that in green vegetables it's the green part that has the nutritional value. If it is not green then what is the sense of eating it? The darker green it is the better it is for you.

NUTRITIONAL VALUES

Mustard Greens (100 g [3 1/2 oz])

> 31 calories
> 0 cholesterol
> 3 g protein
> 1.1 g fiber
> 7,000 I.U. vitamin A
> 97 mg vitamin C
> 0.11 mg B1
> 0.22 mg B2
> 0.8 mg B3
> 183 mg calcium
> 27 mg magnesium
> 377 mg potassium
> 3 mg iron

Chicory Greens (30-40 small leaves)

> 20 calories
> 0 cholesterol
> 1.8 g protein
> 0.8 g fiber
> 4,000 I.U. vitamin A
> 22 mg vitamin C
> 0.06 mg B1
> 0.10 mg B2
> 0.5 mg B3
> 86 mg calcium
> 13 mg magnesium
> 420 mg potassium
> 0.90 mg iron

Cabbage (raw, 225 mL [1 cup] shredded)
    24 calories
    0 cholesterol
    1.3 g protein
    0.8 g fiber
    130 I.U. vitamin A
    47 mg vitamin C
    0.05 mg B1
    0.05 mg B2
    0.3 mg B3
    49 mg calcium
    13 mg magnesium
    233 mg potassium
    0.4 mg iron

Collard Greens (100 g [3 1/2 oz])
    40 calories
    3.6 g protein
    0.9 g fiber
    6,500 I.U. vitamin A
    92 mg vitamin C
    0.2 mg B1
    0.31 mg B2
    1.7 mg B3
    203 mg calcium
    57 mg magnesium
    401 mg potassium
    1 mg iron

Butterhead Lettuce (100 g [3 1/2 oz])
    14 calories
    1.2 g protein
    0.5 g fiber
    970 I.U. vitamin A
    8 mg Vitamin C
    0.06 mg B1 & B2
    0.3 mg B3
    35 mg calcium
    11 mg magnesium
    264 mg potassium
    2 mg iron

Romaine Lettuce (100 g [3 1/2 oz])
  18 calories
  1.3 g protein
  0.7 g fiber
  1900 I.U. vitamin A
  18 mg vitamin C
  0.05 mg B1
  0.08 mg B2
  0.4 mg B3
  68 mg calcium
  11 mg magnesium
  264 mg potassium
  1.4 mg iron

Iceburg Lettuce (head, 100 g [3 1/2 oz])
  13 calories
  0.9 g protein
  0.5 g fiber
  330 I.U. vitamin A
  6 mg vitamin C
  0.06 mg B1 & B2
  0.3 mg B3
  20 mg calcium
  11 mg magnesium
  175 mg potassium
  0.5 mg iron[42]

By looking at the above nutritional breakdowns it is easy to see that the greener the green, the higher the nutritional value. When I teach vegetarian or natural food cooking classes I always instruct the students to eat only green lettuce. If lettuce is pale green or almost white it is not nutritionally useful. Most of the head lettuce is made for selling, not for eating. It can be grown without much trouble. It can be picked, shipped, and stored without much trouble. When it gets to the shelf it can remain there for days without going pale (since it already is) or wilting; in a salad bar it stays crisp for hours under hot lights out in the open. In the store it can be displayed, and after a few days the outer leaves can be removed and the lettuce can still be sold for the same amount. Rough treatment doesn't make too much difference in how it looks. This all means that it is the most economical lettuce for a store or restaurant to use. Even though the nutritional values of the B vitamins are low, heat and light destroy B vitamins, so the longer it stays out the less there are of them in the lettuce we eat. After a while there might not be any B vitamin left at all. If the lettuce is very dark green, then it is a different story.

Just remember my favorite expression: "If God made it, eat it; if man made it, leave it." Pale lettuce is something that man altered, it is not the way God intended it to be.

MELONS, CUCUMBERS, AND OTHER CUCURBITS

We remember the fish we ate in Egypt for nothing, the cucumbers, the melons . . . . Numbers 11:5 (RSV)

Cucumbers and melons are from the same family, so it is no wonder that the names are used in such a way in the Bible as to be interchangeable. *Miqshah* used in Isaiah 1:8 is often translated as "garden of cucumbers," but it is felt that it really should be "the place of the watermelon." (*And the daughter of Zion is left like a booth in a vineyard, like a lodge in a cucumber field, like a besieged city.* Isaiah 1:8) In Numbers 11:5 the word *Quishuim* is used and this can mean watermelon, cucumber, or gourd. It seems to me that it means cucumbers *Cucumis sativus.*[43] If this were not the case why else would there be the two listed: cucumbers and melons. It is not clear whether melons and cucumbers were wild or cultivated, but it seems that there were some of each. This is what was being described in the first chapter of Isaiah.

When gardens or market gardens were grown the farmer built a shelter to sleep near his crop to keep poachers away. When the season was over this fell to ruin and was left as a mass of rubble. Along with the rubble left from the vines of the cucumbers the garden looked desolate. In North America we have the same look in fields when the corn plants are left standing after the corn heads are harvested. Some are broken, and some have fallen.

Hollow gourds were a source of water jugs and vessels for carrying and holding liquids. They are light weight, easy to carry, and don't leak.

Pumpkins and other squash are also in the same family, but are generally not grown in the warmer climates as often as melons and cucumbers. The high water content of melons and cucumbers were necessary for health in the hot climate. The reverse is also true, that water is needed to grow them, and the rivers were used as irrigation to grow these plants. Many poor people lived off cucumbers in the hot weather, so there may have been wild ones growing or cucumbers were very inexpensive!

CUCUMBERS AND BEAUTY

Cucumbers are used for beauty treatments in cleansing creams, rubbed on the skin to improve oily skin, and reduce large pores. They are soothing and help to draw out excess water. Slices of cucumber are placed over the eyelids when in the sun to prevent wrinkles around the eyes and to soothe the eyes from the effects of the sun. Some women put slices over their eyes when they have been crying to remove the redness and puffiness. Others rest with them on their eyes while lying with their feet elevated. There are cucumber beauty recipes that go back to before Cleopatra. Cucumbers have withstood the test of time and are still being used today. I just bought some cucumber hand lotion and soap from one of the "first apothecary shops to open in the new world." It was advertised in their catalogue ". . . to keep skin moist, firm, refreshed." Sarah Bernhardt used this and had some sent to her while she was in Paris 100 years ago.

MELONS

Watermelons were known in the Middle East and it is the *Citrullus vulgaris* that is thought to have been grown as it is still being grown and sold outside the Damascus Gate at Jerusalem.[44] They were green and leathery outside and orange-red and sweet inside. Watermelons are often eaten in the hottest weather due to the fact that they have a high percentage of water. They are also believed to be good for the kidneys and are used frequently as the only food or drink taken during fasting. Because they are very sweet they will furnish calories so that one can continue to work while doing a cleansing fast. (I am not fond of unsupervised fasting of any kind, even with watermelons.)

NUTRITIONAL VALUES

Cucumber (1/2 medium, raw, with peel)
>   8 calories
>   0.5 g protein
>   0.3 g fiber
>   125 I.U. vitamin A (found in the skin)
>   6 mg vitamin C
>   0.01 mg B1
>   0.02 mg B2

0.1 mg B3
13 mg calcium
6 mg magnesium
80 mg potassium
0.60 mg iron

Watermelon (250 mL [1 cup])
50 calories
1 g protein
0.5 g fiber
585 I.U. vitamin A
15 mg vitamin C
0.13 mg B1
0.03 mg B2
0.3 mg B3
0.23 mg B6
13 mg calcium
17 mg magnesium
0.11 mg zinc
0.059 mg manganese
0.28 mg iron
0.051 mg copper[45]

You can see that cucumbers and melons are low in calories and contain many of the necessary nutrients which make them good for every day eating as well as for dieting.

SQUASH

There is no mention of squash in the Bible, although they are in the same family with the melons and cucumbers. Gourds, also in the same family, are mentioned but not in a good light as in Jonah 4:6. It is thought that this plant is really the castor bean not the gourd that we know. Some of the melons mentioned were very similar to squash and many have been hybrid into the squash that we use now. Squash and pumpkin were used in recipes in the first known cookbook that is still in existence. It was written by a man named M. Gabius Apicius who seems to have popularized both the omelet and cheesecake. He lived in Rome around 42 B.C. to 37 A.D. We are not sure if these are the same squash and pumpkin that we know in North America.

We eat squash, carrots, yellow turnip or rutabaga, and other yellow vegetables for the taste but also to have vitamin A in the diet. After reading the section on the bitter herbs and the dark green leafy veggies, we can see that people in the ancient Middle East obtained vitamin A from green vegetables, which they ate often. Because we need more vitamin A in cold climates to keep the mucus membranes healthy that might be damaged by cold climates, we need to eat dark yellow and orange vegetables as well as dark green ones. In very cold climates like the Arctic, people are in the habit of eating reindeer liver to get high doses of vitamin A when they don't have yellow or green vegetables. That they do this naturally indicates to me that we need more vitamin A in colder climates.

Baked Squash

Scrub off any dirt. Cut out any bad spots and rub cut area with oil or butter. Place squash on baking sheet. Pierce it on the top with a knife to let steam escape, this will prevent any accidental explosions. Bake at 425^0F for an hour or so depending on the size and type of squash. A giant hubbard will take longer than a small butternut, since the former is larger and has a firmer flesh. The cut side should be on top so the juices don't drain into the oven or pan. When you think it might be done test it by inserting a sharp knife in the top, if it is easily inserted then the squash is done. You might also want to test it a second way. I generally use two pot holders and gently squeeze the squash, if it gives easily it is done, if not continue to cook for 10-15 more minutes. Remove from oven using the pan underneath.

Once I took a giant hubbard out of the oven after almost 2 hours. I lifted one end with a pot holder and grasped the stem with the other pot holder. Well, you guessed it, the stem came off, the squash plopped to the floor and flattened right there in my kitchen. I carefully lifted up all the squash that was not touching the floor using a pancake turner and put it into a bowl. I was baking the squash to purée and freeze in 1 1/2 cup portions for the Thanksgiving cake in the sweets chapter of *The World's Oldest Health Plan Recipe Companion*. Even then I ended up with about 10 portions or more of frozen squash. This squash was almost as big as the entire oven, it was a good thing that I lost almost half of it. It was easy to laugh at myself for being so stupid as to hold the stem when there was so much squash left anyway. It isn't as easy if you are having one for dinner and drop it this way.

Place the whole squash in a large bowl and cut it open with a long knife. The juices will drain into the bowl and can be used for puréeing if needed. Simply scoop out the seeds and serve portions any way you like. The flesh will be rich, sweet, juicy, and very enjoyable. There will be no peeling of raw squash, no hard work, no dried-out baked squash. Once it is cooked and cut open you can add butter, honey, lemon zest, nuts, brown sugar, or whatever you would have put on it while baking. A dark squash such as turban or butternut could be mixed with pineapple in its own juice and served for dessert once it is baked this way.

This works best with winter squash, those with hard skins like acorn, pepper, butternut, hubbard, turban, pumpkin, spaghetti, and many others.

Squash Soup

4 large	cooking onions cut in 8 pieces each
2 Tbsp.	cold pressed oil or butter
1 medium	squash, seeded and cut into 1 inch squares
	water as needed
1 tsp.	sea salt
2–3 Tbsp.	hard wheat flour
	tamari sauce to taste

Sauté onions in oil or butter in soup pot until golden or just limp, add squash and continue to sauté until soft at the edges. Add water to cover and cook until squash is soft. Drain veggies and reserve the liquid, cool. Peel squash and purée with cooking liquid and onions. For each 4 cups purée add 1 1/2 cups more water. Heat purée and water to the boiling point slowly. In separate pan toast flour until it gives off a nutty smell. Make runny paste with flour and water and add to boiling soup. Cook 10–15 minutes until thickened, stir often. Add salt or tamari to taste after cooking.

Serves 4–6 depending on the size of the squash. Garnish with toasted sesame seeds and/or chopped parsley or cilantro. I often stir in 1 teaspoon of ground cumin for a different taste.

NB: You can peel the squash first if you wish.

Stuffed Squash or Pumpkin

1 medium	pie pumpkin
2 Tbsp.	oil or butter
2	cooking onions

1 clove	garlic
3	mushrooms
1–2 cups	cooked buckwheat or rice
1 cup	Chinese style tofu
1–2 tsp.	dried tarragon or 1 Tbsp. fresh
1 Tbsp.	miso paste
1/2–1 tsp.	sage (optional)

Bake squash in 400°F oven for 30 minutes or until just starting to be done. Pierce top with knife before baking.

Chop onions, garlic, and mushrooms and sauté in butter until golden brown. Blend tofu, miso, tarragon, sage together in food processor or with potato masher. Using plastic blade add remaining ingredients and mix well. (Or mix by hand.) Cut the top off the pumpkin and scoop out the seeds. Stuff pumpkin with filling and replace top. Set in baking dish and bake in 350°F oven for 20-40 minutes until pumpkin is soft and filling is firm.

Serve by cutting into wedges, keeping filling in place. Each person will have a crescent shaped serving. This can be topped with mushroom gravy or served plain. Serve with cranberry sauce, green vegetable and/or salad. One serving contains protein, whole grain, and yellow vegetable. Only green vegetables are needed for a well balanced meal. A dessert of fruit can be served or the cranberry sauce can serve as the fruit serving.

I often serve this when I can prepare it ahead of time and just do the last stage of baking at the time of eating. Many vegetarians have this sort of dish on Thanksgiving or other holidays in place of turkey.

The squash can be stuffed raw and baked for an hour or until done. Cut off top and scoop out seeds. Fill with prepared filling and replace top.

NB: the tofu can be replaced by two eggs if tofu is not available. Ground meat can be included if desired.

NUTRITIONAL VALUES

The United States Recommended Daily Allowance of vitamin A is 5,000 to 8,000 I.U.[46] This would be very easy to obtain if our diets consisted of dark green leafy vegetables, peas and beans, yellow and orange vegetables each day. This is why the governments of Canada and the United States suggest we eat these foods daily.

BETA CAROTENE

Beta carotene is the precursor of vitamin A, which means that our body will make vitamin A from it. Beta carotene is also being shown to protect against cancer, and mucus membrane disorders like bronchitis, asthma, sinus, ear, eye, and throat problems. It is also good for the skin and intestines. That means that most of the body inside and out needs beta carotene to be healthy. Many soldiers in World Wars I and II remember being forced to eat carrots to help them see at night. Then it fell out of popularity to say that one could see better at night if he or she ate carrots. Now science has shown that the rods and cones in the eyes which are necessary for all vision, especially night vision, need beta carotene to function and keep healthy. Funny how the old sayings are being proved true by science, isn't it?

SPROUTS

Sprouts can be made very easily from seeds, grains, beans, and some nuts. When selecting seeds, make sure that they have not been treated to prevent sprouting or molding; this is why it is best to buy the seeds in a grocery, natural food, or other food store. Sprouts can be a good source of vitamins and minerals at a very low cost. For some people it is the only fresh food that they can grow, especially in an apartment. Sprouts can be grown all year long and provide ready fresh vegetables.

HOW TO GROW SPROUTS

A quart or liter jar and an open covering for the top are all the equipment necessary to grow sprouts. I generally use a piece of nylon screening for the cover, some people use old stockings, J Cloths or Handy-wipes, or netting from curtains. Use the jar ring to hold the material in place or use a string or rubber band. A larger jar can be used for more sprouts, this is useful for large groups, not small families. It is better to have several jars of different sprouts growing at various stages to be used over several days than to have one big jar of one kind.

Measure out the amount of seeds or beans needed for the jar. With alfalfa seeds I usually use 2 Tbsp. (30 mL) and kidney beans 1/3 cup (60 mL) for a one liter or one quart jar. This will be enough for the size of the jar. Use smaller measures of small seeds, and larger measures of larger seeds or beans.

Wash and pick over the seeds or beans to remove any rocks, dirt, or sticks. Soak the seeds for 4 to 8 hours and the beans overnight to rehydrate them.

Pour off soaking water and use for plants or soup. Put the soaked seeds into the jar, cover, drain, shake the seeds to spread them out. Leave in a slightly warm, dark place until sprouted. Rinse and drain every 4 to 6 hours or three times a day until they have sprouted. When sprouts form place the jar in the sun for a few hours to allow the little leaves to develop chlorophyll and turn green. It usually takes two or three days for the sprouts to grow to edible size and 20 to 30 minutes for chlorophyll to form. If the place is too hot the sprouts or seeds might rot, mold, or cook. If too wet they might rot or mold. If too cold they won't sprout and might even freeze.

The basement is not always a good idea if the basement is not extremely clean.

When sprouts are finished clean off the unsprouted seeds by floating them away in a bowl of cool water, this also gets rid of the hulls. Drain and keep in the refrigerator in a lightly covered bag or bowl in the crisper.

NUTRITIONAL VALUES

Alfalfa Sprouts (3 1/2 oz [100 g], raw)
> 41 calories
> 0.6 g fat
> 0 cholesterol
> 5.1 g protein
> 1.7 g fiber
> 16 mg vitamin C
> 0.14 mg B1
> 0.21 mg B2
> 28 mg calcium
> 1 mg zinc
> 1.4 mg iron

Mung Bean Sprouts (3 1/2 oz [100 g], raw)
> 35 calories
> 0 cholesterol
> 3.8 g protein
> 0.7 g fiber
> 20 I.U. Vitamin A
> 19 mg Vitamin C
> 0.13 mg B1

0.13 mg B2
0.8 mg B3
19 mg calcium
223 mg potassium
1.3 mg iron[47]

SPROUTS AT EVERY MEAL

Sprouts can be eaten with every meal. There are many commercial breakfast cereals made of sprouted grains. Adding fresh sprouts to meals is often a great way to introduce raw vegetables at every meal. In the 70's many people went on "sprout kicks" and ate sprouts for breakfast. The favorite was a peanut butter, mustard, dill pickle, and sprout sandwich, often with slices of raw garlic or onion as well. I eat sprouts for breakfast on various sandwiches or burritos, or on a bowl of steamed vegetables.

Alfalfa sprouts are sources of vitamin K. We saw earlier that vitamin K is useful in helping to absorb calcium and for prevention of osteoporosis.

POWER GARNISH

Freshly chopped alfalfa, sunflower, or radish sprouts and parsley can be added as a garnish to any meal. This looks great over soup, stews, salads, vegetables, anything. This will give the enzymes that are found in raw veggies, Beta Carotene, calcium, magnesium, B vitamins, minerals, protein, and chlorophyll to the food being eaten. You could even sprinkle it on pizza just before serving it. I'm sure that Superman ate sprouts.

Egg Foo Yong

2	green onions
4	mushrooms
1/4	red or green sweet pepper
1 cup	mung bean sprouts
2	eggs
2 tsp.	cold water
1 tsp.	shoyu or tamari
1 tsp.	corn or arrowroot starch (optional)
	oil or butter for cooking

Cut onions, mushrooms, and peppers into match stick pieces. Heat about 2 teaspoons oil until hot, but not smoking, use medium heat. Sauté veggies until soft and lightly browned. Beat eggs, water, shoyu, and starch together, mix in the cooked veggies and raw sprouts. Wipe a griddle or heavy pan with oil and heat to hot, but not smoking. Spoon egg/veggie mixture onto it cooking until slightly set on the top, turn and cook until firm. This should take no longer than 5–7 minutes. Most of the sprouts should still be crunchy.

Egg Foo Yong can be served in whole grain buns with lettuce, mayonnaise, mustard, catsup, etc. Traditionally it is served as a main course with a gravy made from corn starch and soy sauce or mushroom gravy.

Tofu Foo Yong

Follow the directions for Egg Foo Yong above, but use 1 egg and 200 g of well mashed tofu and 2 tablespoons of corn or arrowroot starch. OR use all tofu of the silken or calcium sulfate/Chinese style and no eggs. You might want to add seasonings to this such as 1/4 teaspoon cumin powder, soy sauce, or cayenne pepper.

Sprout Melt
Whole grain, sprouted grain, or Ezekiel bread slices
Avocado
lemon juice
cayenne pepper
green onions
garlic
parsley
alfalfa sprouts
Edam, Swiss, or white cheddar cheese

Toast bread on both sides and set aside. Mash avocado and lemon juice together using enough lemon juice to make it spreadable. Add chopped onions, garlic, parsley, and cayenne pepper to taste. Spread on toast, cover with sprouts then cheese slices and broil until cheese melts.

SEA VEGETABLES

Sea Vegetables are the most useful vegetables available today because of their great abundance, versatility, and high nutritional values. All known vitamins and minerals can be found in some type of sea vegetable.

DULSE

Dulse, *Palmaria palmata*, has been eaten in Iceland since 961 B.C. It is usually eaten raw or dried as a snack. It is eaten in Ireland and all of the British Isles, the Mediterranean area, Alaska, Canada, Brittany, and the old U.S.S.R. Dulse is very high in protein, fat, and vitamin A. It has a high iodine and phosphorus content. It also contains sugar, starch, Vitamins B6, B12, C, and E, soluble nitrogen, yeast, bromine, potassium, magnesium, sulfur, calcium, sodium, radium, boron, rubidium, manganese, titanium, and trace elements.[48] It is also a source of carrageenan, a thickening agent used in food processing. Dulse is often sold in fish markets in small packages and is dark reddish/purple in color.

AWO-NORI

Awo-nori, *Monostroma latissimum*, is found in the Mediterranean as well as in the Atlantic, Pacific, and other temperate coastal waters. This sea vegetable is used most often dried and ground as a seasoning.

Sea vegetables were highly esteemed in China as far back as 800 to 600 B.C. During the time of Confucius sea vegetables and other algae were mentioned in poems coupled with love, in much the same way as we think of chocolates and love.[49] Sea algal repasts have recently been excavated from sea side dwellings of Stone Age South Africa.

SEA VEGETABLES IN THE BIBLE

There is no mention of sea vegetables in the Bible, but then again there are many foods that are not mentioned in the Bible that were commonly eaten. We know that the area depended on the sea for much of its food. It is very possible that sea plants and algae were regularly eaten as they are in Japan, China, Canada, and other coastal areas that depend on the sea for their livelihood.

Sea vegetables are gaining popularity, once again, due to the abundance of types and the high nutritional values each offers. Kelp is becoming very popular because of its iodine and potassium contents.

Most health or Asian food stores carry several different sea vegetables such as nori, kombu, wakame, hijiki, kelp, and other lavers. They are an easy way to obtain minerals in the diet. They can be added to just about everything or toasted, crushed, and sprinkled on as a condiment. Many salt substitutes contain sea vegetables because they are higher in potassium than in sodium and, yet, have a salty taste.

Algin found in sea vegetables, especially kelp, is used for attracting and removing pollutants from the body. When I worked in the Nutritional and Preventive Medical Clinic in Toronto we used it to remove lead poisoning, cadmium poisoning, and the effects of cigarette smoking (also lead poisoning.) English research done in the 60's showed that many children classed as hyperactive by doctors or schools were children who had lead poisoning from parents who smoked and the lead that comes from certain coal and gas fires. Algin was used to remove it and they were no longer exhibiting signs of being hyperactive. Algin tablets can be found in health food stores alone or in combination with other cleansing ingredients such as garlic, brewers yeast, pectin, and vitamin C. Dark green leafy vegetables and beans also help remove many kinds of toxins. A simple blood test will show levels that are very high. A hair analysis will show levels that are in the beginning stages.

Many cases of mental retardation can be traced to high lead levels in the air or the parents' bodies. If you live in an industrial area, near a highway, or smoke cigarettes, please have yourself and your children checked for high lead levels. Eating apples, dark green veggies, beans, garlic, and sea veggies can help remove the toxins, but an holistic practitioner can design a specific program for detoxifying your system of this ancient and modern curse. Lead pipes, pewter, brightly colored pottery, old paint, synthetic gardening sprays, and automobile exhaust all can contain lead levels high enough to cause a reaction in a child's body.

At the Nutritional and Preventive Medical Clinic we found that many people who came to us for treatment of hardening of the arteries also had high lead levels. There are many good books and pamphlets available on lead poisoning. If you suspect that you might have been in contact with any of these lead sources, please have yourself checked out.

REFERENCES

1. Shewell-Cooper, W.E., *Plants, Flowers, and Herbs of the Bible*, Keats Pub., New Canaan, Connecticut. 1977.

2. Genesis 25:34.

3. Jenkins, Dr., David, "Research Highlights," Dec. 1986, University of Toronto.

4. Hallfrisch, J., R. Andres, J. Tobin, D. Muller, "Fiber Intake, Age, and Other Risk Factors," Gerontology Research Center, NIA, NIH, Baltimore, Maryland., American Journal of Clinical Nutrition, 41 (4) 846 '85.

5. Pennington, Jean and Helen Church, *Food Values of Portions Commonly Used*, Harper and Row, 1980, 1985.

6. Shewell-Cooper.

7. Walker, Winnifred, *All The Plants of The Bible*, Lutterworth Press, London, 1959.

8. Soy Protein In Adult Human Nutrition: A Review With New Data, *Soy Protein and Human Nutrition*, Ed.: H. Wilcke, D. Hopkins, D. Waggle, Academic Press, 1979.

9. Pennington-Church.

10. Anderson, James W., "Cholesterol Lowering Effects of Canned Beans For Hypercholesterolemic Men," Medical Services, Veterans Administration Medical Center and University of Kentucky, Clinical Research 33 (4) A871 1985.

11. Lappé, Frances Moore, *Diet For A Small Planet*, Ballantine, New York, 1971.

12. Williams, Sue Rodwell, *Nutrition And Diet Therapy*, The C.V. Mosby Company, Saint Louis, 1973, p. 229.

13. Williams, p. 14.

14. Airola, Paavo, *The Miracle Of Garlic*, Health Plus Publishers, Phoenix, 1978, p. 25, 27.

15. Shewell-Cooper.

16. Lau, Benjamin, M.D., Ph.D., *Garlic For Health*, Lotus Light Publications, Wisconsin, 1988.

17. Crook, William G., M.D., *The Yeast Connection*, Professional Books, Jackson, Tennessee, 1992, p. 141.

18. Crook, p. 136.

19. Airola, p. 35.

20. Airola, p. 33.

21. Pennington-Church.

22. Pennington-Church.

23. Shewell-Cooper.

24. Maleskey, Gale, "Intensive Healing Diets," Prevention Magazine, Vol. 38, No. 12, Dec. 1986, pp. 77–78.

25. Pennington-Church.

26. Delvin, E.E., "New Perspectives In The Role Of Calcium And Vitamin D In Human Health," Nutrition Quarterly, Volume 10, No. 4, 1986, p. 33 ff.

27. Walker, p. 36.

28. Walker, p. 36.

29. Pennington-Church.

30. Treben, Maria, *Health Through God's Pharmacy*, Wilhelm Ennsthaler, Steyr, 1982, p. 23.

31. Pennington-Church.

32. *U.S.D.A. Agriculture Handbook No. 456*, Nutritive Value of American Foods, 1975.

33. Spoerke, David, Jr., *Herbal Medications*, Woodbridge Press, Santa Barbara, 1980, pp. 91, 92.

34. Pennington-Church.

35. Walker, p. 132.

36. Shewell-Cooper, p. 91.

37. Meyer, Joseph, *The Herbalist*, Clarence Meyer Publisher, USA, 1973.

38. Spoerke, p. 180.

39. Shewell-Cooper, p.122.

40. Lamsa, George M., *Idioms Of The Bible Explained And A Key To The Original Gospels*, Harper and Row, San Francisco, 1931, 1971, 1985.

41. Shewell-Cooper.

42. Pennington-Church.

43. Shewell-Cooper, pp. 99,100.

44. Walker, p. 130.

45. Pennington-Church.

46. Pennington-Church.

47. Pennington-Church.

48. Madlener, Judith Cooper, *The Sea Vegetable Book*, Clarkson N. Potter, New York, 1977, p. 124, 125.

49. Madlener, p. 19.

You will have plenty of goats' milk to feed you and your family and to nourish your servant girls. Proverbs 27:27 (NIV)

In that day, a man will keep alive a young cow and two goats. And because of the abundance of the milk they will give, he will have curds to eat. All who remain in the land will eat curds and honey. Isaiah 7:21, 22 (NIV)

IV

Dairy In The Diet
Dairy Products–
Milk, Yogurt, Cheese, & Butter

Milk products were a staple food in Bible times. It was, however, considered that only children or babies should actually drink milk. Adults generally ate foods made of milk such as buttermilk, cheese, kefir, yogurt or laben, and butter, but they didn't really drink milk. There were many foods that were prepared from milk such as custards, cakes, and even sherbet or a kind of ice cream. Because some of the people were living in tents and moving around, they had different ways of using dairy products. Those people who were in towns and cities were more able to use all dairy products in their cuisine rather than just using cheese, yogurt, and butter. Those peoples who were traveling with a dairy herd, generally sheep or goats, were also able to use dairy products more on a daily basis.

Milk was used to connote abundance throughout the Old Testament and there are at least 17 references to "the land flowing with milk and honey."[1] Throughout the Old and New Testaments milk is used in different ways. Some of the passages refer to the use of milk and milk products as food. But milk is also used figuratively as abundance, to describe the whiteness of the teeth or skin, for Israel's vindication, for excellencies of a loved one, for the rudiments of teaching, and for unfalsified Christian doctrine.[2]

Water, bread, wine, and milk are used as symbols for the life with God. They, as well as the life with God, are no mere luxury or extra; they infer its necessity. These commodities were generally purchased for food and drink, but spiritual food to satisfy spiritual hunger was to be had for free. Isaiah 55:1 is an invitation to all who are spiritually dissatisfied (who thirst) to drink of God.[3]

Ho, every one who thirsts, come to the waters; and he who has no money, come, buy and eat. Come, buy wine and milk without money and without price. Why do you spend your money for that which is not bread, and your labor for that which does not satisfy? (RSV)

It is obvious to see that milk was a very important part of the diet of the times. The milk used most often was goat's, sheep's, or camel's milk. Cow's milk was not as common since there was very little pasture land for feeding cattle. Because of the climate and lifestyle, drinking fresh milk would be not as practical as using cultured, curded, or curdled milk such as yogurt, buttermilk, cheese, or kefir.

MILK

Sheep and goats were first domesticated in 8920 BC in Iraq; the first record of cattle for dairy purposes is in Macedonia in 3000 B.C.[4] From Neolithic times in Egypt the liquids drunk most often with meals were mead, wine, and beer, not milk.[5] In the first century A.D., Virgil wrote *Georgics* in which he is quoted as saying: "Camel's, goat's, and ewe's milk is for humans, cow's milk is for calves."[6] It almost seems to me that there was the same sort of prejudice against cow's milk among the literate then as there is growing again today in Europe and North America.

COW'S MILK

There are those who "feel" that cow's milk should be for cows only and those who can show "scientific" information as to why this is true. The "feelers" say that a cow grows to full maturity in 18 months and a human in 18 years, therefore, the genetic growth message in cow's milk is too strong for humans. They "feel" that this is why so many milk drinkers are so much bigger than those who do not drink milk. On the other side, the "scientifically" based show that there is more than twice as much protein in cow's milk as in human milk; that a newborn human cannot digest it unless it is diluted.[7] Those who advocate breast feeding of infants show that breast milk is used by infants with nearly 100% efficiency, while cow's milk is used with only 50% efficiency. The remainder is excreted. This excretion of excess protein is often mentioned as the cause of strain on an infant's kidneys which could lead to fluid retention.[8] Either way, it still looks like the same prejudice against cow's milk that was expressed thousands of years ago. And yet, cows are still bred, raised, and milked for human consumption, as they have been for 5000 years!

COOKING RULES FOR MILK, YOGURT, CREAM, AND CHEESE

From the nutritional standpoint all protein should be cooked on medium or medium/high heat or less. This includes meat, eggs, fish, milk, and milk products. Protein foods should never be cooked on very high heat, nor broiled closer than 6 inches from the heat source. High heat causes a change in the structure of the proteins, including the milk protein, or casein. The protein molecules might be broken down into smaller fragments, change shape, or clump together from the heat. This is not too bad when you want to have an end product that is lumpy or curdled, but not so good when you are making a white sauce or melted cheese sauce. Moisture is forced out of the protein because of the heat and it can also leave the end product separated or stringy, as in the case of cheese that turns stringy.

This can render the protein very difficult to digest which could lead to many health problems. Some of these problems might be hyperacidity in the stomach, heartburn, burping up sour food matter after eating, gas, belching, constipation, allergies, milk sensitivity, and a bogged down feeling. It is a stress for the body to try to digest improperly cooked proteins, which then might increase the need for more digestive enzymes or for more stress reducing techniques in the form of relaxants or sleep inducers.

Yogurt and sour cream must never be boiled in a sauce or gravy or they might curdle or separate. This is why recipes for stroganoff call for adding the sour cream just before serving after the sauce has already finished being thickened on higher heat. The sour cream or yogurt would just need to be heated.

Cheese sauces should never be boiled or the cheese will separate or, perhaps, become stringy and ruin the sauce. It is very hard to recover protein that has been cooked too much, unless you strain it and press it into cheese and use it for something else.

COW'S MILK AND DIABETES MELLITUS

A study reported in 1992 in the New England Journal of Medicine provided research that showed that an allergy to one specific part of the cow's milk actually was responsible for insulin-dependent diabetes in children. The children all were considered at risk genetically for diabetes. The conclusion of the research, however, was that if these children were never given cow's milk they would not have developed diabetes.[9]

GOAT'S MILK

For nearly 10,000 years goats have been raised for dairy use. Goat's milk has smaller protein molecules and is, therefore, more easily digested. Goat's milk comes already homogenized from the goat. This is good and bad. Good in that it never separates, bad in that without this separation butter cannot be made. A special cream separator is used to do this so that butter can be made as well as low fat goat's milk products. Goat's milk can be frozen and most of the nutrients are retained. When it is thawed it looks curdled, but will go back together when stirred. This is an advantage if goat's milk can only be bought in quantities. I love goat's milk and have even kept gallons of it frozen so that I could have freshly made yogurt, cottage cheese, cream cheese, or custard daily.

GOAT'S MILK FOR HEALTH

Allergy to cow's milk is often the first food allergen newborn babies encounter. Since goat's milk is nearest to human milk, it is often given to potentially allergic children if they are unable to breastfeed.[10] The allergy could manifest in one of three different ways. It could be dermatological in the form of eczema, gastrointestinal, or as nonspecific symptoms such as irritability and failure to thrive. The skin symptoms can be seen as dry patches, or widespread redness, dryness, and peeling. Gastrointestinal symptoms could be colic, distention, gas with vomiting, and either constipation or diarrhea.

If you have a child who is exhibiting any or many of these symptoms and is also taking cow's milk, it is best to check with your doctor to determine if there is any possibility of allergy to cow's milk. There are now lactase supplements that can be added to the milk if the person is lactose intolerant. Many people recommend taking various cultures for milk "allergy" such as L. acidophilus, L. bulgaricus, or bifidum. Either of these would be a good start if you or someone in your family is sensitive to milk. It is, however, essential to have an infant checked for allergies or other medical problems if he exhibits any of the above mentioned symptoms. Don't take a chance with your child's life. Serious aftereffects could result from giving a child anything to which he is allergic.

Dr. Paavo Airola, a noted nutritionist and health writer, often mentioned that goat's milk was closer in composition to mother's milk than cow's milk. This is why so many doctors and nutritionists recommend goat's milk for children who are unable to have breast milk for any reason. Years ago, nearly everybody knew somebody who had to give their child goat's milk for one health reason or another. Now with the advent of synthetic "milks" it isn't as common.

GOAT'S MILK & ARTHRITIS

Many people I have met have told me that drinking a quart of goat's milk a day has kept them free from symptoms of arthritis. Nutritionist Dr. Paavo Airola often recommended up to a quart of goat's milk a day as a cure for arthritis, he had many patients who claimed to have been cured doing this.[11]

I knew a plumber in Goodwood, Ontario who even raised goats so that he could get the milk. He always knew if he had drunk his milk when he was doing physical work. By the late afternoon his elbows would begin to become red, hot, and achy and seize up if he had not had his goat milk ration for the day. If he had drunk his goat's milk he would have no problem with his elbows or any other joints.

NUTRITIONAL VALUES

Cow (whole, 3.5% butterfat, 1 cup)
150 calories
8 g fat
34 mg cholesterol
8 g protein
11 g carbohydrate
0 fiber
0 vitamin A
5 mg vitamin C
0.10 mg B1
0.42 mg B2
0.2 mg B3
0.85 mg B5
0.02 mg B6

12 mcg folic acid
122 mg sodium
351 mg potassium
288 mg calcium
24 mg magnesium
1 mg zinc
0.12 mg iron[12]

Goat (4% butterfat) 1 cup
168 calories
10.1 g fat
28 mg cholesterol
8.7 g protein
10.9 g carbohydrate
0 fiber
451 I.U. vitamin A
3 mg vitamin C
0.12 mg B1
0.34 B2
0.7 mg B3
0.76 mg B5
0.11 B6
1 mcg folic acid
122 mg sodium
499 mg potassium
326 mg calcium
34 mg magnesium
0.73 mg zinc
0.12 mg iron[13]

MILK AS MEDICINE IN BIBLE TIMES

Barley soaked in curdled milk was a remedy used for palpitations of the heart.[14] Goat's milk and barley porridge was used in all forms of wasting away diseases.[15] It's interesting how milk and grains were used as medicine. At our house we used to have cornstarch pudding made of milk, cornstarch, honey, and a little vanilla, if we were ill. When we had our tonsils out we could eat all the gingerale and ice cream we wanted for several days. I didn't have mine out until I was nearly 16 so I didn't care for very much ice cream for fear that the inactivity and calories might put weight on me.

BUTTERMILK

Buttermilk is a by-product of making butter. It is the liquid that is left from the cream that is churned to separate the butter fat from the liquid. The fat, when squeezed of all liquid, becomes butter. The remaining liquid is often a little tart because it is left out overnight to make the butter. It must have been used in Bible times since they made butter, but we have no references to it in any historical data or in the Bible, at least not by that name.

Buttermilk is often drunk in the hot summer as a cooling refreshing drink. Cultured buttermilk is now being made in the dairy. It is generally made of skimmed or partially skimmed milk that is brought to a pasteurizing temperature and then cooled to 100–105°F and a starter or culture is added. It is allowed to culture until it has formed 0.6 % lactic acid. This also allows acidophilus bacteria to grow, rendering it more easily digested by people who are lactose intolerant. The milk is poured into churns and butter is added and mixed in with it to simulate real farm buttermilk. This gives a constant end product for mass marketing. It is almost impossible to find "real" buttermilk unless you make your own butter.

NUTRITIONAL VALUES

Cultured Buttermilk (1 cup)
> 99 calories
> 2.2 g fat
> 9 mg cholesterol
> 8.1 g protein
> 11.7 g carbohydrate
> 0 fiber
> 81 IU vitamin A
> 2 mg vitamin C
> 0.08 mg B1
> 0.38 mg B2
> 0.1 mg B3
> 0.08 mg B6
> 0.54 mg B12
> 0.67 mg B5
> 257 mg sodium
> 371 mg potassium
> 285 mg calcium
> 27 mg magnesium
> 0.12 mg iron
> 1.03 mg zinc[16]

FERMENTED MILK DRINKS

Kefir was made from milk using a fermentation process. It was known for its intoxicating qualities. It was made from mare's milk. Similar drinks were made of camel or yak milk. Kefir is sold now in natural food stores and delicatessens which has been made from fermented rice grains and milk, but the end product is not fermented. Generally this kefir does not contain alcohol. These fermented drinks can often be used by lactose intolerant people with great success without any stomach or digestive distress.

LACTOSE INTOLERANCE

Lactose is the name for the sugar that is naturally present in milk. Lactase is the enzyme in the human body that is responsible for digesting the lactose. If a person has no or very little lactase, he will not be able to digest milk products. About 2/3's of all adults including 90 to 95% of Orientals and 70 to 75% of blacks, have very little ability to digest milk sugar. The symptoms most often associated with lactose intolerance are gas, intestinal or abdominal bloating, diarrhea, constipation, and, sometimes, behavior problems.

In Toronto, Ontario in the 1980's a CTV television network show did an experiment through the school system with children from Negro backgrounds. They were from India, the West Indies, South America, and Africa. All of these children had no background of milk causing distress. All of the children drank milk with meals. When the children were given milk to drink on an empty stomach a very large majority of them exhibited immediate and often severe symptoms from vomiting and diarrhea to stomach cramps. Their conclusions were that the other foods eaten with the milk often masked the symptoms and also helped to digest it somewhat. All of the children who were immediately ill from the milk also were the same children who had frequent colds, runny noses, and other symptoms of their body being out of balance.

If you find that you suffer from headaches, diarrhea or constipation, skin rashes, or other vague symptoms that are not explained by some diagnosed illness, you may wish to switch to fermented milk products only and see if that relieves your symptoms. Or use milk that contains lactase to supply the needed enzyme. You might even want to experiment by going off all milk products altogether. This would mean no butter, margarine, cream, ice cream, yogurt, milk, cheese, or anything that contains any milk whatsoever. (Read every label of everything you eat.) You may even experience a kind of "withdrawal" from dairy products. This could take the form of headaches, a bad cold, or stomachaches, or any number of symptoms.

I have had clients tell me that when they gave up dairy products they developed severe stomach pain, like a fist in the stomach. One client told me she found herself at the refrigerator in the middle of the night with a half pound of cheese in her hand. The problem was that when she went to bed there had been a whole pound of cheese. She was so "addicted" to the cheese that when she was in the withdrawal stage her body craved it so much she sleep walked to the refrigerator and ate some before she could wake up. She had chronic health problems that were attributed to her dairy products "allergy." I knew we were on to something when she told that story. This sounds just like an addict of any kind. They have to have the offending item at any cost. Otherwise, there will be withdrawal and that always brings unease or pain of some kind. This was a severe case. Of all the foods that we eat milk products get the most "bad press."

LABEN OR LABAN, YOGURT BY ANY OTHER NAME

Laben is the Middle Eastern name for yogurt. It is one of the words used for yogurt that signify Life, Long Life, or Health. Persian tradition has it that Abraham was given the recipe for yogurt by an angel and that this alone was responsible for his fecundity and longevity. Almost every Middle Eastern country has a kind of fermented milk product and has had for thousands of years. Yogurt by whatever name it is known has been used for many health prescriptions for thousands of years. It is reputed to have been used against epidemics, tuberculosis, and many gastrointestinal disorders. It is the bacterial culture L. acidophilus that is reported to inhibit the growth of dysentery, food poisoning, and gas-forming yeasts such as candida albicans.

FLORA AND BACTERIA

In order for the B vitamins to be utilized in the intestines there has to be a certain amount of "good" bacteria or intestinal flora present. This flora occurs naturally. Without flora much gas can be produced in the intestines during digestion. Intestinal flora can be destroyed by antibiotics and various illnesses. This is why doctors always suggest taking yogurt when antibiotics are necessary, to replace the needed "good" bacteria. Antibiotic diarrhea is generally unnecessary when you eat yogurt.

"Tourista" or Montezuma's revenge often occurs when foods are eaten that contain more bacteria than one is used to eating. This means there is an imbalance of the intestinal flora. Yogurt is also the remedy here. If you are traveling in places where you might have trouble with the food or water and you can't find yogurt, take yogurt tablets with you to make sure that you don't suffer needlessly. I have successfully avoided problems with food and water in Mexico and India by taking a yogurt tablet each time I ate. Eating yogurt is most likely what kept the people of Bible times healthy even though, as a rule, they had no refrigeration, sterilization, pasteurization, or food preservatives.

Of course you don't want to be foolish and eat rotten or questionable foods. It is possible to eat in those places that are clean and not have trouble with the food. I always drink either bottled, pure water or ask for boiled water. Most times beer and soft drinks are safer than local water, depending where you are. I have seen unscrupulous people put local tap water in a bottle meant for purified bottled water. Use your instinct and senses to look around and assess the situation. Generally bread is cooked, so it is acceptable. Cooked vegetables are usually OK if they are freshly cooked. Raw veggies are often acceptable if they can be peeled, but the yogurt tablets could make up for the water they use to wash them. Or wash them off in pre-boiled water yourself. I try to never eat the meat, mainly because it often has been cooked hours before or is left without refrigeration. Fresh fish or chicken that is cooked at the time you order it is generally acceptable. Still, I would take the yogurt tablets. If eating certain foods gives you problems you may need to avoid them or add more yogurt tablets.

Once in the 1970's I was traveling with a group of Canadians in Mexico on a much needed vacation. We met a woman from the States who had a very sick baby. This woman was a hippie. She was living hand to mouth, had no job, her parents didn't know where she was, and she refused to call them. Her baby had had severe diarrhea for weeks. The baby was weak and listless. The mother seemed to have been on drugs or something (I think) and could not decide what to do nor afford a doctor. I suggested that she give the baby some fresh yogurt. She did and when I ran into her a few days later the baby was playing with some other children. Her life had actually been saved by taking yogurt. I tried to get the woman to go home with her baby and give up that life before they both died.

NUTRITIONAL VALUES

Yogurt (partially skimmed milk, 1 cup)
> 123 calories
> 8.3 g protein
> 4.2 g fat
> 12.7 g carbohydrate
> 294 mg calcium
> 230 mg phosphorus
> 0.1 mg iron
> 125 mg sodium
> 350 mg potassium
> 170 IU vitamin A
> 0.10 mg B1
> 0.44 mg B2
> 0.2 mg B3

Yogurt (whole milk, 1 cup)
> 152 calories
> 7.4 g protein
> 8.3 g fat
> 12 g carbohydrate
> 272 mg calcium
> 213 mg phosphorus
> 0.1 mg iron
> 115 mg sodium
> 323 mg potassium
> 340 IU vitamin A
> 0.07 mg B1
> 0.39 mg B2
> 0.2 mg B3[17]

YOGURT OR YOGHURT

Yogurt is made from milk that is heated to lukewarm (100–120°F), a culture is added, and then is left for 4–12 hours at that heat. Anything that will keep the temperature constant can be used. Most people prefer to use an electric incubator because it keeps the temperature constant. The oven of a gas stove with a pilot light is often warm enough. Before electricity a special box was used that was insulated and often covered with blankets or layers of straw to keep the heated milk warm. I have used each of these methods and found them to work. The hardest part is knowing how long to leave it to incubate. If you are using a commercial starter it will generally tell you how long to leave the first batch. Several batches can be made from this yogurt by saving a few tablespoons of the fresh yogurt to use in starting the second batch. Each batch will take less and less time. So that it might take 12 hours for the first batch, 8 for the second, 4 for the third, and so on. If you use a starter from yogurt that you purchase it must be unflavored and have live culture in it. Both of these can be found out by reading the label. It is possible to keep the saved yogurt in the freezer so that it will work, but I have never done this so I am not sure how well it works.

Yogurt should be placed in the refrigerator as soon as it is thickened. As long as it is warm it will continue to work. If it is allowed to go beyond the "just set" stage it will begin to become tart and to separate. This is why you need to keep track of the time that it is culturing. It is best to use glass, corning ware glass, or ceramic for the culturing. Stainless steel, enamel, or corning ware can be used for heating the milk. Never use aluminum, copper, or enamel pans that are chipped. All the equipment should be very, very clean to avoid adding any unwanted bacteria. For this reason I use a nylon spoon or rubber scraper for stirring rather than a wooden spoon.

Easy Yogurt

3 3/4 cups	water a little hotter than lukewarm*
1 1/2 cups	milk powder
2 Tbsp.	fresh live yogurt

Mix water and milk powder in blender until thoroughly blended. Check for lukewarm.* Stir in starter with a sterile spoon and place in one of the recommended culture places. Check it after 2–3 hours. To check the firmness of the yogurt, tip the container to the side. If the yogurt is as thick as heavy cream (unwhipped whipping cream or pancake batter), then it is ready to be refrigerated. If it has begun to separate, then it has been culturing too long, chill it immediately to stop the process, then refrigerate. If it does not adhere to the sides of the glass or bowl and seems watery, then let it culture for another hour and check again. After you have made it a few times you will get a feel for how long it takes.

*Lukewarm is between 100–120°F on a thermometer. A candy or dairy thermometer will be fine. Or you could use the old fashioned way of dropping a few drops on the inside of your wrist. It should feel comfortably warm. If it feels hot, then it is too hot for yogurt, wait a few minutes until it cools off, stir it a few times to aid this. If you can't feel anything other than something wet, it is not warm enough.

Because yogurt is cultured it is essential that all the utensils be very clean. The outcome of the batch can be changed by the presence of other bacteria or yeasts.

FRESH MILK YOGURT

When you make yogurt from milk that is fresh whether it is pasteurized or raw, it is essential to bring it just to the boil and cool it down before adding the culture. This will destroy the enzymes that might cause the yogurt to curdle. This has already been done to the dried milk powder. When heating the milk always rinse the pan with very cold water first to prevent the milk from sticking or scorching.

SMOOTHIES

Smoothies are drinks that have been called by many names and taken many forms over the years. A smoothie generally is made from milk and/or yogurt and fruit blended in a blender. Banana, peach, apricot, strawberry, blueberry, raspberry, pineapple, watermelon, cantaloupe, kiwi, carob, chocolate, coconut milk, almonds, pistachios, sunflower seeds, and many other ingredients have been used alone or in combinations to make smoothies. Buttermilk could be used. In India a similar drink is made from yogurt or buttermilk. It is served either sweet or salty and is called a lassie. Traditionally, this does not have fruit, but has ice cubes.

SHAKES AND MALTS

Milk shakes are made with milk and ice cream blended up, with or without fruit or other flavors. A chocolate milk shake could have milk and chocolate ice cream and chocolate syrup, or chocolate milk, vanilla ice cream, and chocolate syrup. A malted milk shake is made the same way with the addition of malted barley powder. The secret is to blend it very little so the ice cream doesn't melt, but forms a thick body making a shake so thick that the spoon stands on its own.

MILK AND EGG CUSTARDS

In the book *Apicus, Cookery And Dining In Imperial Rome,* the original of which was believed to have been written around the time of the birth of Christ, there are numerous recipes for custards baked in an oven in a water bath. Many seem to include vegetables, meats especially calf or veal brains and chicken, as well as milk and eggs. One contains milk, pignolia (pine nuts), honey, eggs, pepper, and broth and is very close to a modern nut custard served in Europe today. Asparagus cooked in a custard of milk and eggs with savory seasonings is mentioned several times in this old "cook book" so it must have been very popular among the Romans. We have no way of knowing if the Hebrew people ate something like this.

Baked Custard

2 cups	milk*
3	eggs
1/4 cup	honey
1/4 tsp.	sea salt
1/2 tsp.	vanilla extract
	nutmeg for garnish

Oil or butter** 6 custard cups or a casserole or soufflé dish, setting them in a large pan that will hold water. Blend ingredients together (except nutmeg) and fill the cups within 1/4–1/2 inch of the tops. Pour hot water into the pan so that it comes half way up the custard cups (any more and it might bubble or splash into the custard). Dust with a grinding of fresh nutmeg.

Bake in a pre-heated 325° F oven for 1 hour or until a knife inserted in the custard comes out clean. Serve warm or cold.

*The milk can be scalded or not. There are those who feel that the milk should be so that it doesn't curdle when other ingredients are added. We tried this recipe both with and without scalding and we like it not scalded.

**I save the butter wrapping paper to use for buttering the cups.

It is important to bake the custard in a water bath or in a pie crust to prevent the custard from curdling.

Date or Raisin Custard

2	eggs
2/3 cup	dates or raisins, chopped fine

2 cups	milk
1/4 tsp.	sea salt
1/2 tsp.	ground nutmeg

Beat eggs slightly and whisk in the remaining ingredients. Pour into lightly oiled or buttered custard cups, set in a pan of water and bake for 1 hour at 325° F. Serves 6.

This recipe is the closest to one that might have been made in the Middle East during the time of the Bible. They used honey to sweeten, but dates, figs, and raisins along with other fruit concentrates and syrups were used by the common person in daily life.

CHEESE

Take your brothers an ephah of this parched grain, and these ten loaves, and carry them quickly to the camp to your brothers; also take these ten cheeses to the commander of their thousand. See how your brothers fare, and bring some token from them. 1 Samuel 17:17b, 18 (RSV)

Soldiers in those days were not paid by the government, they were supported by their families. Jesse had to send supplies to his sons and also sent some cheese to the commander of the unit as a token of good will. Bread and cheese were staples in the life of all people and certainly in the life of soldiers. There is no explanation as to whether there were ten cheeses of the same kind or ten different kinds. It does show, however, that cheese was a necessity of life along with bread.

HOW CHEESE IS MADE

For pressing milk produces curds . . . . Proverbs 30:33a (RSV)

Cheese is made by allowing or making the milk curdle. This can be done by leaving the milk exposed to the air for 6 to 24 hours where the normal bacteria will produce lactic acids that will cause the milk to curdle. Or this can be done by adding an acid like lemon juice or vinegar, or a bacterial culture. Another coagulating agent is rennin, which is an enzyme found in the fourth stomach of a calf or goat.[18] This is often called rennet and has been used for thousands of years to aid in cheese making. Rennin produces the firm curd needed for pressed cheeses such as cheddar, brick, or longhorn. Many cheeses use one or the other coagulating agents, some use both. There are vegetable curding agents for those who keep Kosher or vegetarians who do not wish to have animal rennet.

The agent used to form the curds and the temperature at which it is added or kept for a length of time determines the texture and density of the curds. The same processes are used to make most cheeses, the time, temperature, stirring, draining, pressing, and aging make the difference.

Cheese making equipment believed to be about 5,000 years old was recently found in a stone age dwelling in Switzerland.[19]

PROCESSED CHEESE AND PASTEURIZED PROCESS CHEESE FOODS

Processed cheese is made by melting natural cheese and adding emulsifiers and often other dairy products such as milk or whey. These "cheeses" are generally higher in moisture and lower in calories and fat than natural cheese. But as Nikki & David Goldbeck say in their book *The Supermarket Handbook,* processed cheeses are "mild in flavor, melt easily, and are chock full of chemicals—don't choose this" in the supermarket. Pasteurized cheese spread has a higher moisture content so that it is spreadable at 70° F. These have stabilizers added to prevent the separation of ingredients as well as "a number of undesirable ones."

I tend to agree with the Goldbecks, and suggest you don't choose these kinds of products in the store. The cheese, milk, and moisture are not the parts in question here. It is what they add or do to it to make it spread or melt nice that are the undesirable ingredients. I prefer to eat something that I know what the ingredients are, where they come from, and how they are put together. This is natural cheese. We have known about the effects of natural cheese like Swiss or cheddar for hundred of years. We don't know what the effects of the emulsifiers are and I prefer not to ingest them.

REAL CHEESE?

In the late 1980's some pizza places began to advertise that they served "real" cheese on their pizzas. Yes, there were places that were not serving real cheese. They were using a synthetic manufactured cheese that contained additional ingredients so that the cheese didn't have to be refrigerated. We used to call it plastic cheese because it was a very strange texture and consistency, it was sort of rubbery and stringy at the same time. It seemed to snap like a rubber band when you pulled it. It was never fully chewed and seemed like a rubber band when you ate it. This is why I prefer to eat things like this made at home, where I know what goes into them. Look at the label of frozen foods that contain cheese and see if you are eating real cheese or processed cheese. You might not want to eat what is in the processed cheeses.

YOGURT CHEESE

A popular cheese in the Middle East was made from laban or yogurt. Using fresh yogurt let it drain through a fine cloth until all the whey has separated from the solid. Often 2 teaspoons of lemon juice are added to very fresh yogurt to help it separate. Most cheese-making books suggest doing this at room temperature or 72°F; however I prefer to let it drain in the refrigerator. At room temperature the yogurt will become more tart; therefore, the cheese will also be tart. Add a small amount of salt or fresh herbs to the solid matter and store covered in the refrigerator.

UNREFRIGERATED CHEESE

Make the yogurt cheese above and roll it into balls. Leave it on a plate overnight or longer in the refrigerator to dry out on the outside. Then, pack it in a jar of sesame oil or Virgin olive oil. The oil can contain various herbs or spices like garlic, black pepper corns, bay leaf, dried red peppers, thyme, whole cloves, cumin seeds, dill seeds, or caraway seeds. So long as the oil is covering the cheese it should stay fresh. This is a great cheese to take on a trip. When at home it is best to keep it in the refrigerator. Several types of goat cheese, as well as goat and sheep mozzarella, are displayed and sold like this in delicatessens—in large jars with no refrigeration for weeks at a time. Keeping the cheese in oil is the most likely way that cheese was kept fresh in the Holy Land. It is still being done there today, as well as in Italy, France, and North America.

This cheese is traditionally eaten by spreading one ball of cheese on a piece of dark or whole grain bread, then spooning a small amount of the oil over it. Cucumbers, tomatoes, peppers, lettuce, olives, and parsley could also go with this to make a complete meal.

LESS CALORIES & FAT

Yogurt cheese eaten as "cream" cheese or dried and stored in oil as a more firm cheese has less calories than most cheeses that are made from cream. If low-fat yogurt is used there is often one-fifth the calories of regular cream cheese. One tablespoon of 25% butter-fat cream has around 60 calories. One tablespoon of whole milk yogurt has about 7 calories. The same proportions of cream and yogurt are used for the cheeses, so the calories will be in about the same proportions. If you are reducing your fat intake, you could make the yogurt "cream" cheese from skimmed milk yogurt and still have the same satisfaction as you would have had from eating real cream cheese. Or you could reduce the fat even more by mixing the yogurt cheese with tofu "cream cheese" and also reduce the amount of cholesterol in your diet.

GOAT'S MILK CHEESE

Several kinds of cheese can be made easily at home from goat's milk. Cottage and cream cheeses are the most popular, but it is also possible to make hard curd cheeses as well. Many people have an aversion to a certain "goaty" taste and smell that they find in even commercially produced goat cheeses. I, of course, have never been able to notice it, perhaps because I have known lots of goats, studied them extensively, and been in goateries.

CURDS

. . . and because of the abundance of milk which they give, he will eat curds; for every one that is left in the land will eat curds and honey.
Isaiah 7:22 (RSV)

The meaning of the word curds is difficult to determine. George Lamsa, a Bible scholar who was brought up speaking Aramaic in a community that followed customs unchanged since the time of Christ, explains that in this passage "curds" refers to butter.[20]

Then he took curds, and milk, and the calf which he had prepared, and set it before them; and he stood by them under the tree while they ate.
Genesis 18:8 (RSV)

This reference to curds is interpreted in the Interpreter's Bible as meaning leban or yogurt, both of which are still eaten in the Middle East today. Lactose or milk sugar can be difficult for most people to digest because they lack the enzyme lactase to digest it. When milk is made into yogurt the process uses up the lactose and leaves an end product that is easier to digest.

We think of Miss Muffet when we hear "curds" since she was eating curds and whey, which now is called cottage cheese, but it might have been yogurt. In Canada and other places where there has been a British influence curds are often sold and eaten. They are, of course, the curds that were to be pressed into cheese and aged. Generally they are cheddar or longhorn type cheeses.

In Quebec there is a native dish in certain regions called poutine that is made from fresh cheese curds covered with French fried potatoes, peas, and some kind of gravy or ketchup-type sauce. It is very popular and stands are all over at roadsides selling this and soft drinks.

FATS IN CHEESE

Cow's milk generally contains 3.5% fat unless it is skimmed; goat's milk has 4% (human milk also contains 4% fat). Dry skimmed milk cottage cheese contains about 0.3% fat.[21] A 1 ounce piece of cheese contains these quantities of fat:

blue	8.2mg
brick	8.4 mg
brie	7.9 mg
cheddar	9.4 mg
colby	9.1 mg
edam	7.9 mg
gouda	7.8 mg
Monterey	8.6 mg
mozzarella (part skim)	4.5 mg
provolone	7.6 mg
Swiss	7.8 mg
cream cheese	9.9 mg
Neufchatel	6.6 mg[22]

One ounce of cream cheese is 2 tablespoons. Two tablespoons of tofu has 1.2 mg fat. It is possible to blend tofu and cream cheese and reduce the fat, yet still have the flavor of the cream cheese. Two tablespoons of this mixture would have 5.5 mg fat. (For more information on fat, look under Butter in this chapter and in Chapter VI—Alternative Proteins–Meats, Fish, Fowl, & Eggs.)

CHEESE LORE AND HISTORY

Sumerian clay tablets mention cheese as long ago as 4000 B.C. Little pots for making cheese have been found in tombs at Saqqara, Egypt that date from about 3000 B.C. Funerary offerings from 2800 to 2500 B.C. mention cheese. Remains of cheese-making equipment have been found in Greece, Crete, on the island of Therasia, and in most places that date from the Neolithic and Early Bronze Age Periods. A type of cheese was even eaten in China, at least it was reported to have been by Marco Polo.[23] Cheese is not a new food. Processed cheeses and cheese foods are new. Processed cheeses are generally made from a base of cheese which is melted and emulsifiers added. Milk, milk powder, whey, oils, lecithin, or other material are often added.

CHEESE IN DAILY LIFE

Cheese was eaten more often by the Hebrews than was meat. Meat was generally eaten at feasts and on special occasions, but cheese was often consumed daily. Soldiers considered cheese part of their daily rations. So did farmers, herdsmen, and most Romans, who ate cheese for the first and second meals of the day. Cheese, bread, wine, olives or olive oil, figs, and fresh vegetables were daily fare for most people. A typical meal in Saul's days was lentil soup, a small amount of lamb mixed with parched grains and chick peas, cheese, wine, and fruit.[24]

MEDICINAL PROPERTIES OF CHEESE

In 1987, Dr. Mark Jensen, Associate Professor of Dentistry at the University of Iowa College of Dentistry, reported that research that he had done showed that cheddar cheese reverses the early stages of cavity formation. He also found in 1988 that there were 12 cheeses whose medicinal properties were effective in fighting plaque.[25] In the 1989 "Nutrition Briefing" Issue No. 4 an article was published titled: "Cheese and Dental Health." This article reported on testing that showed that cheese protected against dental caries by stimulating saliva and increasing the pH of the plaque which inhibited the demineralization and favored the remineralization through the water-soluble components, probably of calcium and possibly phosphorus. This might be a key to healthier teeth.

MILK, CHEESE, EGGS, VEGETABLES: THE ROYAL COMBINATION

The domestic hen was common in the Mediterranean from the 5th century BC and eggs were a common part of the diet. Apicius is credited with inventing omelets and cheesecake in the first century A.D. or before. The book generally attributed to contain the only written record of recipes of this period and often called the first cookbook, *Apicius, Cookery And Dining In Imperial Rome,* (One of the many translations available), lists at least 3 or 4 recipes that use milk, cheese, eggs, and vegetables together with or without meat or fish. There are dozens more that use vegetables, eggs, and cheese or just eggs and vegetables. It could well be from this trend that quiche, bread pudding, baked custard, and, of course, omelets and soufflés became popular. There are many recipes that include milk, cream, cheese, eggs, honey or other sweetener with nuts to be served as dessert, especially the cheesecake-type recipes. The recipes in this book are in very rough form, there are no measurements, many of the ingredients are unknown, and several translations do not always agree. But it is the first real record of recipes. There are other mentions in historical material that give the fare at certain feasts, but they do not give the ingredients or the recipes.

CHEESE PIE (QUICHE AU FROMAGE)

Traditionally, this open-faced cheese tart is made with butter, eggs, heavy cream, and Swiss cheese or Swiss and Parmesan cheese combined. The pastry is also made with butter. This is very rich, very high in saturated fats, cholesterol, and calories. This traditional recipe, when cut into 6 pieces, has in one piece at least 534 calories and 60 grams of saturated fat not including the crust. Almost all of the calories come from fat. Now we recommend that only 10 to 20% of the calories should or could come from fat. Once in a while this dish is not bad to eat, it tastes great. You might even discover that there is too high a fat content for your taste if you have been eating lower-fat meals. If you had a low-fat day, such as oat bran and fruit for breakfast, or steamed plain vegetables, you may enjoy a salad with no dressing and no-oil crackers for lunch. Choose a salad of very dark green lettuce, watercress or dandelion greens, parsley, and cucumbers with a mostly-lemon and slight bit of olive oil dressing to go with the quiche. If you eat the lower-fat diet suggested in this book as taken from the information in the Bible, you could have this quiche once in a while, however, for frequent eating you will want the new recipes given here.

Pie Crust (Pate Brisée)

8 Tbsp.	chilled butter, cut in 1/4 inch pieces
1 1/2 cups	unbleached white flour
1/4 tsp.	salt
3–5 Tbsp.	ice water

In a large chilled mixing bowl sift the flour and salt together, cut in the butter with a pastry blender or use your fingers. Blend until it resembles coarse meal. Pour 3 Tablespoons of the ice water over the flour mixture and quickly mix in and gather the pastry into a ball. If this is not enough, gradually add a teaspoonful at a time and mix well after each addition until dough can be formed into a smooth ball. (I always use the food processor for this—it goes so much faster and easier.) Lightly dust the pastry with flour and wrap in waxed paper or plastic wrap and refrigerate for up to three hours until it is thoroughly chilled. Remove from the refrigerator about 5 minutes before rolling it out. With the heels of your hands, flatten into a circle about 1 inch thick and roll from the center out to the edge. Lift the dough, turn it a little and roll again. Continue to turn and roll until you have a circle about 11 or 12 inches across.

Place the dough into a buttered 8 or 9 inch false-bottomed quiche pan or use a deep pie pan. Prick the bottom with a fork making sure to not pierce all the way through. Chill it for an hour. Butter a piece of aluminum foil and place it buttered side down on the pastry, pressing it lightly into the sides to hold up the sides of the pastry while baking. Fill bottom with beans to hold it in place if desired. Bake in preheated 400°F on the middle shelf for 10 minutes. Remove from oven, remove foil and reprick bottom, return to oven and bake until lightly browned. Cool on wire cake rack while you make the filling. Reduce the oven temperature now to 375°F to be ready for the final baking.

Quiche Filling (high fat)

2	eggs
2 extra	egg yolks
1 1/2 cups	heavy cream 35% (whipping cream)
1/2 tsp.	salt
pinch	white pepper
3/4 cup	grated Swiss cheese (or Swiss and Parmesan)
2 Tbsp.	butter, cut into little pieces

Preheat oven to 375°F. Whisk together eggs, extra yolks, cream, and seasonings, stir in the cheese. Spoon the mixture into the cooled pie shell to within 1/8 inch of the rim of the shell. Sprinkle the top with dots of butter. Bake in the upper 1/3 of the oven for 25 minutes or until the filling has puffed and browned and a knife inserted in the center comes out clean.

Serve hot or warm with a green salad as described above.

Variations—I would never eat a plain quiche at home. I always follow the early Roman traditions of having vegetables in it. My favorite is leek and mushroom, I also love sweet red pepper and mushroom and onion.

Sauté leeks or onions, mushrooms, and garlic in a small amount of butter until soft or transparent. Spoon it into the pie shell before adding the cheese and milk mixture. Bake as usual.

SUGGESTED COMBINATIONS

- grated carrots, sliced onions, broccoli flowers
- cauliflower, green peppers, onions
- fresh tomato slices, basil, oregano
- zucchini, onion, mushroom
- fresh dill, leeks, and oyster mushrooms
- green onion, fresh rosemary and parsley
- shrimp, green onions, dill
- tarragon, cod fish,
- scallops, green onions, mushrooms
- precooked chicken or turkey, green onions, mushrooms
- asparagus, onion, mushroom

The list is endless. Almost any combination can be used. Just remember that onions, mushrooms, peppers, broccoli, cauliflower, etc. should be steamed or sautéed first. If you find this is too bland add some ground cumin or nutmeg to the mixture. Or if you are really adventurous you could try cayenne pepper, jalapeno peppers, or one of the hundreds of other hot chiles.

Lower Fat & Calorie Cheese Pie

1	prebaked 8–9 inch whole wheat pie shell
3	eggs
1/2 cup	low fat yogurt
1 cup	partially skimmed milk
2 Tbsp.	whole wheat bread flour, toasted
1/8 tsp.	ground nutmeg or cumin
1 cup	low fat cheese, preferably Swiss

Beat together eggs, milk, yogurt, flour, nutmeg. Fold in cheese and spoon into pie shell and bake at 375°F for 25–30 minutes or until puffed and lightly browned.

See Variations above for ideas for additions.

Lowest Fat & Calorie Cheese Pie

1	prebaked 8–9 inch whole wheat pie shell
2 Tbsp.	butter
1 large	leek
4–5	mushrooms
1 cup	tofu
2	eggs*
1/2 cup	skimmed milk yogurt
1/2—1 tsp.	ground cumin
1 1/2 cup	low-fat Swiss or Ementhaler cheese

Slice leek using the white part only, slice mushrooms. Sauté veggies in butter until transparent. Beat or mash tofu and eggs together, add yogurt, milk, and cumin. I use the food processor. Switch to the plastic blade and add the cheese or stir it in with a spoon. Put veggies in bottom of pie crust and spoon on the cheese mixture. Bake at 350°F for 30 minutes or until filling puffs up and browns lightly. Serve with green salad. When cut into six pieces, each piece has approximately 153 calories and 22 grams of fat not including the crust.

*The eggs can be replaced by 2 tablespoons of corn starch, unflavored custard powder or any natural egg replacer if you want to further reduce the fat and calories.

CHEESE SANDWICHES AT ANY MEAL

If you **always** eat lettuce or one of the other bitter herbs with cheese it will be easier to digest the fat and cholesterol. Low-fat cheese when cooked tastes just about the same as full fat cheese. If you are going to eat cheese on a regular basis, and by that I do not mean even as often as daily, but two or three times a week, it is important to pay attention to the other fats in your diet as well as the fats in the cheese. It is also important to pay attention to the quality of the cheese, type, and method of cooking.

My husband and I often have cheese sandwiches for breakfast. By "often" I mean no more than once every three months. We always have vegetables and bitter herbs with them and do them in a sandwich grill with very little fat added or broil them. On the days when we have a cheese sandwich we would never think of having meat or eggs at another meal. We would have whole grains, tofu or tempeh, lettuce, and lots of vegetables. If we are having cheese for dinner we would have oatmeal or oat bran cereal with sea vegetables for breakfast.

When we have fajitas, for instance, we have cheese, avocado, no-fat sour cream or yogurt, red, yellow, and green peppers, mushrooms, fresh cilantro (green coriander leaves), onions, garlic, and tomato based salsa. We don't have meat fajitas, we have marinated tempeh burgers using lime juice and hot peppers instead. And, of course, we use whole wheat tortillas. The cilantro is one of the bitter herbs and the garlic is helpful in breaking up the fat as well. For more information on this please read Chapter III—Our Daily Proteins under garlic and bitter herbs. If we have lasagna we have it vegetarian and just have cheese as our protein. When we eat any kind of animal protein like fish or chicken, which is very seldom at home, we have it in a stir fry with brown rice or whole grain noodles, and lots of vegetables, never with cheese or eggs. This is the way, I think, the Hebrews ate cheese as well. Since many of them followed the Kosher laws and didn't eat meat and milk together it seems to me that this was the normal way of eating for them.

This was not the normal way for the wealthy Romans or Greeks. They often ate to excess in every way and then purged themselves with laxatives, enemas, or forced vomiting. Egyptians (especially between 1900 B.C. and 1400 B.C.) were preoccupied with their digestion and believed that most illnesses had their source in the alimentary canal.[26] With all the rich and fatty foods that they ate to excess, and the huge amount of alcohol that was drunk, it was necessary to be concerned. They were the original "binge and purgers."

Grilled Cheese Sandwiches

2 slices	whole grain bread
	low fat real cheese, cheddar, Swiss, Jack, etc.
1 Tbsp.	chopped fresh parsley, dill, watercress, or cilantro
2 slices	fresh tomato, optional
1–2 tsp.	natural mustard or catsup, optional
	butter wrapper paper or olive oil

Heat sandwich grill, wipe with butter paper or brush with olive oil using a non-plastic pastry brush and put in sandwich. To build the sandwich start with the bread and spread the insides with mustard or catsup. Using a cheese slicer slice the cheese very thin and put some on each slice.

On one side add the parsley or other greens, tomato, and other veggies as desired. Close the sandwich so that the veggies are sandwiched between the cheese and then the bread. Slip into heated grill and cook until the cheese starts to melt. This takes about 4 or 5 minutes. If you are using frozen bread, thaw it first or it will become too dark before the cheese melts.

Other Veggies—slices of onion, green or red peppers, chopped garlic, low salt pickle slices, green or black olives, precooked zucchini or carrots, etc.

NB: This can also be done in a heavy pan. Turn it once during the cooking being careful to keep the sandwich together.

Lower Fat Cheese Sandwiches

Combine equal quantities of mashed tofu and grated cheese and proceed as above.

Broiled Cheese Sandwiches

Build a sandwich on whole grain bread or bagels spread it with mustard or catsup, then add sliced veggies (like onions, olives, garlic, red or green peppers, chopped parsley or dill), then cheese and broil under the broiler. This will be an open face sandwich and can be served for breakfast, lunch, or dinner. Serve this with a fresh green salad for lunch or dinner. I usually grate the cheese and mix it with the mustard, greens, onion, olives, and other veggies, then broil it.

Cheese Sauce

When I make a cheese sauce I first make a roux sauce then add grated cheese when the sauce is thickened, and heat it just until the cheese melts, then serve it. This generally allows a sauce to be made that tastes like cheese, but has less fat and more fiber because of the whole wheat roux.

BUTTER

His speech is smooth as butter, yet war is in his heart; his words are more soothing than oil, yet they are drawn swords. Psalms 55:21 (NIV)

Butter is made by setting cow's milk out until the cream rises to the top. Often it is left to ripen or develop a lactic acid content that would culture the milk. The heaviest cream is then churned at a temperature of 53–64°F until the fat of the cream is congealed together. It is then pressed or hung to remove the remainder of the liquid milk matter. Salt is added as a preservative and it is then chilled or it is chilled without the salt. Salted butter is known as butter, unsalted butter is known as sweet butter or unsalted butter. It must be refrigerated as soon as it is made to avoid rancidity. It is best to keep it either frozen or refrigerated until just before use.

When I was a child milk was not always homogenized, but had the cream that rose to the top. One of our school projects was to make butter at school. Everybody brought a little cream and we mixed it together and shook it in a jar until we had butter.

Margarine was much cheaper than butter, but a lot of work. It came in a sealed bag, it was white and there was a color packet that we had to work into the fat if we wanted it yellow. This was as much work as churning butter, I thought, and the taste was not as nice as butter. If we had kept a cow we might have had butter all the time. We had butter on special holidays and whenever my mother made fresh bread. There was nothing better than fresh warm bread with butter and leaf lettuce just picked from the garden in a sandwich for lunch. Once again, we naturally ate the bitter herb (lettuce) that helped to digest the fat.

Butter was not as well known in Biblical times as oil for the obvious reason that they didn't have quantities of cows, they used mostly goats, sheep, and mares, and the butter was more difficult to make because the cream does not naturally separate to the top in their milk. Butter also had to be kept cold to keep it for any length of time.

As I was in the days of my youth, when the secret of God was upon my tabernacle . . . When I washed my steps with butter, and the rock poured me out rivers of oil. Job 29:4, 6 (KJV)

Butter was used medicinally and was eaten mostly by the rich. This is why most of the quotes in the Bible use butter to connote wealth. George M. Lamsa says that the above passage means "When I was very wealthy" in the old Aramaic idiom.[27]

Margaret Visser sums up the current feeling towards butter in her book *Much Depends On Dinner*: "Butter is irreproachable, unique, and irreplaceable. In this it is like salt, except that salt, as earth, is strange in being edible, whereas milk's prime function is to feed. Corn, as we now normally eat it, is either white or yellow.

Salt is white. Milk is white, butter yellow, honey gold. For us the colours white and gold have distinct meanings, but they both signify purity, delectableness, even heavenliness."[28]

BUTTER FOR COOKING

Butter has been used for cooking for thousands of years. Generally it is added for taste or is used to sauté foods after it has been clarified. Often it is made into a roux and used to thicken. This was a common use of butter in Biblical times, when it was available.

Clarified Butter

1 lb.   unsalted butter

Melt slowly over low heat. The pilot light on a gas stove is excellent. Pour into a large measuring cup and allow to cool or chill in the refrigerator. Separate the whey and the milk solids from the clear, golden, butter oil. Save the solids for use in soup, salad dressing, or cereal. The solids are the parts that burn during cooking, so they will not be used for this. This method is the traditional French way of making clarified butter.

BUTTER IN ANCIENT INDIA

Clarified butter was the major cooking medium in India from 3,000 to 1,000 BC, and it still is in popular use today. The Indian clarified butter is called ghee and is made in a different manner.

Indian Ghee

1 lb.   unsalted butter

Melt over a low flame using a heavy pot. After it is melted it will begin to simmer, keep the heat at the simmer level and allow it to simmer for about 45 minutes. (It might take more or less time depending on the amount of water in the butter.) Continue to cook until all the solids turn brown and cling to the edge of the pan or fall to the bottom. Stir often and keep a close eye on it so that the butter doesn't brown or burn, only the solids do. Strain through several layers of cheese cloth. In this method the liquid in the milk solids is boiled off and the solid protein is discarded, leaving the butter oil. Pour into a jar and cover and refrigerate

Since butter is saturated fat it can be balanced by adding mono-unsaturated fats to it. The most common ones are olive, peanut, and canola oil.

Balanced Butter

| 1 lb. | softened butter |
| 3/4 cup | mono-unsaturated oil, olive, peanut, or canola blended or alone |

Beat the butter until it is creamed with an electric mixer or food processor. Add oil and continue to mix until well blended. Store in covered containers. Keep one for daily use in the refrigerator and store the rest in the freezer. This will have the taste of butter but less saturated fats and less cholesterol, and it will spread better than cold butter.

COOKING WITH BUTTER

Clarified butter will not burn as easily as regular butter so it is good for sautéing, browning, and other cooking where the butter would ordinarily burn. Clarified butter is best to use when cooking an omelet or scrambled eggs to prevent that very browned appearance.

Clarified butter can also be made into herb or garlic butter for cooking use and stored in the refrigerator, covered, for instant use. This can also be used on garlic bread, melted and brushed on.

Balanced butter is suitable for cooking on medium or low heats and is not recommended for stir fry. Clarified butter mixed with peanut oil would be good for stir fry type dishes where a butter taste is desired. Traditionally, butter and olive oil are used in many French recipes.

If you are heating butter to cook and are distracted so that the butter browns, it might be best to pour it out, clean and cool the pan and start over. Unless you are making a recipe that specifically calls for browned butter, and there are a few, although I don't think it is a good idea to eat this often.

BUTTER AND DEGENERATIVE DISEASES

According to Udo Erasmus in his book *Fats And Oils*, "Butter has been used since cows were domesticated. Degenerative diseases on a large scale are more recent in origin, having risen from rarity to epidemic proportions in the last 100 years, so it is unlikely that either butter or the cholesterol that it contains or the cows and goats that provide us with both are to blame for the meteoric rise of degenerative diseases."[29]

BUTTER AND CHOLESTEROL

Butter is always being blamed for all kinds of health problems, now it is high cholesterol levels. Of course we never knew about high cholesterol or even how to measure it until recently. But we did know about butter for thousands of years. If butter is eaten in moderation there will be no health problem. In a society where the average person eats large quantities of saturated fats in meat, poultry, eggs, and butter daily and very little amounts, if any, of the things that help to digest the fats such as greens, whole grains, and raw vegetables, why do we try to blame the butter for the problem?

This same society is blaming a food that has been eaten for thousands of years for diseases that are relatively new. Eating large amounts of high fat meats is also relatively new in the lifestyle of the average North American. Most cultures around the world eat less meat than North Americans. Cheese, whole grains, vegetables, wine, beer, and salads were the main diet of most people for thousands of years, a little oil, butter, or meat or fish was added to this diet along with fruit at different seasons of the year. This is the optimum health diet. This is the World's Oldest Health Plan.

There are several other factors that seem to be left out of the picture. Pollution of the water, food, and air (especially from cigarette smoke) contribute to the stresses that can raise the blood cholesterol. Highly refined "foods" have been around about as long as the high amount of degenerative diseases, could this be the cause? Agricultural chemicals were unknown to farmers until the last hundred years. Have they been the culprits in encouraging degenerative diseases? Have our habits of eating highly processed foods, that are often rancid, added to our own downfall? Do we eat too fast, so fast that we don't have time to even digest the food let alone get any nutrients out? If cows ate natural food, drank pure water, and were allowed to live a natural lifestyle, like they did for thousands of years, we might not be able to find anything wrong with eating cheese and butter in moderation. Isn't it possible that we need to clean up more than just our own diet in order to save the health of our bodies? If we eat food as pure as we can get it we will be on the way to better health. Remember my favorite expression: "If God made it, eat it; if man made it, leave it alone." This still applies. Cheese, butter, cream, milk, olive oil, are foods made by God to be eaten. Refined foods, margarine, processed cheeses of all kinds, artificial milk and cream substitutes were made by man. These foods were made with profit and convenience foremost in mind.

I have always felt this was the case and Udo Erasmus now says the same thing: "Butter contains cholesterol, about 1 gram per pound. Cholesterol is required for the proper functioning of every body cell, but the average North American diet, severely deficient in the vitamins and minerals and fiber required for the metabolism of cholesterol and fats, becomes overloaded with cholesterol, which we find deposited in arteries and associated with cardiovascular problems and deaths from heart attack, stroke, and kidney and heart failure. It is not the fault of butter that the North American diet is so poor in vitamins and minerals but butter itself does not contain the factors required for its own metabolism (oil seeds and fresh seed oils do contain these factors)."[30] He also says that "used in moderation, neither butter nor coconut fat creates any health problem."

ROUX IN COOKING

Roux is made from fat and flour, generally toasted. Butter is used in traditional French cooking as well as oil. In early Rome roux was used in much food preparation. It utilized butter, lard, oil, and other fats. It is difficult to tell exactly how it was made or of what fat due to translation difficulties.

Roux is used to thicken soups, sauces, gravies, and other dishes where thickening is needed, even desserts. We know it as gravy with a roast, but there are many other ways it can be used.

Basic Roux

Use clarified butter or oil and heat it in a heavy pan over medium heat. When it is melted begin adding whole wheat hard or bread flour. Use a fork to mash and stir the flour into the butter. All the oil should be saturated with flour and all the flour should be coated with oil. Let this cook until it bubbles up, stir constantly. Cook this mixture carefully for 15 to 45 minutes. As it cooks longer it will toast more and become darker. 15 minutes is "blonde" roux used for cream sauces and light gravies, 30 minutes is "brunette" roux used for heavier sauces, and 45 minutes for very dark sauces and gravies. Cover and store in the refrigerator to keep the flour fresh. This can be kept for several months.

USING ROUX

Add a tablespoonful to soups or broths to thicken, more depending on the amount of liquid and thickness desired. A quick soup can be made from leftover veggies and meat. Just put all the veggies and meat in water and when it boils add a tablespoon or more of the roux, stir and cook until thickened, add the seasonings, especially summer savory or marjoram, just before serving so they don't boil.

TOASTING FLOUR

When using flour to thicken sauces or gravies it is best to use whole wheat bread flour. Rice, barley, triticale, or buckwheat could be used, but you might have to experiment more with them. Toasting the flour before adding it to the fat will quicken the cooking time of the sauce and avoid that raw or uncooked taste to the flour. The flour for a white sauce can be toasted ahead of blending if roux is not used.

Once you know how to make a white sauce you can make cream soups, noodle casseroles, cheese sauces (don't let the sauce boil after adding cheese), and a wide variety of quick easy dishes. Cheese sauce on toast is an old fashioned Sunday evening meal, just add a green salad and you are set. Make a white sauce using water and some lemon juice, add grated lemon peel, and pour the thickened sauce on steamed asparagus, green beans, broccoli, Brussels sprouts, or mixed vegetables. Add some whole grain noodles or brown rice and you have a quick meal.

White Sauce With Roux

1 cup	milk or water
2 Tbsp.	light roux
	salt optional

Mix in blender then heat until thickened. Pour over vegetables.

Roux Cheese Sauce

Make white sauce when thickened add 1/2 to 1 cup shredded cheese, stir until cheese melts. Serve over veggies or noodles or use in casseroles.

Traditional White Sauce

1 heaping Tbsp.	whole wheat bread flour

1 Tbsp.	clarified or regular butter
1/4 tsp.	sea salt, optional
1 cup	milk, water, or other liquid

Toast flour until it gives off a nutty smell. Use a heavy pan and stir often over medium heat or in a slow oven. Blend toasted flour with softened butter, liquid, and salt. Using medium heat cook until almost boiling and allow to thicken. Stir often. This makes a thin sauce. To make a thicker sauce add more fat and flour for the one cup of liquid. Traditionally a thin sauce used 1 tablespoon of fat and flour each with one cup liquid, medium used 2 tablespoons, and thick sauce used 3. Depending on the purpose of the sauce you can choose the amount.

Vegetable Gravy

2 Tbsp.	clarified or regular butter (or oil)
1	cooking onion
2 cloves	garlic
6–8	mushrooms
1/2–1 tsp.	shoyu or tamari, optional
	whole wheat bread flour

Melt butter over medium/high heat. Slice or chop onions, garlic, and mushrooms and sauté in butter, stirring often, until slightly browned. Add flour to coat all the veggies and soak up any butter, stir to coat. Cook until the flour is toasted and starts to give off a nutty smell. Add 1 cup cold water all at once and stir quickly. Add more warm or hot water as needed to desired consistency. Add shoyu or tamari if using. Serve over noodles, rice or leftover meats. Add precooked veggies if desired.

NB: I often make this with white wine to serve over tofu dinner loaf or baked potatoes. This gravy made with the addition of tempeh or tofu served over a baked potato and garnished with fresh parsley or cilantro is a meal. It will also reduce the fat if you generally would have lavished butter on the potato.

Basic Quick Dinner

4 Tbsp.	butter or butter and oil mixed
1	onion
2 cloves	garlic
4–5	mushrooms
1	carrot, diced

1	stem of broccoli in match stick pieces*
1/8–1/4	cauliflower, cut in small pieces
2–4 Tbsp.	whole wheat flour
1 tsp.	shoyu or tamari
1 tsp.	ground cumin
1-3 cups	water
	broccoli florets cut in small pieces

Slice onions and mushrooms, chop or press garlic. Melt butter and add onions, garlic, carrots, and mushrooms, stir. Cook a few minutes then add broccoli stems and cauliflower pieces, stir. Cook and stir until the stems turn darker green, then sprinkle on flour one spoonful at a time, stirring to coat all the veggies with flour. Add as much flour to coat veggies and soak up the butter. There should be no dry flour in the pan. Cook until the flour starts to brown and smell nutty, add cumin, stir. Then add 1 cup cold water and stir immediately, add shoyu. Continue to stir and add more water as needed until thickened. When almost thickened add broccoli florets, stir. Serve over brown rice, whole grain noodles, or other cooked grains. Serve with a green salad.

*Match Stick Pieces are cut in small pieces like kitchen matches. Slice broccoli stem into 4 or 5 even pieces about 1 or 1 1/2 inches long, slice those lengthwise and cut the slices into strips.

Noodles and Basic Quick Dinner

Make the above dinner in the following order. (1) put on noodle water in large pot, (2) heat butter while you chop all the veggies and arrange on a plate, (3) get out flour, shoyu, cumin, and noodles, (4) add noodles to boiling water, (5) sauté onions, garlic, carrots, mushrooms, stems and cauliflower, (6) stir noodles and test for doneness, (7) add flour to veggies and stir, (8) add seasonings and water OR drain noodles depending which is needed, (9) drain noodles and add broccoli florets to basic dinner, (10) put noodles on plate and spoon on thickened veggies and sauce, (11) top with chopped parsley or serve with salad which you can get someone else to make while you do the basic meal. This should take about 25 minutes or less from the minute you start until you are ready to eat.

VARIATIONS TO THE BASIC MEAL

Now the fun begins. You can use any combination of veggies that you happen to have and any noodles or grains.

Italian—Onions, garlic, mushrooms, zucchini, red peppers, tomato juice, 1 teaspoon each basil and oregano. Serve over whole grain pasta.

East Indian—onion, garlic, mushroom, potato, carrot, chick peas, green peas, water or creamed coconut and water, 1 tablespoon mild curry. Serve with brown rice or whole wheat chappatis.

New Mexican—onion, garlic, potato, green pepper, hot green or red chile pepper, precooked black or pinto beans. Top with grated cheese and serve with whole wheat or corn tortillas.

Blender Hollandaise Sauce

1/2 cup	butter (1 quarter pound stick)
3	egg yolks, room temperature
2 Tbsp.	lemon juice
1/4 tsp.	salt
	white pepper

Melt butter over low heat, do not let it brown. Put egg yolks, lemon juice, and salt in blender, cover and blend at low speed. Immediately remove the cover and slowly pour in the melted butter in a steady stream. When all butter is added, turn off motor. This makes enough for 4 servings.

Serve over steamed vegetables like broccoli, asparagus, cauliflower, green beans, fiddle heads, spinach, etc. One serving of this sauce has about 250 calories and 27 grams of fat. If it were eaten with vegetables and whole grain noodles it will reduce the fat to calories ratio.

Mock Hollandaise Sauce

1 Tbsp.	melted butter
3 Tbsp.	lemon juice
1	egg yolk
1/2 cup	tofu
2–3 Tbsp.	water
	salt, optional

Place butter, lemon juice, egg yolk, and salt if using in blender and blend at medium speed. Remove cover and add tofu. Add water as needed for pouring consistency. Serves 4. One serving would contain 84 calories and 9 grams of fat. When compared with the regular hollandaise above it has less calories and fat. This would be the one to use on a regular basis if you are concerned with fat and/or calories.

Eggs Benedict

1	whole grain or Ezekiel English muffin
2	poached eggs*
2 pieces	low fat ham or turkey ham
1 serving	mock hollandaise

Poach eggs, toast muffin. Place ham on muffin, cover with egg, then pour hollandaise sauce over it. Serves one. It is not necessary to butter the muffin.

*See Chapter VI—Alternative Proteins–Meat, Fish, Fowl, & Eggs for directions on poaching eggs.

BUTTER VERSUS MARGARINE

Butter is a food that has been used for thousands of years, margarine has only been around for 100 years. Although many margarines advertise that they are made with polyunsaturated fats and are therefore better for you to eat, the research is not conclusive. Many scientists and nutritionists feel that margarine is not as good to eat since the process of hydrogenating the oil to make it harder damages the structure of the fats and renders them less digestible. For more on this subject look in Chapter VI—Alternative Proteins–Meats, Fish, Fowl, & Eggs.

I prefer to eat butter! It fits my basic rule: "If God made it, eat it; if man made it, leave it alone."

REFERENCES

1. Buttrick, George Arthur,(Commentary Ed.), *Interpreters Dictionary of the Bible*, Vol. 3, Abington Press, New York, 1962, p. 379.

2. Buttrick, p. 380.

3. Interpreters Bible, Vol. V.

4. Tannahill, Reay, *Food in History*, Stein & Day, NY, 1973, pp. 40, 41.

5. Tannahill, p. 58.

6. Bouquet, A.C., *Everyday Life in New Testament Times*, Charles Scribner's & Sons., New York, 1954, p. 79.

7. Aihara, Herman, "Milk a Myth of Civilization" The George Ohsawa Macrobiotic Foundation, 1977 (3rd printing), p. 11.

8. Pryor, Karen, *Nursing Your Baby*, Mc Graw Hill Co., NY, 1970.

9. Jukka Karjalainen and others, "A Bovine Albumin Peptide as a Possible Trigger of Insulin-Dependent Diabetes Mellitus," New England Journal of Medicine, Volume 327, Number 5, July 30, 1992, p. 302 ff.

10. Dehejia, Harsha V. M.D., The *Allergy Book*, Personal Library Publication produced for John Wiley & Sons, Toronto, 1980, p. 80.

11. Airola, Paavo, Ph.D., N.D., *How to Get Well*, Health Plus Publishers, Phoenix, 1974. p. 43.

12. Pennington & Church, p. 115.

13. Pennington & Church, p. 116.

14. Daniel-Rops, Henri, *Daily Life in the Times of Jesus*, Hawthorn Books, Inc., New York, 1962, p. 368.

15. Bouquet, p. 174.

16. Pennington & Church, p. 115.

17. US. Department of Agriculture, *Agriculture Handbook No. 456*, Nutritive Value of American Foods, p. 174.

18. Carroll, Ricki & Robert, *Cheese Making Made Easy*, Garden Way Publishing, Charlotte, Vermont., 1982, p. 19.

19. Erasmus, Udo, Fats and Oils, *The Complete Guide to Fats and Oils in Health and Nutrition*, Alive, Vancouver, British Columbia, 1986, p. 219.

20. Lamsa, George M., *Idioms of the Bible Explained*, Harper & Roe, San Francisco, 1985, p. 28.

21. Erasmus, p. 205.

22. Pennington & Church, pp. 16, 17.

23. Alth, Max, *Making Your Own Cheese & Yogurt*, Funk & Wagnalls, New York, 1973, pp. 2–4.

24. The Readers Digest Assoc., Inc., *Great People of the Bible & How They Lived*, Pleasantville, New York, 1974, p. 159.

25. Jensen gave me this information in a telephone interview in 1989.

26. Tannahill, pp. 66–68.

27. Lamsa, p. 16.

28. Visser, Margaret, *Much Depends on Dinner, The Extraordinary History and Mythology, Allure, and Obsessions, Perils, and Taboos of an Ordinary Meal*, Collier Books, McMillan Pub., Co., New York 1986, p. 86.

29. Erasmus, p. 240.

30. Erasmus, p. 116.

And the woman said to the serpent, "We may eat of the fruit of the trees of the garden; but God said, 'You shall not eat of the fruit of the tree which is in the midst of the garden, neither shall you touch it, lest you die.'" Genesis 3:2,3 (RSV)

V

Special Treats
Fruits, Nuts, Sweets, & Oils

The Fruit In The Middle Of The Garden

Of all the fruits mentioned in the Bible, and there are many, this fruit is the one most people remember. It is also the most controversial. Biblical scholars seem to differ on the translation and, therefore, the name of the fruit. Some feel it is the quince, others the apricot, and some the pomegranate. Some are sure it is the peach while others know it is the orange. It seems that the apples we know in North America did not grow in the Holy Land, and if they did they were very small, very hard, and not suitable for eating in any way. Apples are mentioned in Apicius, along with quince, pomegranate, pear, peach, fig, plums, cherries, citron, mulberry, and grapes.[1] It is the same problem with translation that we have seen before, the translator has to know what existed before he or she can give a name to it. If the translator is not a cook, gardener, or botanist, it is possible that somewhere along the way things did get lost or mixed up. Apple may well have been a word like "corn" was. There was no grain that was really corn as we know it today, but the word "corn" was used to describe many kinds of grains. Golden apple often refers to apricot in the Middle East and many of the verses in the Bible that mention "apple" use it generically rather than meaning any special fruit.

FIG

Then the eyes of both of them were opened, and they realized they were naked; so they sewed fig leaves together and made coverings for themselves. Genesis 3:7 (NIV)

The first fruit that is named in the Bible is fig *Ficus carica*, in Hebrew *teenah*. In this first mention only the leaves were spoken of, but it is well-known that fig trees yield figs. Figs were a staple food and were generally eaten fresh. They were also dried and threaded on strings to take when traveling. This is known as a "cake of figs" and is mentioned in 1 Samuel 25:18:

Then Abigail made haste, and took two hundred loaves, and two skins of wine, and five sheep ready dressed, and five measures of parched grain, and a hundred clusters of raisins, and two hundred cakes of figs, and laid them on asses. (RSV)

It is obvious that fruit, grains, and bread were the main portion of the diet of a traveler.

Figs are unique in that the fruit often appears before the leaves. A fig wasp is needed to fertilize the blossoms for without this no seeds could be made. The fig tree also needs proper cultivation, fertilizing, and watering to produce fruits, as is mentioned in Luke 13:8, so they were a lot of work. Some fig trees, however, were known to live as long as four hundred years, the hard work paid off.[2] The fig tree represented the Tree of Life to the Egyptians, could this be the Tree of Good and Evil as well? There must have been fig trees in the Garden of Eden, where else would they have gotten the leaves?

FIGS AS MEDICINE

Then Isaiah said, "Prepare a poultice of figs." They did so and applied it to the boil, and he recovered. 2 Kings 20:7 (NIV)

Isaiah cured King Hezekiah of anthrax or a malignant ulcer with a poultice of figs. (Please don't do this yourself, see a doctor for more modern medical treatment if you have a boil.)

Syrup of figs is often taken as a remedy for constipation. Ten dried figs have 9 grams of fiber, whereas ten dried dates have only 4.2 grams.[3] Figs are considered a high fiber food. They contain the indigestible food fiber lignin, which holds water and helps to bulk up the stool therefore making it easier to pass. Figs also contain pectin which helps to remove toxins from the body and encourage bowel movements.[4]

They are also good sources of carbohydrates, iron, calcium, and potassium. Four small dried figs contain slightly more potassium than a cup of orange juice.

When choosing figs for your daily use make sure that they are "unsulfured." Many people who have adverse reactions to sulfites may react to the compounds used to keep dried figs from turning dark. Sulfating agents are often responsible for triggering asthma and asthmatic-like reactions. Always try to purchase dried fruits that state "no sulphur," "no sulfites," or "no preservatives." This is especially true if you have allergies, asthma, sinus trouble, or are chemically sensitive.

Fresh figs are soft, fleshy fruits that come in green, brown, or purple, and they are all delicious. They are not as sweet tasting as they are when dried. Fresh figs can be eaten, after being washed, easily without any trouble. They do, however, have very small seeds, so remember to chew them well.

NUTRITIONAL VALUES

Fig (1 medium raw)
> 37 calories
> 0.2 g fat
> 0.1 g polyunsaturated fatty acids
> 0 cholesterol
> 0.4 g protein
> 9.6 g carbohydrate
> 0.6 g fiber
> 71 I.U. vitamin A
> 0.03 mg B1
> 0.03 mg B2
> 0.2 mg B3
> 0.15 B5
> 0.06 mg B6
> 1 mg vitamin C
> 1 mg sodium
> 18 mg calcium
> 8 mg magnesium
> 0.07 mg zinc
> 0.064 mg manganese
> 116 mg potassium
> 7 mg phosphorus
> 0.18 mg iron
> 0.035 mg copper

Figs (10 dried)
    477 calories
    2.2 g fat
    1.0 g polyunsaturated fatty acids
    0 cholesterol
    5.7 g protein
    122.2 g carbohydrate
    9 g fiber
    248 I.U. vitamin A
    0.13 mg B1
    0.17 mg B2
    1.3 mg B3
    0.81 B5
    0.42 mg B6
    14 mcg folic acid
    20 mg sodium
    1331 mg potassium
    269 mg calcium
    111 mg magnesium
    0.94 mg zinc
    0.726 mg manganese
    128 mg phosphorus
    4.18 mg iron
    0.585 mg copper

FAMILIAR FIGS

Most people have eaten fig newtons, they were a lunch box favorite when we were children and children still love them. They are cookies, and yet they are not as sweet as other cookies. They have almost no fat, and one has 53 calories compared to 336 calories for a brownie. They are even higher in fiber when they are made with whole wheat flour.

Always try to brush your teeth after eating any kind of sticky fruit like dried figs, dates, raisins, or apricots. Research is now showing that foods that stick to the teeth can cause tooth decay more readily than foods that do not. Eating figs with lettuce, celery, or carrot sticks helps to "brush" them off the teeth.

Figs were eaten for breakfast or lunch in Bible times. I often eat figs for breakfast stewed with prunes, apricots, or other dried fruits and a zest of lemon peel. Sometimes we put them in the cereal while it is cooking. This adds a sweetness to the cereal that we usually don't have, but once in a while something sweet for breakfast is nice.

I prefer the dried black mission figs. They usually don't have sulfur added to prevent them from turning black since they are already black.

FIGS AS SWEETENER

Fig syrup was used as a sweetener in Bible times as well as date, raisin, and carob syrups. Any dried fruits can be made into a sweet syrup by chopping them very fine and soaking them in hot or boiling water for 15–20 minutes. I generally put them in a heat-safe glass measuring cup and pour enough water over them to cover and when they are rehydrated, I blend them until smooth. Sometimes the fruit soaks up all the liquid, if not just drain it off before blending. I have used this in cooking for years. In 1992 articles were being written in the popular press that used puréed prunes to replace the fat in cake recipes. This is not new, it was done in Bible times. In my weight loss classes we use puréed fruit to replace all of the sweetener and part of the fat. Blended tofu replaces the remaining fat.

CAROB, ST. JOHN'S BREAD, HUSKS

Now John wore a garment of camel's hair, and a leather girdle around his waist; and his food was locusts and wild honey. Matthew 3:4 (RSV)

Carob is the name of the fruit of the Locust Bean tree, *Ceratonia siliqua*. The locusts and wild honey that John the Baptist is described as eating in Matthew 3:4 and Mark 1:6 is now thought to be carob beans. They are very sweet and high in minerals and fiber. They grow all over the Holy Land and are easy to find. In the East and Middle East holy men did not go about plucking the wings off insects let alone eating them. So there is no doubt in my mind that this is what John ate. Others were so sure they have nicknamed the tree's fruit after him: St. John's Bread.

Carob pods are used in the Mediterranean to make syrup and wine. I have eaten the syrup and it is very pleasant. It has a taste somewhat like molasses in that it is thick, dark, and filled with minerals. It is not very easy to find so I will not include recipes for using it in this book.

Carob powder or flour, on the other hand, is very easy to find. It is sold in several forms at almost every health food store. The roasted or toasted powder has a taste somewhat like chocolate and contains none of the caffeine of chocolate. This is why it is so popular! Many people are now refusing to give their precious children caffenated products to help keep them calm at home and school. Cocoa contains the central-nervous-system stimulant caffeine and the muscle stimulant theobromine, this is what causes the adverse reactions in most children. Carob has no caffeine or theobromine. Carob baked goods replace the chocolate products that children love. Carob hot drink mixes can be found in most health food stores as well as brownie and cake mixes. Unsweetened carob chips are also available to use in cookies.

HOW TO USE CAROB

Carob can be used to replace cocoa in most recipes with a few changes. Since carob is sweeter than chocolate, the sugar or honey should be reduced in the recipe sometimes as much as 1/3 cup. This is easier to judge in shakes and puddings than in cakes, but you can experiment or compare carob and chocolate recipes and see what the average difference is. Look at the carob pie recipe below for some comparisons. No matter how you first begin to use carob in your cooking or baking, don't tell your family you have made the switch until they have eaten and enjoyed the food. This prevents any reaction to a change or a change to something that is "good for you." If your children are already used to not having chocolate, then you will have to tell them so that they will feel free to eat. The average serving of chocolate cake contains 14 mg caffeine, 2/3 cup chocolate ice cream has 5 mg, 2 tablespoons chocolate syrup only 4 mg, 1 tablespoon dry powdered cocoa a whopping 11 mg. Compared to a cup of brewed coffee which contains from 108 to 137 mg it is minor.[5]

Very few children can drink coffee without getting revved up, imagine how many are getting little amounts of caffeine in chocolate products. This might be the reason why some grade school students are staging protests to have chocolate milk in the lunch rooms at schools. Caffeine is an addictive drug. If a student has it for breakfast he is going to want it again soon, like for lunch or before. This is why most schools removed it in the first place from the lunch rooms.

Carob or Chocolate Cream Pie
(crust)

3/4 cup	whole wheat pastry flour
3/4 cup	slivered or finely ground almonds
6 Tbsp.	melted butter
1 Tbsp.	honey, warmed

Add honey to butter and mix. Blend together flour and almonds and pour honey/butter mixture over. Mash together with a fork, or use a food processor to mix everything all at once. Press into a 9 or 10 inch pie pan and bake at 400°F for 10–12 minutes. Cool.

(filling)

3 cups	firm tofu, drained very well*
3/4 cup	melted butter
3/4 cup	honey
pinch of	sea salt
3/4 cup	roasted carob flour
1 Tbp.	brandy or rum (optional)

Blend tofu and add remaining ingredients and blend until smooth and creamy. Pour into the cooled pie crust and chill several hours or overnight. I use the food processor for this, but a blender will work just as well.

If using chocolate use 1 cup honey. * Wrap tofu in several layers of toweling and press the water out with a weight.

This was the second prize winning recipe at a "cheesecake" bake off at a soy foods convention. I didn't get the name of the winner whose recipe it was, nor would they give out the first prize recipe. I have taken this pie to parties and watched it disappear in minutes, even after people knew they had been eating tofu. It is so great that it could be a first tofu recipe to spring on your family.

Carob Cake

1 1/2 cup	whole wheat pastry flour
3 Tbsp.	carob flour, toasted
1/2 tsp.	sea salt
1 tsp.	baking soda
1 tsp.	baking powder
1 tsp.	pure vanilla extract
5 Tbsp.	oil or melted butter
1 tsp.	apple cider vinegar
2/3 cup	honey
3/4 cup	water

Grease or butter a 9 inch square cake pan. Mix honey and water together. Sift the dry ingredients into the pan and spread evenly. Make three depressions in the flour mixture with the back of a spoon, using a teaspoon for two and a very large spoon for the third. Put the oil into the large depression and the vanilla and vinegar in the small ones. Pour the honey and water over it and mix. Use a rubber spatula so that you don't scrape up the butter from the pan. You will also want to check the seams and corners for any unmixed ingredients.

Bake in a preheated 325°F oven for 35 to 40 minutes.

If using cocoa use 3/4 cup honey.

This cake can be mixed in a bowl by sifting dry ingredients into bowl and mixing liquids together and pouring them over the dry. For 15 or 20 years I did it in the pan and then found out I could do it quicker in a bowl. This cake does not work in high altitudes, there is not enough fat in it.

Carob Fudge Sauce

1 Tbsp.	butter
1/4–1/2 cup	milk or cream
1/4 cup	honey
1/3 cup	carob powder

Mix together in a sauce pan. Heat over low/medium heat until bubbly and thick. Stir constantly. Serves 3–4. Serve over ice cream or fresh fruit. This would make a good topping for the cake above, as well.

NUTRITIONAL VALUES

Carob flour (1 cup)
>   452 calories
>   2 g fat
>   6.3 g protein
>   113 g carbohydrate
>   10.8 g fiber
>   493 mg calcium
>   113 g phosphorus

Carob flour (1 Tablespoon)
>   14 calories
>   0.4 g protein
>   0.1 g fat
>   28 mg calcium
>   6 mg phosphorus[6]

GOODLY FRUIT

And you shall take on the first day the fruit of goodly trees, branches of palm trees, and boughs of leafy trees, and willows of the brook; and you shall rejoice before the Lord your God seven days. Leviticus 23:40 (RSV)

This quote is taken from the Revised Standard Version. There is some discrepancy in the various translations as to whether it says the fruit or the boughs of the goodly tree. The New International Version says to take "choice fruit from the trees," but gives no indication of the kind of fruit. In *All The Plants Of The Bible*, Winifred Walker lists the goodly fruit as the citron, *Citrus medica*.[7] Citron is mentioned often as a cooking ingredient in *Apicius* so it is a fruit that was eaten then. It is still being eaten, for that matter, in North America. Yes, citron is the melon that is used to make certain kinds of candied peel that is used in fruit cakes and dessert breads.

Melons were covered in Chapter II in depth along with cucumbers so I will not spend any space on them here. Except to say that cantaloupe and watermelon are the main melons eaten in the Middle East.

CHOOSING MELONS

It is very important to select melons that are not moldy, mildewed, or soft in any way. You never get a bargain when you buy any fruit that is already spoiled. "Yes," you might say, "I can cut off the spoiled parts," and you can. But mold is insidious and can seep into the fruit. Mold is a health hazard that is explained in Chapter III—Our Daily Proteins and Chapter VIII—The Secrets of Good Health.

There are no sure ways to tell if melons are ripe. Some say to thump the bottom to listen for a hollow sound to determine ripeness, others say this in ineffective. Then there are those who say to depress the blossom end. If it gives, the melon is ripe. Shaking melons is never recommended as a test for anything. Smelling a melon could be dangerous if it turned out to be moldy. This isn't much help to those wishing to select melons. I have used all the methods with some success, smelling, thumping, depressing, and even gentle squeezing of the melon. Looking for uniform color and raised mottling is about the best way to start looking for a melon.

Melon Supreme

1 envelope	unflavored gelatin
1/4 cup	cold water
1 medium	cantaloupe, very ripe OR watermelon
1/8 cup	liquid honey or sweeter fruit juice concentrate like orange, peach, apple, or apricot
1/2 cup	non-fat dry milk powder
1/2 cup	ice water

Soften gelatin in cold water. Purée enough melon pulp, without the seeds of course, to yield 2 cups. Combine with gelatin and honey or fruit juice concentrate in a small pan and heat over low heat until gelatin dissolves, about 3 minutes. Chill until a slight thickening appears. Combine milk powder and ice water in mixer bowl, and beat at high speed until the consistency of whipped cream. Fold* into the thickened gelatin mixture. Spoon into a lightly oiled 1 quart ring mold, and chill until firm. Serves 8. This is generally served with sprigs of fresh mint as a garnish. It is cool and refreshing.

*Fold—to mix a very light substance with a heavier one so as little lightness as possible is lost. The mixture must be lifted up from beneath and folded over, not stirred in a circle.

DATE PALMS

The righteous flourish like the palm tree . . . . They are planted in the house of the Lord, they flourish in the courts of our God. They still bring forth fruit in old age, they are ever full of sap and green, to show that the Lord is upright. Psalms 92:12-14. (RSV)

Palms are mentioned many times in the Bible. Some give shade and some give fruit. The date palm which provides the fruit is known as *Phoenix dactylifera*. These trees often attain a height of 100 feet and many of them live for over 100 years, many as long as 200 years. A date palm is not even considered a mature tree until it is at least 40 years old. The average date palm produces 100 pounds of dates a year for sixty or more years. A really good tree often produces 150 pounds of dates a year for almost 100 years.[8] Dates are a variety of colors: red, brown, yellow, or mahogany.

Dates were eaten fresh. The juice was pressed out and evaporated into a thick syrup to be used as a sweetener. They were often the base of fermented drinks or soft drinks. Dates were dried and compressed to be used in the winter for cooking. The sap was drained from old trees and made into syrup or palm toddy, a type of strong drink.

When a tree became old and refused to bear fruit the palm branches were cut and a small head of sprouts would grow, this was harvested and eaten like Brussels sprouts or cabbages. Then the sap was drained, and finally the tree was cut down and used for wood.

The dates on the date palm ripen at different intervals over the season so that dates are always ready to be eaten or made into syrup or wine. This sure makes it nice to have a tree next to the house providing sweetness for many months in many different ways.

SAFE DATES

Most of the chopped dates sold for cooking contain sugar to keep them separated or preserved. It is hard to tell why they do this. Read the package to see if they have sugar to determine if they are safe for you to eat. If you do not want to eat cane sugar or refined sugars, you would be better off purchasing dates that were pitted and chopping them yourself in a blender or food processor, or even with a knife. Sugar is hidden in many foodstuffs used in cooking and baking without it even being suspected. **Read, read, read!** I guess I have said this before, but it is very important to do if you are going to be in control of your diet, life, and health.

NUTRITIONAL VALUES

Dates (10 dried)
> 228 calories
> 0.4 g fat
> 0 cholesterol
> 1.6 g protein
> 61 g carbohydrates
> 1.8 g fiber
> 42 I.U. vitamin A
> 0 vitamin C
> 0.08 mg B1
> 0.08 mg B2
> 1.8 mg B3
> 0.65 mg B5
> 0.16 mg B6
> 10 mcg folic acid
> 2 mg sodium
> 541 mg potassium
> 27 mg calcium
> 29 mg magnesium

0.24 mg zinc
0.247 mg manganese
33 mg phosphorus
0.96 mg iron
0.239 mg copper[9]

Dates (1 cup chopped)
488 calories
3.9 g protein
0.9 g fat
130 g carbohydrates
90 I.U. vitamin A
0.16 mg B1
0.18 mg B2
3.9 mg B3
2 mg sodium
1,158 mg potassium
105 mg calcium
112 mg phosphorus
5.3 mg iron[10]

FRUIT AND GRAINS TOGETHER?

There are those who say that fruit and grains together is a bad combination. These are the people who espouse the theory called Food Combining. The idea is that grains have higher amounts of fat and protein and will, therefore, take longer to digest in the stomach. While the stomach is waiting to digest the grains, the fruit will have a good chance to ferment producing alcohol among other things and causing digestive disturbances.

My theory is that if you are healthy you can digest any combination of foods together as long as they are well chewed. You notice that this does not eliminate their theory nor condone it. I pooh-poohed this food combining theory for years, then I found that I had trouble digesting fruit and grains together, especially with protein, and had had trouble all along. So for years I stopped eating fruit and grains together and I felt great! Then again, I felt great before so that was really no test of the theory. What I have found through newly published research is a few reasons why a person might have trouble digesting fruit and grains or fruit and protein together.

LOW BLOOD SUGAR

A person who has trouble keeping their blood sugar levels stable may find that when they eat fruit it causes a rise in blood sugar that can trigger the digestion to slow down either from producing too much insulin or from a drop in blood sugar signaling the fight or flight response which will slow down or stop digestion. This will be explained in greater detail in *The World's Oldest Health Plan, Diets, Health Tips, Poultices, Medicines, Etc.*, as we are planning to call it now.

YEAST SYNDROME

This is the latest "dis-ease" in the holistic health world. Many people have been affected by yeasts, molds, and the like so that yeasts are living in their body. Yeasts live off sugar and starch and in return they make toxins. One of the toxins is alcohol. If a person has yeast living in their body and they eat fruit or fruit and grains together the yeast can turn their body into a very large still and produce alcohol along with other toxins that can cause health problems of many kinds as well as headaches, stomachaches, and indigestion or poor digestion, or no digestion. So it is possible that people with these problems would not be able to tolerate fruit and grains together.

Low blood sugar and yeast problems are indications that the person is not in the best of health and needs to seek medical help in correcting these problems before they could become major problems. If you have problems digesting fruit and grains together, I suggest you have yourself tested at a holistic practitioner who can help you if you have problems with low blood sugar, blood sugar swings, pre-diabetes, or yeast infestation. It is an indication of something out of balance in your body. There is also the possibility that an allergy could be present.

The Israelites often ate bread, cheese, fruit, olives or olive oil, and wine for lunch or breakfast. They never seemed to complain of poor digestion from this. But they had foods with higher nutritional values, no pollution from chemicals in the food or water, no automobile and airplane exhaust, no nuclear waste, so perhaps they were stronger.

SUGAR, HONEY, OR FRUIT CONCENTRATE?

Sweets are to be eaten as special treats, not as every day foods. Some people find that one type of sugar is easier to digest than another. There are many reasons for this including the two major ones mentioned above. Honey and concentrated fruit syrups or juices have been used for several thousand years as sweeteners. Honey is natural as it comes in the container. Fruit concentrates or syrups like maple or birch syrup have been dehydrated to remove some of the water from them. This can be done in the sun as it was in the ancient Middle East and still is today, or it can be boiled, as we do with maple syrup to drive off the liquid, this, too, is a pretty natural process. In these cases most of the original food value of the fruit or juice is still maintained. There is a type of sugar that is being sold in health food stores and delicatessens that is just the juice of sugar cane, dried, this too, is natural, it still contains most of the original nutrients.

White sugar, however, has been denatured by having the nutrients removed during the process of making it into sugar. The part that is removed, the molasses, contains all the B vitamins. The B vitamins are necessary for the digestion of the sugar. If the B vitamins have been removed from the sugar where will they come from to help with digestion? the other food being eaten? a pill? where? This can eventually lead to a certain stress on the body, always trying to digest without the proper nutrients necessary to do so. For this reason I suggest that you consider switching from white sugar to something more whole when you choose to eat sweets. That is why these recipes contain honey or fruit concentrate, not just because they didn't have white sugar in Bible times.

APRICOT, PEACH, PEAR, PLUM, AND PRUNE

Although apricots, peaches, pears, plums, and prunes were not mentioned specifically in the Bible we know they were grown and eaten. Apicius has many recipes containing these fruits mixed with each other in a compote, baked into a sweet or pie type dessert, or stewed in with meats, generally lamb or chicken.

It is no secret that of the locally grown fruits, peach is my favorite. I'm in good company since it is said that the peach was the highly favored fruit of Bible times as well, although it is not mentioned in the Bible. It is a fruit to be eaten fresh or cooked into some pudding, cobbler, or pie. They do not store well, and were eaten dried in Bible times. I have been known to buy a large freezer just to keep goat's milk during the off season and peach slices ready to make into pies at a moments notice. People would often come to my house from hundreds of miles to visit, enter the door in travel weariness and gasp "peach pie, peach pie." I loved it. I would go to the freezer and thaw a bag of peaches ready for the pie and within an hour and a half we would be eating hot peach pie and drinking freshly brewed decaffeinated coffee and sharing stories of what had transpired since we were last together.

Fruit Snacks

Use fresh dried fruit that is soft and moist. Get the pitted ones, which means the pits have been removed. Gently open up fruit on the cut line and insert filling. Arrange decoratively on a fancy plate. Choose from dates, apricots, prunes, or figs (you will have to cut them open since they are not a stone fruit and won't have been pitted).

Fillings

Fresh or toasted almonds, pecans, pistachio nuts, walnuts, pinon nuts, blue cheese, peanut butter, or a mixture of chopped nuts and nut butter.

These fruit snacks can be served to adults or children with ease and confidence. You will know that they will like them and that they are good for them.

Fruit Plates

The fruit snacks can be served on a plate interspersed with fresh fruit slices which have been dipped in lemon juice to keep them from turning dark, as well as fresh bunches of grapes. Cut the grapes into very little bunches with scissors so that there are three or four grapes on each stem. Serve pear halves, cored, with a filling in the hollow made from blending blue cheese and a small amount of mayonnaise to give a creamy consistency.

Fruit Squares
(filling)

1 pound	dried fruit, dates, figs, apricots, etc.
3/4 cup	honey or fruit juice concentrate
2/3 cup	water
1 Tbsp.	butter
1/2 tsp.	ground cinnamon, nutmeg, or allspice
	grated lemon rind

Chop fruit very fine if you use fruit other than dates. Mix everything together and cook over low heat until thick and creamy. Cool.

(Base & Topping)

1 1/2 cups	whole wheat pastry flour
1/2 tsp.	sea salt
1 tsp.	baking soda
1/2 cup	butter
3/4 cup	warm honey
1 3/4 cups	rolled oats

Sift flour, salt, and soda together. Mix butter, honey, and oats together and then mix in flour mixture. Divide in half. Pat half in bottom of 9 x 9 or 9 x 13 inch pan. Spoon filling over top and sprinkle remainder of topping over. Bake at 350°F for 30–40 minutes or until no longer soft on top. Cool and then cut into squares.

You can use all dates, all apricots, all figs, or even all raspberries. Or you can use a mixture. If you use figs or dried fruit other than dates, they must be chopped very fine to break down the high fiber skins so that they will mush together.

Peach Pie
(crust)

2 cups	whole wheat pastry flour
1/2 tsp.	sea salt
2/3 cup	unsalted butter, chilled
6 Tbsp.	ice water

Sift salt and flour together, cut in butter until mixture resembles coarse meal. Using a fork begin fluffing up the flour and slowly adding the water, fluffing and mashing quickly until all the water is added and you can gather the dough into a ball. Cut it into two pieces one a little bigger than the other. Roll the larger piece out rolling from the edges until you have a circle larger than the pie pan you will be using. It is best to roll the dough on a pastry cloth so that you can use it to put the crust in the pan. Lift the edges and gently press the dough into the corners of the pan so that the filling will not stretch the dough and allow the juice to leak through. Cut the extra dough off leaving enough to seal the crust. Roll out top piece and keep it ready.

(filling)

4–6	fresh peaches, washed and dried
1/2 – 3/4 cup	honey
3 Tbsp.	cornstarch or whole wheat flour
1/2 tsp.	grated fresh nutmeg
	grated peel of 1/4 lemon, or more to taste

Slice peaches and put into bowl. Slice enough to fill the size pie pan you are using. Heat honey enough to melt it, pour it over peaches and add the remaining ingredients and stir. Pour into pie shell. Wet the edges of the crust with cold water. Cover with remaining pastry. Press top crust into bottom, cut off excess dough, and flute edges. Cut slashes in top crust to allow steam to escape. Place on cookie sheet to catch any drips that might occur. Bake in preheated 425°F oven for 10 minutes to set the bottom crust. Turn heat to 375°F and bake until crust is browned and filling is thickened. About 45–50 more minutes.

I never peel the fruit for a pie, cobbler, or crisp, except oranges, of course. This way there is more fiber along with the wheat bran and the fiber of the fruit.

I always use the food processor to make pie crust. Put the flour, salt, and butter in and process until it is like coarse meal. Add 2/3 of the ice water and process by pulsing off and on. Gradually add a little more as needed until the pastry dough comes together in a ball. It generally takes less liquid with a food processor, sometimes even a tablespoon less. If you are using a firm fruit like apples or pears, you can even slice them in the food processor.

Fruit Rolls or Balls

1/2 cup	sesame seeds
1/2 pound	dried apricot, peach, or pear
1 pound	pitted dates
1/3 cup	raisins or currants
2 Tbsp.	liquified honey
1 tsp.	finely grated lemon or orange peel, optional

Toast sesame seeds in oven at 300°F for about 6 minutes or until just browned. Shake often to toast evenly. Chop fine or grind fruits, drizzle honey over fruit and peel and mix together. Form into balls and roll in seeds or form into long roll and coat with seeds then slice into rounds.

My step-grandfather used to have my grandmother make this in the '50s. She used dates, figs, prunes, walnuts, and lemon peel with honey. He used to make a sandwich with the slices and they looked about like salami so it didn't seem strange to me.

Fresh Fruit Cobbler or Shortcake Base

2 cups	whole wheat pastry flour
1/2 tsp.	sea salt
5 Tbsp.	chilled butter
1 Tbsp.	sweetener, honey, syrup, concentrate, etc.
1/2 cup	milk

Sift flour and salt together and cut in butter until consistency of coarse meal. Mix sweetener and milk together and blend into the dough. Knead, gently, for about 1 minute, fold over. Roll out on floured cloth and cut into rounds about 3 inches. Bake on ungreased baking sheet close together for 10–15 minutes in preheated 425°F oven. Cool. Split open and serve covered with fresh fruit and drizzle with lemon juice or concentrated fruit juice. Makes 1 dozen.

I often serve this with ice cream, yogurt, or whipped cream, and even add nuts or seeds, especially pecans and pistachio. But that would be all that we eat at that sitting. This would be the entire meal. Fruit, whole grains, nuts or seeds, butter, milk, yogurt, this would give a variety of foods from several food groups.

Cobbler I

Use the same dough and place over prepared fruit and bake in 375°F oven for 20 minutes until browned and fruit soft. Prepare fruit by slicing it into bowl, dust with flour or corn starch and concentrated fruit juice, cinnamon or nutmeg and mix well. Place in baking pan about 9 x 13 and put sweet biscuits on top.

Cobbler II

Use the same dough but use 1 cup of milk. Prepare fruit as in Cobbler I. Drop dough by spoonfuls onto the fruit and bake as above.

Once I did this on the TV segment I was doing on *100 Huntley Street* in Toronto. Val Dodd was with me and he always got to eat everything we were talking about. I did the Cobbler II using mangos as the fruit. He thought they were peaches because they had a beautiful orange color and were firm when cooked, just like peaches. It took a lot of talking to really convince him it was mangos and not peaches. Often I would use the Ezekiel-type blended flour for this to give a rich, nutty taste to the pastry.

NUTRITIONAL VALUES

Apricot, raw (3 medium)
>51 calories
>0.4 g fat
>1.5 g protein
>11.8 g carbohydrate
>0.6 g fiber
>2769 I.U. vitamin A
>11 mg vitamin C
>0.03 mg B1
>0.04 mg B2
>0.6 mg B3
>0.25 mg B5
>0.06 mg B6
>1 mg sodium
>313 mg potassium
>15 mg calcium
>8 mg magnesium
>0.28 mg zinc
>0.084 mg manganese
>21 mg phosphorus
>0.58 mg iron
>0.094 mg copper

Peach, raw (1 medium)
>37 calories
>0.1 g fat
>0.6 g protein
>9.7 g carbohydrate
>0.6 g fiber
>465 I.U. vitamin A
>6 mg vitamin C
>0.02 mg B1
>0.04 mg B2
>0.9 mg B3
>0.15 mg B5
>0.02 mg B6

3 mcg folic acid
0 sodium
171 mg potassium
5 mg calcium,
6 mg magnesium
0.12 mg zinc
0.041 mg manganese
11 mg phosphorus
0.10 mg iron
0.059 mg copper

Pear, raw (1 medium)

98 calories
0.7 g fat
0.2 g polyunsaturated fatty acids
0.7 g protein
25.1 g carbohydrate
2.3 g fiber
33 I.U. vitamin A
7 mg vitamin C
0.03 mg B1
0.07 mg B2
0.2 mg B3
0.12 mg B5
0.03 mg B6
12 mcg folic acid
1 mg sodium
208 mg potassium
19 mg calcium
9 mg magnesium
0.20 mg zinc
0.126 mg manganese
18 mg phosphorus
0.41 mg iron
0.188 mg copper

Plum, raw (1 medium)

36 calories
0.4 g fat
0.5 g protein
8.6 g carbohydrates
0.4 g fiber
213 I.U. vitamin A
6 mg vitamin C

.03 mg B1
0.06 mg B2
0.3 mg B3
0.12 mg B5
0.05 mg B6
1 mcg folic acid
0 sodium
113 mg potassium
2 mg calcium
4 mg magnesium
0.06 mg zinc
0.032 mg manganese
7 mg phosphorus
0.07 mg iron
0.028 mg copper[11]

WHAT'S SO GOOD ABOUT FRUIT?

Look at the nutritional values for the fruits mentioned in this chapter. You might notice some things you never knew before. Like the high content of vitamin A in some of the fruits, or the high amounts of calcium or iron. It is especially good to see a food low in fats and sodium and high in potassium. If you have trouble making yourself eat dark green leafy vegetables and/or deep orange vegetables, you might find that eating your vitamin A in the form of fruit is more pleasant. I hope you don't think this is an excuse to give up these veggies, they are full of nutrients that you really need to keep alert.

WHY POTASSIUM AND SODIUM

These two minerals are very important in the functioning of your body and mine. To keep it simple: sodium retains fluids, potassium releases them. It must be obvious by now that if you have a water retention problem you, generally, have too much sodium in your body or diet and too little potassium. The best way to help with this is to eat foods high in potassium and low in sodium. Fruits are great for this. It is thought by some that eating fruit flushes toxins out of the body as the water is released. So even though the Hebrews may have eaten salty cheeses and olives, they also ate fruits which helped to balance their diets.

POMEGRANATE

Saul was staying in the outskirts of Gibeah under the pomegranate tree which is at Migron. I Samuel 14:2a (RSV)

The pomegranate, *Punica granatum*, is highly regarded in the Middle East. The Hebrew name is *rimmon* and there are many towns that have rimmon in their name signifying that the fruit grew near there. Pomegranate is mentioned thirty times in the Bible. In Exodus they were on the hem of the High Priest's ephod, in I Kings and Jeremiah they adorned the temples, in the Song of Songs they are mentioned again and again. The spies brought back pomegranates to show them to Moses in Numbers 13:23, and as the fruit was greatly esteemed, we find that Moses extols the virtues of the Promised Land by pointing out that pomegranates grew there in abundance.[12]

The fruit was loved for its versatility and taste. The juice was and is still used as an indelible blue stain. In Morocco leather is tanned with the juice. The juice is made into a syrup called grenadine that is used in mixed drinks and confections. The first sherbet was made from the juice and snow brought down from the mountains. And, of course, it was made into wine, alone or mixed with grapes. The blossoms are used in a preparation used in treating dysentery. Pomegranate fruits even appeared on the currency in 143 to 135 B.C.

The fruit is not much to look at. It is a round ball about the size of an average orange with a leathery maroon skin. Inside there are many seeds encased in a bright red jelly-like substance that is the fruit. The seeds are in various compartments sectioned off by a membrane. It is not easy to eat when very ripe because the seeds often fall out in groups from each section. The juice of pomegranate is very refreshing and slightly tart. Even a room temperature pomegranate can be cooling on a hot day.

... I would give you spiced wine to drink, the juice of my pomegranates. Song of Solomon 8:2 (RSV)

... your cheeks are like halves of a pomegranate behind your veil. Song of Solomon 4:3b (RSV)

Pomegranates seem to be in poetry, on gowns, in parts of buildings, on coins, and generally highly regarded. This seems strange to me for a fruit that only yields juice and is often made into wine and other drinks. Even its nutritional values are so low that very few are even mentioned. Now don't get the idea that I don't like pomegranates, I do, I eat them.

You will see the value and beauty of pomegranates if, on a hot day, when you want to be refreshed, you reach for a pomegranate and peel back the leathery shell to reveal the seeds covered with pure succulent refreshment. Bite into the compartment and allow the juice to cool you, refresh you, and relax you all at the same time. This is the benefit of pomegranates. Spit out the seeds and take yet another and another mouthful of the ruby red refreshment of the Middle East, beloved for centuries by all the people we read about in the Bible. My nutrition class in Santa Fe, New Mexico was equally split on whether to eat the seeds or spit them out. I voted for "spit them out."

GRAPE (VINE)

When they reached the Valley of Eshcol, they cut off a branch bearing a single cluster of grapes. Two of them carried it on a pole between them, along with some pomegranates and figs. Numbers 13:23 (NIV)

Vines and vineyards are mentioned nearly 500 times in the Bible.[13] This means that grapes were grown on these vines, and that grapes are the most frequently mentioned, albeit indirectly, fruit in the Bible. Grapes, *Vitis vinifera*, were used mostly to make wine, the main drink of the Israelites. There are many mentions of raisins, so grapes were also eaten dried as well as fresh. White grapes were never watered, but the red grapes required watering and plenty of other care such as pruning, fertilizing, tying back, and other types of horticultural activities.

Grapes were grown on the sides of the average person's house. It was considered an advantage if a person had a well-kept yard, grape vine, fig tree, watering device, and palm trees for shade. Grape vines have been known to live for three hundred years or more when they are properly tended. This is why there are so many references in the Bible to vines and strength and longevity.

They found an Egyptian in the open country, and brought him to David; and they gave him bread and he ate, they gave him water to drink, and they gave him a piece of a cake of figs and two clusters of raisins. And when he had eaten, his spirit revived; for he had not eaten bread or drunk water for three days and three nights. I Samuel 30:11,12 (RSV)

Raisins were a fruit that people carried with them. They are always handy to eat if you have some with you. Many raisin packages come in special small packages that are handy for lunches or for carrying in the purse or briefcase. If you have a time when you are worn out, or your attention flags, raisins are a good pick-me-up, much better than cigarettes or caffeine.

Raisins are a good source of iron. Iron is best absorbed when vitamin C or other acid is taken at the same time as the iron. Raisins come with vitamin C in them, so the iron is usable.

Raisin Pie

2–3 cups	raisins*
1/4–1/2 cup	honey or concentrated orange juice
1 tsp.	grated lemon peel
1 tsp.	ground cinnamon
1/8 tsp.	ground nutmeg
1 Tbsp.	cornstarch
2 Tbsp.	cold water
	water as needed
	2 whole wheat pie crusts

Mix raisins, honey, spices, and lemon peel together in small sauce pan. Heat over low heat until honey dissolves. Blend cornstarch and water together and stir into raisins, continue cooking until mixture starts to thicken. Pour into pie shell, cover, and bake at 425°F for 12 minutes, reduce heat to 375 F and continue to bake until crust is golden brown, about 40 minutes.

*Measure the amount of raisins needed by pouring them into the pie pan before cooking them. Fill the pie pan with the raisins until they are just level with the top of the pan, they will expand with cooking.

NUTRITIONAL VALUES

Grapes—American-Slip Skin, raw (1 cup)
     58 calories
     0.3 g fat
     0.1 g polyunsaturated fatty acids
     0 cholesterol
     0.6 g protein
     15.8 g carbohydrate
     0.7 g fiber
     92 I.U. vitamin A
     4 mg vitamin C
     0.09 mg B1
     0.05 mg B2

0.3 mg B3
0.02 mg B5
0.10 mg B6
2 mg sodium
176 mg potassium
13 mg calcium
5 mg magnesium
0.04 mg zinc
0.661 mg manganese
9 mg phosphorus
0.27 mg iron
0.037 mg copper

Grapes—European Adherent-Skin raw, (1 cup)
114 calories
0.9 mg fat
0.03 mg polyunsaturated fatty acids
1.1 g protein
28.4 g carbohydrate
0.7 g fiber
117 I.U. vitamin A
17 mg vitamin C
0.15 mg B1
0.09 mg B2
0.5 mg B3
0.04 mg B5
0.18 mg B6
6 mcg folic acid
3 mg sodium
296 mg potassium
17 mg calcium
10 mg magnesium
0.09 mg zinc
0.093 manganese
21 mg phosphorus
0.41 mg iron
0.144 mg copper

Raisins—Seedless (2/3 cup)
302 calories
0.5 g fat
3.2 g protein
79.1 g carbohydrate
1.3 g fiber

8 I.U. vitamin A
3 mg vitamin C
0.16 mg B1
0.09 mg B2
0.8 mg B3
0.05 mg B5
0.25 mg B6
3 mcg folic acid
12 mg sodium
751 mg potassium
49 mg calcium
33 mg magnesium
0.27 mg zinc
0.308 mg manganese
97 mg phosphorus
2.08 mg iron
0.309 mg copper

OLIVES

For the LORD your God is bringing you into a good land, a land of brooks of water, of fountains and springs, flowing forth in valleys and hills, a land of wheat and barley, of vines and fig trees and pomegranates, a land of olive trees and honey, a land in which you will eat bread without scarcity, in which you will lack nothing . . . Deuteronomy 8:7,8,9 (RSV)

Yes, olives are considered fruits. See how they are grouped above with the other fruits and honey. The olive, *Olea europaea*, was a very useful fruit. The fruit provided food fresh and dried, as well as pickled, it also provided oil which was used for cooking, medicine, ointments, beauty treatments and preparations, as well as for the oil in lamps and soap. A full-sized tree can often yield a half ton of oil yearly. The wood of the tree was also used for posts and doors in the temple as well as for the Cherubim. Olive wood is finely grained and turns a rich amber color when cut, planed, and oiled. Of all the fruit trees olive trees seem to be the most useful.

In the Middle East a gardener can expect two crops a year for each producing tree. Even an old tree often yields 20 gallons of oil from the pressed fruits.[14]

Olive trees grow in very rocky terrain, just the places where there is no grass or pasture land to raise cattle, sheep, or goats for milk. Without milk there will be no butter. Most of the dairy production was used for cheese, as we saw in the last chapter. This means that many people used olive oil for cooking and eating in these areas, just as they do today in Spain, Greece, southern Italy, and the Middle East.

OLIVE OIL IS MONOUNSATURATED

Nutritionists are studying the effects of the three major kinds of fats on health. Saturated fats are generally found in animal fats, unsaturated fats are generally found in plant fats. This used to be all we needed to know. Now, however, there is new research showing that we need several kinds of fats for different reasons for the health of our body. These are saturated fats, monounsaturated fats, and polyunsaturated fats. Everyone seems to agree that the consumption of saturated fats should be kept low to prevent coronary or arterial problems, including high cholesterol. Most research has shown that consumption of a high saturated fat diet, exclusively, can produce problems such as high blood pressure, obesity, and a tendency to diabetes, as well as the unwanted "bad" fats, low density lipoproteins (LDL). LDL's, it is speculated, are sloppy and sticky and attract things to them while they are themselves sticking to the walls of the arteries. HDL (high density lipoprotein), the "good" cholesterol, is not sticky and does not, generally, lodge in the arteries or anywhere else.

If a person has a high enough ratio of HDL to LDL their chances of heart disease are much lower. That is as long as their overall cholesterol levels are within the accepted range generally considered to be under 200. Obesity, polyunsaturated fatty acid consumption, and high-fat with low-carbohydrate diets all have been shown to lower the HDL cholesterol concentration, which can produce a health risk. Monounsaturated fatty acids, on the other hand, do not lower the HDL concentrations. Furthermore, vigorous exercise also raises the HDL concentration.[15] Olive oil is the main monounsaturated fatty acid, in use for thousands of years.

THE MEDITERRANEAN DIET

Research published in the Journal of the American Medical Association in February 1990 showed that consumption over a lifetime of a diet that included large amounts of vegetables and grains and small amounts of butter and cheese, small amounts of meats and fish, and olive oil as the major fat for cooking and eating resulted in benefits to blood pressure and glucose metabolism. Both men and women reported lower levels of systolic blood pressure, blood glucose, and blood cholesterol.[16] The key word is primary. The primary source of fat in the diet should come from monounsaturated fats, secondary fat sources can come from saturated or polyunsaturated fats. What hasn't been determined, though, is whether the other foods in the diet contribute to the metabolism of the saturated fatty acids along with the monounsaturated fatty acids. I contend that a grain-based diet that includes bitter herbs has more to do with the way the body handles all the fats. This is why the Mediterranean diet is so healthful. This is why the World's Oldest Health Plan is so healthy.

MONOUNSATURATED FATS

Olive oil is the main source of natural monounsaturated fats. I call this natural because most of the olive oil is expeller pressed (previously called cold pressed) so it is in its natural state. Virgin olive oil is from the first pressing. Extra virgin olive oil is also high in monounsaturated fatty acids. I would not rely on olive oil that is not virgin or extra virgin, it could be chemically extracted oil from the residue, it could also be a blend of almost any kind of oil and a small amount of olive oil, which you do not want to eat no matter what the cost if you are at all concerned with your health. Peanut oil and canola (rapeseed) oil are also good sources of monounsaturated fatty acids. These oils also contain polyunsaturated fatty acids in much lower percentages than the monounsaturated fatty acids.

POLYUNSATURATED FATTY ACIDS

For years we have been told to eat less saturated fats and more polyunsaturated fats to help lower cholesterol. The latest research is showing that high consumption of polyunsaturated fatty acids can reduce the HDL cholesterol and promote the formation of cholesterol gallstones. Animal studies have shown that high consumption of polyunsaturated fatty acids can suppress the immune system and predispose one to tumor formations.[17]

In a personal interview with Dr. Donald McNamara, a lipids researcher at the Department of Nutrition and Food Science at the University of Arizona, Tucson, I discovered some interesting information on polyunsaturated fats. He has found that skin cancer patients have a higher concentration of polyunsaturated fatty acids in their fats than non-cancer patients. His research also agrees with that published in the trade journal Circulation, that changes in the fat due to consumption of high amounts of polyunsaturated fats can alter the immune response and therefore increase the amount of cancers and tumors found.

DO WE NEED FATS?

Fats supply a concentrated energy source. Fats and oils also provide the fat-soluble vitamins A, D, and E. Without fats we cannot absorb the fat-soluble vitamins. The functioning of the adrenal glands and the sex organs and glands rely on some fats. Unsaturated fatty acids are given to overcome various kinds of skin problems, an overactive thyroid gland, and can be useful in the reduction of hypoglycemia symptoms in cases not related to diabetes. It is very important to have a diet that contains the right amounts of fats. In North America most people consume way too much fat for the needs of their body. Most people consume the wrong kinds of fats at the wrong times. There will be more on fats in Chapter VI—Alternative Proteins–Meat, Fish, Fowl, and Eggs.

Mayonnaise

1 cup	virgin olive oil
1 large	egg*
2 Tbsp.	apple cider vinegar, lemon juice, or both
1/2 tsp.	sea salt
1/4 tsp.	dry mustard powder OR
1 tsp.	Dijon mustard
1/4 tsp.	paprika, optional

All ingredients **must** be at room temperature. Place 1/4 cup of the oil and the remaining ingredients in a blender or food processor fitted with the plastic blade. Blend until well mixed. Remove feeder tube and, with motor running, slowly pour in remaining oil in a steady stream. Process or blend until thick. Store, covered, in the refrigerator.

*The entire egg can be used or just the yolk. If using medium eggs use two.

Garlic or Herb Mayonnaise—Follow the directions for Mayonnaise above and add pressed garlic or crushed herbs with the first ingredients. Tarragon, basil, dill, or curry are nice.

Pesto

2 cups	basil leaves*
1 tsp.	salt
1/2 tsp.	freshly ground black pepper
2-3	cloves fresh garlic
2 Tbsp.	pine nuts or sunflower seeds
1-1 1/2 cups	virgin or extra virgin olive oil
1/2 cup	freshly grated Parmesan or romano cheese

*To measure the basil leaves strip them from the stems, coarsely chop them and pack them into a measuring cup. Flat Italian parsley prepared as for basil and combined with 2 Tbsp. dried basil can be used. Or cilantro can be used in place of the basil.

Place leaves, salt, pepper, garlic, and nuts in blender or food processor and blend turning the motor off and on, until finely chopped. Add olive oil and mix, then add the cheese and mix together. Use spatula to push leaves into blades often. Blend until smooth or leave coarse.

If you want the end product to be coarse, blend the garlic and nuts first so that they are fine, then add the remaining ingredients following the basic recipe.

This is served in Italy over hot pasta. Traditionally, the pasta is coated with a small amount of butter, then about a tablespoon of the pesto is added to each serving and mixed in. Pesto is used in many ways in today's cooking. Sometimes it is the filling for ravioli, or the sauce for fish as well as other kinds of pasta such as fettuccini, fusilli, or shells.

Olive Pesto

1/2 cup	olives, green or black*
2 cloves	fresh garlic
2 Tbsp.	pinon or pine nuts
1-1 1/2 cups	virgin olive oil
1/2 cup	freshly grated Parmesan or romano cheese

Remove pits from olives. Blend all ingredients until smooth. This is generally mixed with a whole grain pasta.

*Greek or Italian olives work best for this. This means that the olives have been in brine and are preserved in some way. These are not the regular cocktail olives or canned black olives we usually use in North America.

NUTRITIONAL VALUES

Olives (2 Large black)
    37 calories
    4 g fat
    0 cholesterol
    0.2 g protein
    0.6 g carbohydrates
    0.3 g fiber
    14 I.U. vitamin A
    150 mg sodium
    5 mg potassium
    21 mg calcium
    3 mg phosphorus
    0.30 mg iron

Olives (2 medium green)
    15 calories
    1.6 g fat
    0 cholesterol
    0.2 g protein
    0.2 g fiber
    40 I.U. vitamin A
    312 mg sodium
    7 mg potassium
    8 mg calcium
    2 mg phosphorus
    0.20 mg iron

Olives (3 medium Greek)
    67 calories
    7.1 g fat
    0 cholesterol
    0.4 g protein
    1.7 g carbohydrates
    0.8 g fiber
    658 mg sodium
    6 mg phosphorus

Olive Oil (1 Tbsp.)
    119 calories
    13.5 g fat

      1.1 g polyunsaturated fat
      0.01 mg zinc
      0.05 mg iron[18]

Olive Oil
      13.5% saturated fatty acids
      73.7% monounsaturated fatty acids
      8.4% polyunsaturated fatty acids

Peanut oil
      16.9% saturated fatty acids
      46.2% monounsaturated fatty acids
      32% polyunsaturated fatty acids

Canola (rapeseed oil)
      6.8% saturated fatty acids
      55.5% monounsaturated fatty acids
      33.3 % polyunsaturated fatty acids

Soybean oil
      15% saturated fatty acids
      45% monounsaturated fatty acids
      39% unsaturated fatty acids

Butter
      50.5% saturated fatty acids
      23.4% monounsaturated fatty acids
      3% polyunsaturated fatty acids[19]

THE WORLD'S OLDEST HEALTH PLAN

The World's Oldest Health Plan is my interpretation of the diet that was followed by people in the Bible times in the Middle East and Mediterranean. The saturated fats in cheese, butter, meat, fish, and poultry should be the lowest fats consumed. The monounsaturated fats from olives, peanuts, and other monounsaturated sources should be the highest amount of fat consumed and the polyunsaturated fats from other sources such as nuts and seeds should be somewhere in the middle. I advocate that when cooking, use a combination of butter and a monounsaturated fat or all monounsaturated fat. This is what is being done in all good cooking from France, Italy, Spain, the Middle East, India, and China. The use of a mixture of butter and monounsaturated fats for eating is acceptable when the butter is the only saturated fat in the meal. If other saturated fats are being eaten, then try to stick to monounsaturated and polyunsaturated blends.

Make your own mayonnaise with olive oil to use with eggs, tuna, or other meat salads. Better yet make the mayonnaise with olive oil and reduce the fat by using the mono- and polyunsaturated fats in tofu, the recipe is in Chapter III—Our Daily Proteins. If you are having a meat sandwich use mayonnaise, mustard, or olive oil on the bread not butter or margarine. Always use lettuce, watercress, or parsley for the minerals, B vitamins, fiber, and effect of the "bitter herbs" when you are eating saturated (animal) fat.

Many Middle Eastern and Italian sandwiches are made without meat or cheese using beans, humus (chick peas), falafel, roasted red and green peppers, eggplant, or even that old English tradition, cucumber sandwiches. Tofu and tempeh sandwiches are wonderful to eat to reduce the cholesterol and saturated fats in the diet. Most natural food stores, Oriental groceries, or gourmet stores carry a variety of tofu and/or tempeh meat substitutes such as sandwich slices, burgers, hot dogs, or other recognizable tastes and shapes of sandwich fixings.

It is essential to eat a balanced diet, and this is especially true in the area of fats. A very low fat diet is not recommended. This would be a diet with less than 10% fats of any kind in the diet. A moderate fat diet that consists mainly of mono- and polyunsaturated fats and small amounts of saturated fats if desired, is the best approach for total health. This is the diet that was eaten by the Israelites. This is truly the World's Oldest Health Plan.

OLIVE OIL–THE FOUNTAIN OF YOUTH?

There is a currently held theory that free radicals running wild in the body can cause destruction that leads to aging, and in some cases, the formation of carcinogens or cancer causing agents. It is generally held that polyunsaturated fatty acids in the presence of oxygen trigger chain reactions of radical formation. Other factors that play a part in influencing the production of free radicals are pollution, radiation, and other environmental toxins. Cigarette smoke produces free radicals by oxidizing polyunsaturated fatty acids in the body.

Free radical quenchers or scavengers exist in nature that help keep the body balanced. They are vitamin E, vitamin A, beta carotene, vitamin C, and garlic. Dark green leafy vegetables and yellow vegetables are the best sources of carotene. The problem begins when the free radical scavengers are busy protecting the body from the pollution, toxins, and unstable vegetable oils in such a way that they cannot do their regular work in deactivating the free radicals that form normally.[20] This leads to a breakdown in the tissues and cells that has become known over the years as aging. Since olive oil is not a polyunsaturated fatty acid it is not known to contribute to this free radical/aging problem. I can't go so far as to say that using olive oil instead of polyunsaturated oils will help slow the aging process, but I will say it looks like it could help.

OLIVE OIL AS MEDICINE

But a Samaritan, as he traveled, came to where the man was; and when he saw him, he took pity on him. He went to him and bandaged his wounds, pouring on oil and wine . . . . Luke 10:33;34 (NIV)

Olive oil was used to pour into the wounds of the man on the road by the good Samaritan, after cleaning the wound with wine. An Egyptian medical text of 1550 B.C. mentions olive oil approximately 700 times as appropriate either to be taken orally or to be rubbed on the body. Oil was generally used as a shield against infection. Ground olive leaves were used to cause fever abatement and also were used to combat malaria. They contain salicylic acid, the active ingredient in aspirin.[21]

In North America there are many folk remedies that use olive oil to "cleanse" the liver or soften and expel gallstones. The oil is generally taken with or mixed with fresh lemon juice. Although the people who use these remedies feel that they are safe and effective, I would not use one unless supervised by and recommended by a health care professional.

ALMONDS

Then their father Israel said to them: "If it must be so, then do this: take some of the choice fruits of the land in your bags, and carry down to the man a present, a little balm and a little honey, gum, myrrh, pistachio nuts, and almonds." Genesis 43:11 (RSV)

Almonds were eaten often, but they were also used for hidden or double meanings. Almond, *Amygdalus communis*, is also *shaqued* in Hebrew which means "hastening." Hastening can mean "hurry up" or it can mean "watch" or "waken." The almond blossoms appear on the tree before any leaves, which also gives meaning to the word hasten or quickly. Almonds were highly prized as food and for their oil. One hundred and fourteen pounds of almonds will yield fifty pounds of oil. Throughout the Era of the Maccabees the almond was the design used on the shekel.[22]

Almonds like most other nuts are high in fat and protein. The protein is, however, incomplete because it is low in lysine. It is not suitable for people with cold sores or other types of herpes to eat nuts since it has been shown that lysine is needed to prevent these outbreaks. Nuts should be eaten in the same day or same meal with beans or peanuts which are legumes and are high in lysine to balance the protein.

All nuts are freshest when first shelled. When buying nuts it is best, if they are shelled, to buy them from a place that keeps them refrigerated, sealed in cans, or in very dark packages to prevent light, heat, or oxygen from causing them to become rancid. It is never good to eat rancid nuts or seeds. They will look oily or discolored when they are rancid, have an off taste, or taste very strong. Nuts in the shell last longer than nuts that have been shelled. I always keep nuts and seeds in the freezer to slow the process of rancidity.

HOW TO USE ALMONDS

Almonds are used chopped, sliced, or ground in baking. Blanched almonds are almonds that have had the brown skin removed. This is done by plunging the nuts in boiling water for a few seconds and then rinsing them with cold water. The skin will be loosened and slip off very easily. The skin of the almond is high in fiber so it is best to use whole almonds whenever possible. The skin, when intact, helps to slow the process of rancidity by keeping light from getting to the nut as easily as when it is blanched.

ALMOND OIL

Almond oil is often used in baking, on salads, and for beauty treatments. Sweet almond oil is often used around the tender eye area to reduce or remove wrinkles, crows feet, and other dry skin. It should be used very sparingly. Place a few drops in the hand. Using the fingertips gently pat the oil onto the eye lids starting on the upper lid near the nose and working toward the outside, tapping the oil onto the skin. Then add more oil to the fingertips and apply it to the underside of the eyes using the taping motion starting at the outer edge and working toward the nose. Never, never, pull, rub, or stretch the delicate skin around the eyes. This skin has less elasticity and may not tighten back up. If the skin is very dry or very wrinkled, splash warm water on after the oil to moisturize the skin. The oil will help to hold the moisture in.

NUTRITIONAL VALUES

Almond oil (1 Tbsp.)
  120 calories
  1.1 g saturated fatty acids
  9.5 g monounsaturated fatty acids
  2.4 g polyunsaturated fatty acids[23]

Almonds (12–15 Nuts–unroasted, unsalted)
  90 calories
  8.1 g fat
  2.8 g protein
  2.9 g carbohydrate
  0.04 mg B1
  0.10 mg B2
  0.7 mg B3
  104 mg potassium
  38 mg calcium
  71 mg phosphorus
  0.70 mg iron

PISTACHIO NUTS

Pistachio nuts, *Pistacia vera*, were grown in Syria which is why Jacob's son carried them to Egypt as a special treat. Pistachios are used in many confections that come from the Middle East and Mediterranean such a baklava and other nut pastries, as well as in puddings, and halvah, a blend of ground sesame seeds, honey, and pistachios or almonds. Many custard or pudding type desserts have pistachios sprinkled on top for the contrast of their beautiful green color against the pale cream of the custard. The shells are naturally pale brown or beige, but are often dyed red to make them sell better. The red is a vegetable dye, but I prefer to eat them with the natural shell color. The shells were dyed around the turn of the century when some enterprising Middle Eastern pistachio grower found that he could sell the nuts in North America by dying the shells and selling them by the handful in a special machine. They caught on quickly. The shells split open when the nuts are roasted. If they do not come open use a nut cracker to open, never use your teeth. Save half a shell from one nut to open the others. The nuts should fit snug inside the shells, if they are loose, they are often no good. Pistachio nuts should be bright green, never brown. Follow the instructions under almonds for keeping them.

COOKING WITH PISTACHIOS

Many desserts are made with pistachio nuts. They are used in sweets that have a pastry crust and honey and nut filling. They are used in custards and puddings made with grains. Rice pudding with raisins, honey, milk, coriander or cinnamon, and pistachio nuts is a common dish still eaten in the Middle East today. Some recipes call for eggs and/or cream to be blended into the baking pudding, but that might make it too rich or too high in fat and calories. Pistachio nuts can be used in baked apples, pies, cookies, or even in salads or casseroles. Generally rose water is used in a traditional dish that uses bulgur or millet, raisins, cream, honey, and pistachio nuts with the rose water poured on the top just before serving. These types of desserts can be made from pre-cooked grains and assembled and then baked. They can be made from uncooked grains that are cooked with the seasonings in the oven or on top of the stove, either way is traditional. Records of excavations show that the stoves had ovens as well as several top "burner" openings for cooking. They had ceramic and cast iron pots for casseroles as well as for stove top cooking.

NUTRITIONAL VALUES

Pistachio nuts (30 nuts)
>   88 calories
>   8 g fat
>   1.6 g polyunsaturated fatty acids
>   2.9 g protein
>   2.8 g carbohydrate
>   0.3 g fiber

WALNUTS

I went down to the grove of nut trees to look at the new growth in the valley. . . . Song of Songs 6:11 (NIV)

Walnut *Juglans regia, Egoz* in Hebrew, was the nut raised by Solomon in his garden. The word for nuts used in other parts of the Bible is the Hebrew word *botnim*. The passage above distinguishes the reference to nut as walnut in the Hebrew. Walnuts are still grown in Israel today and are used for dyes, cooking, oil for cooking, and eaten from the shell.

Walnuts are best when eaten from the shell or shelled and eaten immediately. Walnuts tend to go rancid very fast once they are shelled so it is best to shell them before use or buy them in a sealed container. It is best to buy from a store that removes them from the sealed container and puts them in refrigeration. If you must buy walnuts in a package please be sure that it is in a darkened area of the store not in the sun or other bright lights. Always look for a code date to see when they were packaged, if the date is more than two or three months old, don't buy them.

In North America we have two kinds of walnuts generally available: the black walnut and the English walnut. They have very different tastes. It is the black walnut that is most often used for dye here, the outer casing of the nut is used. You will know what a powerful dye it is if you have ever tried to remove this outer layer from the nut. It looks like a thick green pith or husk, but quickly turns fingers, nails, anything it touches, brownish.

WALNUT OIL

Walnut oil is a popular gourmet item in most areas of the country. Walnut oil is most often used in a fresh salad with Boston or bibb lettuce, toasted walnuts, orange slices, orange or lemon juice and walnut oil. It has a wonderful taste in a clean salad like this.

CARING FOR OILS

Look for oils that are expeller pressed, previously called cold pressed, when buying oils. Oils should be sealed so that they cannot be opened by shoppers. Each time they are opened, the chance of rancidity increases. Many oils are now sealed in cans to keep the light and oxygen away from them. Nitrogen packed oils are good. Generally oils have vitamin E added as an antioxidant, that is OK. I try to never buy oils that have anything added "to ensure freshness." As soon as the oil is opened it should be refrigerated. The top, neck, and rim of the bottle and cap should be kept very clean and never touched by human hands or fingers. If you pour out too much oil, never return it to the bottle. This could turn the entire bottle rancid if the oil has touched something that contaminated it. If oil spills on the side of the can or bottle, wipe it off with a clean paper towel. The most common thing that can cause oil to "go off" is the oil on your hands. This is why it should never be touched with your hands and replaced in the bottle. This is true even if you have just washed your hands.

WALNUTS AND CHOLESTEROL

Polyunsaturated fatty acids have been reputed to lower cholesterol and serum triglycerides through research using pigs fed with peanut oils. Now research using humans has shown that consumption of walnuts several times a week has caused a reduction in cholesterol levels, including a reduction in the LDL, increase in the HDL, and reduction in the ratio of LDL to HDL.[24] This is good news. The studies showed that men who took walnuts in place of some of the dietary fats but remained on a cholesterol-lowering diet had a better chance of lowering cholesterol than those who only followed the cholesterol-lowering diet. Many people experienced a 18.2 mg per deciliter or 16.3% reduction of the LDL levels and a serum triglyceride reduction of 9.5 mg per deciliter. And this was after only 4 weeks on the walnut diet. In this study 20% of the calories from fat were from walnuts. This means that they also reduced the amount of fats eaten from all other forms of fat such as meat, fish, eggs, oil, margarine, or butter. See Chapter VI—Alternative Proteins for a formula for calculating percentage of calories from fat in the diet. The control group followed the same diet but did not eat the walnuts. The consumption of up to 28 grams a day of walnuts (and appropriate reduction in total dietary fats) could be very helpful in lowering cholesterol and triglycerides. This is about one ounce of walnuts or a quarter cup. The nuts were added to cereals, muffins (great with oat bran added), casseroles, and salads.

English walnuts have a very high ratio of polyunsaturated to saturated fats, 7:1. They also have 23% of their total fat as monounsaturated fat.

In another study reported in 1992 with Seventh Day Adventists, they found that the consumption of nuts helped to reduce the risk of coronary heart disease. Some of the people in the study ate meat and other animal products, others did not. When nuts were eaten with the majority of the daily bread being whole wheat the chances were even greater of reducing the risk of coronary heart disease. [25]

If you have a history in your family of coronary heart disease you owe it to yourself to change your diet to include whole wheat bread (or make sure that all the bread is whole wheat) and to include nuts, especially walnuts, as part of the fat allowed daily. This could help you and your family live longer and happier. This is very close to what was eaten in Bible times. They ate whole grain bread, nuts, fruits, vegetables, herbs, eggs, cheese, olives, and yogurt. The study also showed that when nuts were eaten the desire for larger amounts of food was also reduced in a way that eating saturated fats did not do. Let me warn you that you must reduce the total calories from fat, you cannot just add nuts to an already high fat diet and have beneficial results.

NUTRITIONAL VALUES

Walnuts, English (8–15 halves)

> 98 calories
> 9.7 g fat
> 7.2 polyunsaturated fatty acids
> 2.3 g protein
> 2.3 g carbohydrate
> 0.3 g fiber
> 5 I.U. vitamin A
> trace vitamin C
> 0.07 mg B1
> 0.02 mg B2
> 0.2 mg B3
> 68 mg potassium
> 12 mg calcium
> 57 mg phosphorus
> 0.30 mg iron

Walnuts, Black (8-10 halves)

> 94 calories
> 8.7 g fat
> 4.8 g polyunsaturated fatty acids
> 2.7 g protein
> 2.8 g carbohydrate
> 11 I.U. vitamin A
> 0.90 mg iron[26]

Walnut oil (1 Tbsp.)

> 1.2 g saturated fatty acids
> 3.1 g monounsaturated fatty acids
> 8.6 g polyunsaturated fatty acids[27]

Walnut Bread

1	package dry yeast (1 Tbsp. or 15 mL)
2 cups	warm water
2 Tbsp.	liquid honey
1 tsp.	salt substitute
2 Tbsp.	Extra Virgin olive oil
4 1/2 cups	whole wheat and spelt flour mixed*
1 cup	walnut pieces (actually you need 115 g, a scant cup)
	oil
	corn meal
	cold water

Dissolve yeast in 1/4 of the luke warm water and let it set for 10 minutes or until it foams up. Add the remaining water, honey, salt substitute, and oil, and beat with an electric beater, whisk, or hand mixer for 1 minute. Add 3 cups of the flour and continue to beat for 1 minute after all the flour is mixed in. Remove the beaters and add the remaining flour and walnuts and beat by hand with a wooden spoon for 1 minute after all the flour is mixed in.

Cover it with a non-terry cloth towel. I prefer to rinse it with hot water and ring it out first, but you can do it dry. Put it in a warm, draft free place to rise for 1 hour. After the first 15 minutes remove the towel and stir up or beat the dough for 1 minute. (This requires patience and a strong arm. I use a wooden spoon which I keep in a glass of water.) Replace the towel and put the bowl in a warm draft free place to rise. Do this again after the second 15 minutes and the third 15 minutes also, so that you work through the dough 3 times in the hour it is rising. After the hour is up turn the dough onto a lightly floured cloth and divide in two. Shape each piece into a ball and cover with a cloth and let rest for 10 minutes. Oil a baking sheet and generously sprinkle it with the corn meal to rest the bread on. Roll each ball on the floured cloth into a rectangle 12 x 9 inches. Start with the long side and, using the cloth, roll the dough up like a jelly roll. Seal the edge by pressing on it with your hands. Turn the ends under to seal them. Place the roll, seam sides down, on the corn meal covered baking sheet on one side. Do the same with the other loaf and place it next to the first loaf. Both loaves will expand so leave room.

Make 3 or 4 diagonal slashes in the loaves, cutting just a half inch into the bread or less. This will keep the bread from cracking when it expands. Brush loaves with water and leave in a warm place to rise until double in bulk, about 30 minutes.

Place loaves in a pre-heated 375°F oven and bake for 35 to 45 minutes. You could brush the loaves with cold water and place in a draft to cool, if you want a crispy crust.

The research using walnuts to reduce coronary heart disease found that up to 28 grams a day of walnuts reduced the serum level of LDL cholesterol by 6% in two months, when included in a cholesterol-reducing diet already at the 10% of calories from fat level. One half of each of these two loaves contains that amount of walnuts.

*I like to use spelt and whole wheat half and half in breads. The spelt has a very unique taste that I like. If you prefer you may use all whole wheat. This is a basic recipe that you can adapt easily to a variety of whole grain flours, just make sure that there is some wheat in it since the research is showing that wheat helps the walnuts in the cholesterol lowering process.

SEEDS

And God said, "Let the earth put forth vegetation, plants yielding seed, and fruit trees bearing fruit in which is their seed, each according to its kind, upon the earth." And it was so. Genesis 1:11 (RSV)

Then God said, "I give you every seed-bearing plant on the face of the whole earth and every tree that has fruit with seed in it. They will be yours for food." Genesis 1:29 (NIV)

Of all the times seeds are mentioned, only three seeds are mentioned by name in the Bible: flax, *Linum usitatissimum;* coriander, *Coriandrum sativum;* and mustard, *Brassica nigra.*

Flax stems were used to make linen threads which were then woven into linen to be used for garments. The clothes were made of crudely spun woven linen, much like the raw silk fabrics we have today, or fine linen like we might use today in a business suit or dress. Linen was used to make the wicks for lamps, curtains for the Tabernacle, and was forbidden to be mixed with wool. Flax seeds were pounded and the resulting oil used as an addition to breads, just as they still are in some European health breads. Flax seeds are called linseed when used in food or oil.

Coriander is the seed that is used to describe the taste of manna that was sent to the Children of Israel in the wilderness as their food. Coriander is used in cooking in breads, pastries, and various savory dishes like curry and Chinese stir fry. Coriander will be discussed in more detail in Chapter VII—Drinks–Water, Juice, Wine, Beer, & Teas.

MUSTARD

It is like a grain of mustard seed which a man took and sowed in his garden . . . . Luke 13:19a (RSV)

Mustard seeds were used as seasonings, ground and made into a condiment similar to the mustard we known today, and the ground seeds were used for plasters and poultices. Mustard greens, both the wild and cultivated ones were eaten as a green vegetable. Mustard greens are somewhat bitter and might be considered a bitter herb. Mustard greens can be used in soups, stews, curry, and many other interesting dishes. I often use them in stir frys, putting them in near the end of cooking so they are wilted but not mushy.

NUTRITIONAL VALUES

Linseed oil (1 Tbsp.)
> 1.3 g saturated fatty acids
> 2.7 g monounsaturated fatty acids
> 9.0 g polyunsaturated fatty acids[28]

Mustard powder (1 tsp.)
> 9 calories
> 0.6 g fat
> 0.5 g protein
> 0.3 g carbohydrate
> 3 I.U. vitamin A
> 11 mg potassium
> 5 mg calcium
> 12 mg phosphorus
> 0.12 mg iron

Mustard seed (yellow, 1 tsp.)
> 15 calories
> 1 g fat
> 0.8 g protein
> 0.2 g fiber
> 2 I.U. vitamin A
> 23 mg potassium
> 17 mg calcium
> 10 mg magnesium
> 0.19 mg zinc
> 28 mg phosphorus
> 0.33 mg iron

Mustard greens (1/2 cup cooked)
    23 calories
    0.4 g fat
    2.2 g protein
    4 g carbohydrate
    0.9 g fiber
    5800 I.U. vitamin A
    48 mg vitamin C
    0.08 mg B1
    0.14 mg B2
    0.06 mg B3
    18 mg sodium
    220 mg potassium
    138 mg calcium
    32 mg phosphorus
    1.80 mg iron
    3 1/3 oz contains 2.01 mg vitamin E
    2 mg choline
    2.5 mg myo-inositol[29]

HONEY

They are more precious than gold, than much pure gold; they are sweeter than honey, than honey from the comb. Psalms 19:10 (NIV)

Honey is used in the Bible to connote abundance and richness. It came from bees, dates, and figs. Honey was the main sweetening in most of the breads, cakes, pastries, custards, and desserts. It also was used to preserve fruits and fresh meats. Honey was used in wounds for healing.

Apicius has a recipe for a sweet dish that consisted of removing the crusts from bread, soaking the bread in milk and beaten eggs, frying it in hot oil, covering it with honey and serving it hot. Sounds just like what we call French toast doesn't it? Another sweet eaten by Romans was to make a stiff or hard porridge, spread it into a shallow pan and leave it to cool. Cut into small pieces like small cookies, fry them in oil and dip in warmed honey. Sounds just like what my mother did with leftover corn meal mush. Honey and spiced wine were often drunk together to eliminate the fatigue of travelers.

Many of the Middle Eastern sweets are made from ancient recipes that include honey as the sweetener. Generally they are made with nuts, pastry or custard, honey, and often rose water. You can be sure that these kinds of sweets were not eaten every day by the Israelites or the Romans. Just as we should not eat them every day.

HONEY IN BAKING

I generally use honey in most of my baking. I prefer it because it is a whole food. There are those who say that honey is changed into the same kind of "sugar" as white sugar is once the honey has been heated. This is still a controversy. White sugar has been refined in such a way that the B vitamins have been removed. Carbohydrates, especially sugars, need B vitamins for their digestion and assimilation. If they are removed from the food how will it be digested? Honey as a rule is still in its natural state. Just be sure when you purchase honey that it is pure honey and not honey-flavored syrup. There are some new kinds of sugars on the market now that are just dried or dehydrated sugar cane juice, in its entirety, these I find equally as acceptable as honey from bees, dates, or figs.

HONEY IN PLACE OF SUGAR

When substituting honey for sugar in a recipe you must reduce the amount of sweetener called for since honey is more concentrated and you must reduce the liquid in the recipe. If a recipe called for 1 cup white sugar you would use 2/3 to 3/4 cup honey or less and decrease the liquid by 1/4 cup. This is easy in cakes, pies, puddings, things where there is enough liquid to reduce. In cookies it is a little more difficult. You will also find that the baked goods made with honey tend to brown more so you must reduce the temperature a little, say 25°F. Most honey baked goods bake at 350° or 375°F. This is not the same with pies where the crust does not have honey.

If you are making cookies it is best to use creamed or solid honey, this will give a better texture. Creamed honey and butter "creamed" together will yield the same texture as butter and sugar "creamed" together.

Shortbread Cookies

1/2 cup (125 mL)	butter, unsalted at room temperature
1/2 cup (125 mL)	honey
1 1/4 cup (310 mL)	whole wheat pastry flour
1 tsp. (5 mL)	ground ginger
1/4 tsp. (1 mL)	salt

Cream butter. Add honey and cream until fluffy. Sift dry ingredients into creamed mixture and stir in with a wooden spoon. Form into ball and place on ungreased cookie sheet. Flatten ball and dust lightly with flour. Dip fingers into flour and press into a circle 7–8 inches (17–20 cm) in diameter. Flour hands and gently press around the edge to make a smooth-sided circle. Dip fork into flour and prick through cookie to make 16 wedges. (Cookie will break along these marks after baking.) Lightly prick remainder of cookie for design effect if desired. Bake at 300°F (150°C) for 35 to 40 minutes. Re-prick wedges as soon as it comes from the oven and cool completely before removing from the sheet and breaking wedges apart.

Food Processor: Cream butter with steel blade, add honey, when thoroughly creamed add sifted dry ingredients and process until a soft ball is formed.

To roll into cookies chill first and roll out on floured cloth, baking time will be reduced depending on thickness of cookie rolled.

Mia Bars
(filling)

1 oz. (200 g)	dried apricots
2 oz. (50 g)	blanched almonds
1/4 cup (50 mL)	liquid honey

Cover apricots with boiling water and leave for 30 minutes.

(short bread base)

6 1/2 oz (180 g)	butter, room temperature
1/4 + 1/8 C (75 mL)	creamed honey (or liquid)
8 1/2 oz. (240 g)	whole wheat pastry flour
1 tsp. (5 mL)	ground ginger
1	egg, separated

Cream butter with wooden spoon until light. Add honey in 3 additions and cream until fluffy. Sift dry ingredients into creamed mixture and stir in with wooden spoon. Divide dough into 3 equal portions. Press 2 into an ungreased 9 inch (25 cm) square pan and prick all over with a fork. Press the remaining 1/3 into a 9 inch rectangle on waxed paper, wrap, and chill. Chill base for 30 minutes in the freezer or 1 hour in the refrigerator.

Drain apricots. Using the fine blade of a grinder or the steel blade of a food processor, grind or finely chop 3/4 oz. (20 g) of the nuts and set aside. Then grind the remaining nuts and apricots together, blend in the honey.

Add 1 tsp. (5 mL) water to the egg white and blend. Add 1 tsp. (5 mL) cream or milk to the egg yolk and blend.

Brush base with enough egg white wash to cover it. Spoon filling on and spread around to get an even layer.

Roll out remaining dough on lightly floured surface into a thin rectangle. Cut into strips and arrange over filling. Brush entire surface with egg yolk wash and sprinkle with ground almonds.

Bake in 300°F (150°C) oven for 45 to 50 minutes or until golden. Remove from oven and cut into 36 or 42 bars and leave to cool on rack in the pan for 15 to 20 minutes. Remove from pan and cool on rack until set. The longer they cool, the crisper the crust will become.

Rolled Honey Shapes

1 cup (250 mL)	butter
1 cup (250 mL)	honey
2	large eggs
4 1/2 cup (1L)	whole wheat pastry flour
1 tsp. (5 mL) each:	baking powder, baking soda, salt
1/2 tsp. (2 mL)	nutmeg or mace
4 Tbsp. (60 mL)	soy flour (optional, use whole wheat)
3/4 cup (185 mL)	yogurt
1 1/2 tsp. (7 mL)	pure vanilla

Cream butter, add honey and cream until fluffy. Add an egg at a time beating until fluffy again. Sift dry ingredients and add alternating with liquids. Place on a large rectangle of waxed paper and press into a rectangle about 12 x 15 inches (30 x 38 cm) and chill until firm.

Roll on a floured board or cloth to 1/4 in. (1 cm) thick. Cut with floured cookie cutters and bake on ungreased cookie sheet at 350°F (180°C) for 12 to 15 minutes until lightly golden. Makes about 6 dozen.

NB: These are the same as "sugar" cookies and are great for Christmas cookies.

Basic Icing For Cookies & Cakes

2 Tbsp. (30 mL)	soft butter
1/4 cup (60 mL)	honey
4 Tbsp. (60 mL)	milk or light cream
1 tsp. (5 mL)	pure vanilla
2/3 cup (165 mL)	whole milk powder or more as needed

Put ingredients in blender in order listed except for milk powder. Blend until smooth. With blender running remove top and gradually add sifted milk powder until spreading consistency. Color or flavorings can be added. It should be slightly soft and very spreadable, almost runny, as it will firm up as it sits. Divide it in small bowls before adding coloring if using more than one color. This is great for frosting santas, trees, stars, gingerbread people, valentine hearts, and cakes as well as squares.

Chocolate Or Carob

Make icing as above and replace 1 tsp. to 3 Tbsp. (5 mL to 45 mL) of the milk powder in the beginning with the same amount of cocoa or carob powder to taste. Carob is sweeter than chocolate.

Special Decorations—This icing recipe can be used to pipe decorations on cookies or cakes. Due to the nature of natural foods, there are no exact quantities that can be given. As it sits it becomes stiffer. I have used it in icing bags for making roses, sweet peas, and forget-me-nots as well as various braids and trims, and in metal icing tubes with equal success. It is one of the few recipes that doesn't use icing sugar to form the base of the recipe, thereby reducing the amount of sweetening agents in the finished product.

Egg Paint Icing For Cookies

Mix egg yolk with food coloring and paint onto cookies before baking. Bake at recommended temperature. Remove from oven immediately to avoid over-cooking paint. This is great for drawing designs on cookies. It is also a no sugar way to decorate cookies. They will be very shiny and look like stained glass. Be careful to add just enough food colors as too much can make the finished cookie very dark and then green and blue will look almost the same. Often I write peoples' names on cookies with this paint. At Christmas I use this method of painting onto stars, bells, hearts, and circles words like "peace," "joy," "love" with various colors. Often I decorate my house with these kinds of cookies and offer them to guests. A gingerbread camel painted with swags and a saddle is very impressive when done this way. If one were very ambitious one could make stained glass windows from thinly **Rolled Honey Shapes** (p.249) recipe and paint them with this paint. This makes a great rainy day project for children that they can do and be creative, and still eat it later.

Ginger Bread Cookies

1/2 cup (125 mL)	each–molasses, honey, butter
2 2/3 cup (665 mL)	whole wheat pastry flour
2 tsp. (10 mL)	ground ginger
1/2 tsp. (2 mL)	salt
1 tsp. (5 mL)	baking soda
2 Tbsp. (30 mL)	yogurt
1/2 cup (125 mL)	milk less 2 Tbsp. (30 mL)

Cream first 3 ingredients until light and fluffy. Mix yogurt and milk together and remove another 2 Tbsp. (30 mL). Add remaining milk mixture to the creamed mixture alternating with the sifted dry ingredients.

Press into a rectangle on waxed paper, wrap and chill for several hours or overnight. Roll on floured cloth to 1/4 in (0.5 cm or 1/2 cm) thickness. Cut with floured cutters and bake on ungreased sheets at 350°F (180°C) for 12 to 15 minutes. Cool and decorate. Makes 5 to 6 dozen. Small pieces of currants can be used as eyes on people or animals. Add decorations using **Basic Icing Recipe** (p.249) and either frost or pipe them on or use the special **Egg Paint For Cookies** (p.250) recipe.

SPECIAL COOKIE NOTES

The **Rolled Honey Shapes** (p.249) and **Ginger Bread Cookies** (p.251) dough can be stored in the freezer and thawed as needed for almost instant cookies. This is almost a must in households where there are children, especially for a rainy day project or bake sale.

Pressed Cookies

1 cup (250 mL)	smooth peanut butter
1/2 cup (125 mL)	softened butter
3/4 cup (180 mL)	honey
1	egg
1 tsp. (5 mL)	pure vanilla
1 1/2 cup (375 mL)	whole wheat pastry flour
1/2 tsp. (2 mL)	salt
1/2 tsp. (2 mL)	baking soda
1/2 cup (125 mL)	soy flour, defatted

Cream first 3 ingredients until fluffy. Add egg and vanilla and beat well. Sift in dry ingredients and blend well. Press through cookie press onto ungreased baking sheet and bake at 350°F (180°C) for 8 to 10 minutes depending on size of cookie. Chilling is optional, it does make a nicer shaped cookie. Makes about 6 dozen small cookies.

All ingredients should be at room temperature for mixing. Creamed honey is best to use for these cookies. Tahini and almond extract can be used to replace the peanut butter and vanilla for a fancier cookie. Soy flour can be replaced by brown rice flour or sifted whole wheat flour.

Rolled Oat Cookies

3/4 cup (180 mL)	butter or oil*
2/3 cup (165 mL)	honey
2	eggs
2 tsp. (10 mL)	vanilla extract
1/2 tsp. (2 mL)	salt
1 cup (250 mL)	whole wheat pastry flour
2 tsp. (10 mL)	baking powder
3 cups (750 mL)	rolled oats
3/4 cup (180 mL)	sunflower or pumpkin seeds or chopped nuts

Cream butter and add honey and continue to cream. Add eggs and vanilla. Sift in salt, baking powder, and flour. Add oatmeal and mix well. Add nuts and mix again. Drop from rounded teaspoon onto greased cookie sheet. Bake at 325°F (170°C) for 10 to 15 minutes or until browned around the edges and golden on top. Remove immediately to wire rack to cool. The cookies will be soft until cooled so don't stack them while cooling or they will be bent. Makes 6 dozen.

*If using oil and creamed or solid honey you will get almost the same results as with butter and honey or sugar, the texture of the finished product will be similar.

Matrimonial Cookies Also Known As Date Squares
(filling)

1/2 lb. (225 g)	dates
1/4 cup (60 mL)	honey or fruit juice concentrate
1/2 cup (125 mL)	chopped nuts or seeds
1/2 cup (125 mL)	water

Mix all ingredients; bring just to a boil. Cool before spreading between layers.

(cookie layers)

1/2 cup (125 mL)	honey
1 1/4 cup (310 mL)	rolled oats
1 1/2 cup (375 mL)	whole wheat flour
1 tsp. (5 mL)	baking soda
1/4 tsp. (1 mL)	salt
3/4 cup (180 mL)	softened butter

Combine all ingredients; mix with fingers into fine crumbs. Put half the mixture in 9 in (23 cm) square pan and press down. Spread on cooled date mixture. Top with remaining crumb mixture, lightly pat down. Bake at 350°F (180°C) for 20 to 25 minutes. Cut into squares. Makes 12 squares.

NUTRITIONAL VALUES

Honey (1 Tbsp.)
> 61 calories
> 0 fat
> 0 cholesterol
> 0.1 g protein
> 16.5 g carbohydrate
> 0.01 mg B2
> 0.1 mg B3
> 1 mg sodium
> 10 mg potassium
> 1 mg calcium
> 1 mg magnesium
> 1 mg phosphorus
> 0.10 mg iron

Sugar, white granular (1 Tbsp.)
> 46 calories
> 0 fat
> 0 cholesterol
> 11.9 carbohydrate
> trace of calcium[30]

REFERENCES

1. *Apicius, Cookery and Dining in Imperial Rome,* edited and translated by Joseph Dommers Vehling, Dover Publications, New York 1977, p. 52.
2. Shewell-Cooper, W.E., *Plants, Flowers and Herbs of the Bible,* Keats Publishing, New Canaan, Connecticut, 1977, p. 54.
3. Pennington & Church, p. 227.
4. Rinzler, Carol Ann, *The Complete Book of Food,* World Almanac, New York, 1987, p 141.
5. Pennington & Church, pp. 223, 224.
6. Nutritive Value of American Foods, *US Department of Agriculture, Handbook No. 456,* p. 456.
7. Walker, Winifred, p. 92.
8. Tannahill, p. 65.
9. Pennington & Church, p.76.
10. Handbook No. 456, p. 76.
11. Pennington & Church, pp. 74–79.
12. Shewell-Cooper, p. 71.
13. Shewell-Cooper, p. 78.
14. Shewell-Cooper, p.59.
15. Grundy, Scott, et. al., "Basis For Dietary Treatment" Circulation, Vol. 80, No. 3, September 1989, p. 732.
16. Trevisan, M., V. Krosh, et. al., "Consumption of Olive Oil, Butter, and Vegetable Oils and Coronary Heart Disease Risk Factors," Journal of the American Medical Association, Feb. 2, 1990, Vol. 263, No. 5, pp. 688-691.
17. Circulation, p. 730.
18. Pennington & Church, pp. 162, 163.
19. U.S. Department of Agriculture Science & educational Administration, *Agriculture Handbook, No. 8-4,* Composition of Foods, Fats and Oils.
20. Ballentine, MD., Rudolph, *Transition to Vegetarianism,* The Himalayan International Institute, Honesdale, Pennsylvania, 1987.
21) Visser, p. 244.
22. Walker, p. 12.
23. *USDA Handbook No. 8-4,* p. 24
24. Sabate, Joan, M,D,, et al, "Effects of Walnuts on Serum Lipid Levels and Blood Pressure in Normal Men," The New England Journal of Medicine, Vol. 328, March 4, 1993, pp. 603–607.
25. Fraser, Gary E., M.D., Ch.B., Ph.D., FRACP, et al, Archives of Internal Medicine, Vol. 152, No. 7, July 1992, pp. 1416-1424.
26. Pennington & Church, p.119.

27. *USDA Handbook, No. 8-4,* p.60.
28. ibid, p. 34.
29. Pennington & Church.
30. Pennington & Church, pp. 143, 144.

And God blessed Noah and his sons and said to them . . . Every moving thing that lives shall be food for you; and as I gave you the green plants, I gave you everything. Only you shall not eat flesh with its life, that is, blood.
Genesis 9:1a, 3, 4 (RSV)

VI

Alternative Proteins
Meat, Fish, Fowl, & Eggs

A Change In Diet?

So Elisha left him and went back. He took his yolk of oxen and slaughtered them. He burned the plowing equipment to cook the meat and gave it to the people, and they ate . . . .1 Kings 19:21 (NIV)

The typical Hebrew was almost exclusively vegetarian. Meat was allowed to be eaten on special occasions such as a family festival, the visit of an honored guest, or a sacrificial meal at the local sanctuary. The very rich often ate more meat than the average people as a show of their wealth.[1] Noah was the first person who was allowed to eat meat as you can see in the quote from Genesis at the beginning of this chapter. This didn't mean that they ate meat every day, every week, or even every month.

The World's Oldest Health Plan is in agreement with this. The main proteins in our diet should come from vegetable sources. This is why this chapter on animal proteins is called—Alternative Proteins.

The very rich had ice houses and could keep all animal products cool. People in general, such as soldiers, farmers, shepherds, shopkeepers, merchants, etc., did not have this luxury. As we read in the preceding chapters, the average diet consisted of whole grains or whole grain bread; vegetables, some raw, some cooked; beans; cheese or yogurt; spices; fruit; and wine. Olive oil was the main fat eaten, supplemented with a small amount of butter depending on their location.

Goats, lambs, oxen, calves, fish, fowl, and eggs were available to be eaten almost as a condiment, or special feast food. Salted and dried, smoked, or pickled fish were probably the most frequently eaten animal protein, since they didn't require ice to keep them fresh. This is the kind of fish that was carried when people were traveling, and the fish probably used to multiply in the "loaves and fishes story." People would not have carried raw fish, let alone given it to someone else to eat after it had been carried for several hours or days.

The Romans ate much more meat than the Hebrews; but they still ate mostly vegetables, grains, fruits, cheese, and eggs. Romans were obsessed with feasting, shows of wealth, digestion, and purging. Many wealthy Romans had special feasts that continued for several days. Food was brought in to the reclining guests. After a certain number of courses, the vomit vessel was brought around so the diners could relieve themselves of the previous food to make room for more food. There were even rooms known as "vomitoriums" for that same purpose. I mentioned before that the early Romans must have been the first "bingers and purgers." This does not make it right to binge and purge. This is very dangerous for your body and mind, and may be part of the reason for the downfall of the Roman Empire.

RULES FOR EATING FAT AND BLOOD

The Lord said to Moses, "Say to the people of Israel, You shall eat no fat, of ox, or sheep, or goat . . . For every person who eats of the fat of an animal of which an offering by fire is made to the Lord shall be cut off from his people. Moreover you shall eat no blood whatever, whether of fowl or of animal, in any of your dwellings." Leviticus 7:22a,23,25,26 (RSV)

The rules for eating fat and blood were outlined in various chapters of the Old Testament, mostly Leviticus and Deuteronomy. Fat was not to be eaten, neither was meat with the blood still in it. This should still be true today, as we are seeing in the latest health and medical research. Dietary fat is now being considered the greatest health problem related to foods in North America.

The priest shall burn them on the altar as food, an offering made by fire, a pleasing aroma. All the fat is the Lord's. This is a lasting ordinance for generations to come, wherever you live; you must not eat any fat or any blood. Leviticus 3:16,17 (NIV)

This quote clearly states that fat and blood should not be eaten in the home "wherever you live," but can be eaten in religious places when properly sacrificed, and eaten within the allotted time. The New King James Version puts it this way in verse 17:

This shall be a perpetual statute throughout your generations in all your dwellings: you shall eat neither fat nor blood.

In the Mosaic Law "all the fat is the Lord's" referred to the animal fat that was sacrificed as part of an offering. This is the fat that is found around the kidneys and liver to act as a cushion for these delicate organs. (The very fat now used to make lard and/or beef suet or tallow.) The blood of a sacrificed animal was to be let out and then thrown at the altar.[2] It is from this information that we developed the method of killing animals and letting the blood before eating them. Generally, this is done with all animals and fowl, whether they are commercially or custom processed.

The fat, along with the liver, is the place where toxins are stored. For this reason, in our highly polluted environment it is advisable to eat animal foods with very little fat. Young animals like veal, lamb, and goat kids have less toxins stored in the fat and less fat since they are young and have not had time to store much body fat. The Old Testament rules against fat are now the same as the scientific information available on eating fats. Don't eat the heaviest, thickest, most condensed fats from animals or even vegetable fats that have been made into the same kind of fats. Once again, we can see that the Bible has the latest scientific information on health and nutrition. It has taken us several thousand years to prove it, but we now have proven it.

Today's trend is toward raising animals in such a way that there is less fat in the muscles and therefore less fat in the meat that we eat. This is good, since fat tends to go rancid very easily and rancid fat is very unhealthy to eat. It is the change of fat through oxidation, or rancidity, that produces the free radicals that are reputed to be causing health problems of all kinds, including cancer and aging. (See Chapter V—Special Treats under oil) In the 1990's all kinds of fats are being implicated as health risks, including polyunsaturated fats from vegetable sources and hydrogenated fats used to make margarine and cooking fats. Thus, it is important to pay attention to the amount, quality, and type of fats eaten.

CIVILIZED PEOPLE'S DIET

Until about 3,000 B.C. many people were nomadic and ate whatever they could hunt or gather. They ate meat when it was easy to kill, but not often or on a regular basis. Some anthropologists believe that through the use of the new tools now available to scientists, ancient man was more a gatherer than a hunter. This is the same kind of diet that Dr. T. Colin Campbell of Cornell University found in his research, and as a result of a nutrition survey he did in China.

Until modern times, most people ate large amounts of roots, barks, vegetables, cereals, and fruits. When they began living in settlements, villages, and even cities, they ate more cereals, vegetables, and fruits which were grown through agricultural means. They also added chicken, eggs and milk products in small quantities. This removed the problem of relying on whatever they could find for food and allowed people to spend more time in social and spiritual pursuits.[3] As people began to eat more animal products their rate of death from heart disease, diabetes, and cancer also went up. Exactly the findings of the Chinese research.

FAT IN THE DIET IN THE '90S

The American Heart Association and the Surgeon General's Report recommend that no more than 20 to 30% of the calories in the daily diet should come from fat. (Holistic health practitioners prefer 10 to 20%.)

To calculate the allowed grams of fat in your diet use this simple formula:

1. Determine the total calories per day by adding up the calories in what you expect to eat. This requires planning ahead what you are going to eat for the day or week.
2. Multiply the total calories times the desired percentage of fat in the diet. This should be from 10 to 20%. This gives the total fat calories.
3. Divide the total fat calories by 9 (There are 9 calories in 1 gram of fat.) to see how many grams of fat you should be eating a day to comply with the recommended percentage.
4. Look up the grams of fat and total them. Does this match the total grams of fat you should be eating as determined in #3?
5. If you are eating more grams of fat than recommended, you will have to begin cutting back by choosing more calories from nonfat sources such as grains, legumes, and vegetables and less calories from animal and dairy products.

For Example—If you determined that you were going to eat 1400 total calories, you would multiply it by 0.20 (20%) which would give you 280 total fat calories. Then divide this by 9 to get 31.1 total fat grams a day. Next add up the grams of fat in the foods and see if this matches. If the grams are too high you will have to reduce the fat intake, but not the calories from other sources. You may need to add more carbohydrates from non-fat sources. Or eat the same food in a "no-fat" food. This would mean substituting no-fat sour cream for regular, or low-fat cheese for regular, and so on.

THE LATEST FAT FINDINGS

During the first half of 1990 two studies were released that showed that a diet that had 10% of the calories as fat was healthful and helped to prevent or reverse many diseases. One was done in the United States by Dr. Dean Ornish. The other, mentioned briefly above, was done in China by Cornell University researcher Dr. T. Colin Campbell.

Dr. Ornish's plan can be found in his book on the program: *Dr. Ornish's Program For Reversing Heart Disease*, Random House. Of the 22 people in the treatment group, 82% had some reversal of coronary blockages. His diet is a vegetarian one that includes grains and grain products, fresh or dried fruits, vegetables and greens, beans, sprouts, egg whites, tofu, tempeh, and one cup of skim milk or nonfat yogurt a day. It did not include oils, fats, nuts, seeds, or other high fat vegetable foods, caffeine, or nicotine.[4]

Dr. Campbell's research surveyed 6,500 Chinese people in every province. The healthiest subjects ate less than 20% of their calories from fat sources, generally from 10 to 15%. They also had fiber intakes of from 33 grams to 77 grams a day and exhibited no signs of anemia or mineral loss. Their average cholesterol levels were 88 to 165 milligrams per 100 milliliters of blood plasma. (The average American levels range from 155 to 274 milligrams of cholesterol per 100 milliliters of blood plasma.) The Chinese people with the low cholesterol levels had no cancer, diabetes, or heart disease. Those from the more affluent areas where more meat and refined and fatty foods were eaten had high incidences of cancer, diabetes, and heart disease, although not as high as in the United States, due to the high amounts of plant fibers and grains.[5]

When I spoke with Dr. Campbell he explained that the intent of the original research was to explore dietary causes of cancer. Once the study was underway it was evident that it was necessary to expand the findings to include heart, metabolic, and infectious diseases.

The average Chinese diet in the provinces surveyed included small amounts of animal protein in the form of fish, eggs, and animal meats. The highest protein came from vegetable sources such as soy products like soy milk, tofu, soy sauce, and other fermented bean products. The large amounts of fiber (by United States standards) actually prevented iron-deficiency anemia and calcium-loss diseases such as osteoporosis because it included large amounts of dark green leafy vegetables. As we read in Chapter III—Our Daily Proteins–Legumes and Vegetables, these are excellent sources of B vitamins, Beta carotene, calcium, iron, folic acid, and other minerals.

ECOLOGY

Because the area of the Middle East was often rocky and somewhat barren, or partially desert in the outlying areas, only those animals were raised that could be sustained on the available grasses and fodder. These were mostly sheep, goats, chickens and other fowl, along with horses, camels, or oxen for use as beasts of burden.

Today, there are groups of ecologists who point out that it takes about 4,200 gallons of water to feed a meat-eater, but only 300 gallons to feed a vegetarian person. With water in short supply in many parts of the United States, it is no wonder that people are encouraging the return to vegetarianism. Francis Moore Lappé (*Diet For A Small Planet*) often points out that there is no shortage of protein foods to feed the world. The problem is that the grains and legumes are being fed to animals to convert into inefficient muscle protein. If the same amounts of grains and legumes were grown and fed to the peoples of the world instead of to animals there would be no starvation problems. Now it is rumored that the rain forests in Brazil are being cut down to raise cattle to send to the United States to make fast foods. The rain forests provide the oxygen we breathe. A pound of hamburger represents 55 square feet of rain forest burned off.[6] I would rather breathe and be a vegetarian than eat meat and run out of oxygen. It is just a matter of time and priorities. Perhaps this high meat consumption in the last 50 or 60 years will not deplete our oxygen, but what about our children and grandchildren? Perhaps we should consider going back to the Old and New Testament lifestyle of eating meat only for special occasions.

This would help each person become healthier and also help the economy of world food become more efficient. There would even be more jobs created by a society that grew grains and legumes for human use.

METHANE DANGER

The average cud-chewing animal emits about 400 liters of methane gas a day. This makes cattle responsible for about 12 to 15 percent of all methane emissions, according to the Environmental Protection Agency report, co-authored by Michael Gibbs, and published in early 1990. Methane is the second most important gas in causing the greenhouse effect of the destruction of the ozone layer. Reducing the use of all products from ruminant animals would help to prevent further destruction of the ozone layer, along with the reduction of other known sources of destruction, aerosol sprays and the refrigerant in air conditioners, especially automobile types. Please don't misunderstand me, I am not against meat eating as such. I am just opposed to people using so many animal products that they harm themselves, each other, and the environment.

I have done nutrition education programs with hundreds of people who have health problems directly related to over consumption of animal protein and fat, and over consumption of fast foods containing high fats. It breaks my heart to see children from wealthy homes so fatigued that they can't live a normal life. And yet they live on nutritionless food. It is not just the third world that is suffering from health problems due to malnutrition. It is one of the biggest epidemics in North America.

BALANCED DIET

A balanced diet utilizes a variety of foods. These include grains, vegetables, legumes, and fruits. A balanced diet might also contain milk, yogurt, cheese, and other dairy products, as well as animal flesh. But they are not really necessary to sustain life. The World's Oldest Health Plan is a balanced diet that includes small amounts of animal proteins, small amounts of fat, and high amounts of grains, vegetables, legumes, and fruits. This is the diet that was followed by the Israelites when they were following the life that was the healthiest and the most spiritual. It shows me that "a healthy body helps to contribute to a healthy mind," if I may quote that old phrase we heard in the '40s, '50s, and '60s.

PROTEIN RECOMMENDATIONS

The Food Guide Pyramid, A Guide to Daily Food Choices issued in 1992 recommends 2–3 servings per day of protein foods. This means two servings of 2–3 ounces of lean cooked beef, pork, lamb, veal, fish, poultry, or egg and one serving of 1/2 half cup cooked legumes, dry peas, or beans, is a daily portion. More than this is considered too much. The Food Guide Pyramid also recommends 2–3 servings of low-fat dairy foods daily. This is four or five servings of protein foods. This is a sensible amount of protein for most people to work down to. A serving of 2–3 ounces of meat is much less than most people now eat, so this is a great improvement Adding the grains and vegetables required is also a great improvement for most people and can help give a diet with less fat, more nutrients, and more bulk.

The newest research shows that the high consumption of protein from animal sources, including the fat occurring in the meat, helps to promote the diseases of civilized peoples: cancer, diabetes, and heart disease. The Bible seems to promote eating less meat and fat than we are currently eating. This is the same amount found to be health-giving by those people in areas of the world where the agriculture is not animal based, but is grain or vegetable based.

PROTEIN AND FAT COMPARISON CHART

Amount	Food	Protein	Fat	Unsaturated fat
1 cup	cooked lima beans	12.9 g	0.9 g	
1 cup	cooked kidney beans	14.4 g	0.9 g	
100 g	chick peas	10.2 g	2.4 g	2 g
250 g	butter beans	12.0 g		
100 g	ground chuck	26.0 g	23.9 g	
100 g	porterhouse steak	25.4 g	14.7 g	0.7 g
46 g	lamb loin chop	12.5 g	5.5 g	0.2 g
53 g	ham	19.6 g	4.7 g	0.8 g
100 g	veal loin chop	22.7 g	35.9 g	1.1 g
100 g	baked rabbit	30.9 g	5.0 g	
100 g	roast venison	29.5 g	2.2 g	0.2 g
1 cup	skim milk	8.4 g	0.4 g	0.3 g
100 g	chicken w/o skin	28.9 g	7.4 g	1.7 g
100 g	light turkey	29.9 g	3.2 g	0.9 g
100 g	dark turkey	28.6 g	7.2 g	2.2 g
95 g	broiled cod	26.1 g	5.0 g	
125 g	broiled halibut	31.5 g	8.8 g	
1 large	boiled egg	6.1 g	5.6 g	0.7 g

A blank space means that figures are not available. This does not mean that there is no content.

This table was compiled from the sources listed in the references Pennington & Church and Dept. of Agriculture Handbooks.

EATING MEAT FOR THE EGO

In the '40s and '50s it was thought that eating meat was a sign of a good provider, since in the '30s people were not able to have meat. After the war many Americans equated having money to buy meat with the end of hard times. The ideal was to own your own home, have two cars, and eat meat at every meal. Such a shallow way to determine your worth, through material things! It was even suggested that "real men eat meat," and "sissies eat vegetables." The opposite is just the case as we are finding out now. Many people the world over are very healthy, very active, and physically strong without eating large quantities of meat.

In my family this was carried to an extreme. My parents were both youngsters during the depression and often told us stories of the lack of food, and hard times that many people experienced. A common scenario when I was a teenager would go like this: "Dad, may I have a monogrammed cashmere sweater?" "No." "But, Dad, Barbara and Sharon have them." "They may have fancy sweaters, but we eat meat at every meal," was the reply. No more could be said about the subject. I would rather have had the sweater. I could never figure out why it was so important to people who had lived through the '30s to eat meat at every meal. Or why men felt that their masculinity or ability as a provider was threatened if they didn't provide and eat meat. By the way this did not end with the 50's and '60s, people still believe that eating meat means something. It seems very strange to me that people were talked into believing that meat was for "real" men to eat, and yet we are finding that high meat consumption is directly responsible for many of the diseases that take away a man's ability to perform his daily work, such as cancer, hardening of the arteries, high blood pressure, heart disease, and diabetes.

MEAT THE FORBIDDEN FOOD

Throughout the ages, meat was often considered the forbidden or the desired food. Just like beans came to be known as "poor people's food," meat was known as "rich people's food," or at least, the food of a person with money to buy it.

Now the Spirit expressly says that in later times some will depart from the faith by giving heed to deceitful spirits and doctrines of demons, through the pretensions of liars whose consciences are seared, who forbid marriage and enjoin abstinence from foods which God created to be received with thanksgiving by those who believe and know the truth. For everything created by God is good, and nothing is to be rejected if it is received with thanksgiving; for then it is consecrated by the word of God and prayer.
1 Timothy 4:1-5 (RSV)

It is obvious by the above quote from the New Testament that it was expected that it would be just a matter of time before new Christians would be tempted to follow some of the popular Middle Eastern and Eastern ideas that eating certain foods interferes with a spiritual life. Some of these foods are stimulating herbs like black pepper, ginger, and black tea, and animal products where the animal has to be killed in order to provide the food. Some groups even say that milk and honey should not be eaten because they are animal products. So it goes, from the mild to the severe, in suggestions of abstinence to these foods. During New Testament times there were people who were sure that Christ would return so soon that they were telling their followers to avoid marriage and eat special foods so that they would be purified for the return of Christ. It is this situation which the above verses speak to, an actual situation that was occurring at the time. Always be suspicious of anyone who tells you that you will be "less spiritual" or "less holy" if you eat meat or other animal products. This is directly against the teachings of the Bible. If you find that eating meat gives you high cholesterol and then a heart condition because of it, then you will be wise to reduce your meat intake and increase your vegetables and grains intake. This is a health matter for your particular body, not a spiritual matter.

MEAT ALLERGY?

There are reasons why a person might not want to eat certain foods. The food might be difficult to digest, it might cause a reaction such as a rash, hives, depression, elation, eczema, headaches, backache, swelling, etc. It would be foolish to continue to eat such foods if this were the case. Many non-foods often cause these kinds of reactions. These include food colorings, preservatives, thickening agents, MSG, and various sugar and salt derivatives. In *Not All In The Mind, How Unsuspected Food Allergy Can Affect Your Body And Your Mind,* Dr. Richard Mackarness talks about three patients who tested allergic to broccoli. One was allergic to the spray used in the growing of the broccoli, one was allergic to frozen broccoli only, and the third was truly allergic to broccoli itself. This is what makes it so hard to tell whether it is the food itself causing a reaction.

A friend of mine told me a story of when he was working in a factory in California in the early '60s. He developed a strange rash and they sent him to the company medical clinic to check it out. The doctor looked at it and said: "Did you eat lunch at so and so's place down the street and have a hamburger?" "Yes," was the reply. "Oh, that's easy," said the examining doctor, "This is a penicillin reaction, I see lots of them from that place. They get meat that still has some residue of penicillin in it." The laws and restrictions have changed and this is not supposed to happen now, but you can see what I mean about exploring all the possibilities of where the food came from and what might be actually causing the problem.

MEAT IN NEW TESTAMENT TIMES

But the father said to his servants. "Bring quickly the best robe, and put it on him; and put a ring on his hand, and shoes on his feet; and bring the fatted calf and kill it, and let us eat and make merry; for my son was dead, and he is alive again; he was lost, and is found." And they began to make merry. Luke 15:22, 23, 24

Even in New Testament times meat from animals was not eaten regularly. It was eaten on special occasions, as in this story of the Prodigal Son. This was a special ritual, not an everyday occurrence. How did this get translated into eating meat daily?

MEAT OR FOOD?

There are five different words translated in the New Testament as "meat" in the King James Bible.[7] None of them means meat in the sense that we do now. In Mark 7:19 for instance the King James Version of 1611 says: *. . . Because it entereth not into his heart, but into the belly, and goeth out into the draught, purging all meats?* In the New King James Version of 1982 we read: *. . . because it does not enter his heart but his stomach, and is eliminated, thus purifying all foods?* This same text is translated in the Revised Standard Version as: *since it enters, not his heart but his stomach, and so passes on? (Thus he declared all foods clean.)* It is easy to see how some people misunderstood the language of the earlier translation as meaning meat or animal flesh, as we mean it now.

In John 4:32, 34 in the KJV we read: *But he said unto them, I have meat to eat that ye know not of . . . Jesus saith unto them, My meat is to do the will of him that sent me, and to finish his work.* In the RSV these same two verses are translated as: *But he said to them, "I have food to eat of which you do not know" . . . Jesus said to them, "My food is to do the will of him who sent me, and to accomplish his work."* The NKJ reads: *But he said to them, "I have food to eat of which you do not know" . . . Jesus said to them "My food is to do the will of Him who sent me, and to finish His work."*

It is easy to see that neither "meat" nor "food" in the physical sense of these words is meant. This expression might be similar to our expression "he has too much on his plate" meaning he has taken on more work or responsibility than he can do, not that he filled his plate too full at the buffet, which might be a more literal interpretation.

Meat in the KJV was used to denote food, the act of eating, eatable, nourishment, to eat, and at table or in the process of eating.[8]

BEEF, FATTED CALF, VEAL

Beef is the most commonly eaten red meat in North America. It has to be raised in a large area such as a farm because the animals are so large. Buffalo and beefalo also need this same amount of room for feeding. Smaller animals such as chickens and goats can be raised in smaller areas. Most of the cattle known in Bible times were used as beasts of burden. This is why the prodigal son's father asked for a calf, a young offspring of a work animal.

Beef is now being bred that is lower in fat than it was a few years ago. It was popular to have highly marbled fat in meat to have top quality meat. Now due to consumer pressure meat is being raised that is tender and contains less fat and no visible marbling of fat throughout the muscle. Tastes change, so do ideas of what is first quality. Farmers are generally willing to produce the kinds of foods that people will buy. Consumer demand can rule the marketplace.

I eat beef about four times a year. It is almost always the kind that I prefer to eat or I don't eat it. This is known as chemical free, organically grown, free range beef. I generally don't eat beef if I eat out because I like it cooked very rare and it is very difficult to have it cooked that way. It is also not a good idea to eat beef very rare if you are not in control of the storage and cooking. There is a growing concern about salmonella in meat and cooking is the only way that one can be sure that there is no contamination from it. The unfortunate part is that the less meat is cooked the better it is for you from a nutritional standpoint. And the more it is cooked the better it is for you from a bacterial standpoint. This makes it very hard to decide how to cook your meat. The one thing that is obvious is that cooking it on very high heat can cause cancerous mutations so this is not recommended. (See: Meat and Cancer (p.273)

IS MEAT SAFE?

All meats sold in the United States and Canada are supposed to be Government inspected. Either the meat itself or the packing plant. This is our assurance that meats of all kinds are safe. All meats must be kept cool or cold. If this is not done, it could harbor many different kinds of bacteria or fungus. So it is important for us to look at the places where we purchase our protein foods from. Is it clean? Is it refrigerated? Are the knives sharp? Does the meat cutter wash his or her hands? Do they clean up with soapy water between types of meats when cutting them? Do they pull everything apart and disinfect it daily? Is the meat a uniform color? If there are dark, hard looking spots on the meat it may have been exposed to the air too long, or be old. Does the meat or fat have a perfumy smell? This often happens from freezer burn. Has the meat been previously frozen? This is no problem unless you are buying meat to store in the freezer. In short, you are responsible for what you put in your body. You are responsible for making sure that you know how to handle, store, cook, and serve all foods that you eat or give to your family. So it is essential that you read about it. Call your local extension office, or agricultural commission for the foods in question. In the last few years things have changed a lot in food storage and preparation. Get the latest information.

A WORD ABOUT PORK

In Old Testament times people were told not to eat pork. Pork has changed! It is generally raised in such a way that it is lower in fat than ever before. The farms are almost meticulous in the way the animals are kept clean and healthy. Pork is no longer the unsafe, fatty meat it once was. The pork producers have listened to consumers and responded. The New Testament says that all foods are good if eaten with thanksgiving, this includes pork. However, I still wouldn't eat lard. The fat is not the kind I want to eat. If I came to your house and you served me a pie with a crust made of lard I would give thanks for it, eat it, enjoy it, and be glad for food and companionship with you. I am obligated not to hurt your feelings if you eat something I do not. I am also obligated to not make a show of being so holy as to point out to you how I don't do this. This is very hard, but I still do it. Food is not supposed to be bad or something we argue over.

NATURALLY GROWN?

For many years I have researched "natural" methods of growing plants and animals. The theory is that if the plant or animal is truly balanced and healthy it will not have diseases for which antibiotics and other drugs need to be given. This allows healthy animals and plants to be eaten which are not treated with growth stimulants to make them grow faster or fatter, have unbalanced fertilizers used that rape the soil and eventually ruin it, or that rob the soil of roughage or humus and never replace it. So many farmers today are realizing that soil is a precious commodity that should be treated with the best of care to get the maximum use from it. If the soil on which a plant is grown is only fed the exact nutrients that make the plant grow big and tall, but have no taste or disease resistance, it will not be giving the plant all the needed nutrients that we expect to be eating when we eat it. The nutrient levels of the foods we eat are quickly going down and down. The foods we buy in the store today do not have the same nutritional values that they had in the 1920's. This is mainly due to using fertilizer that does not contain all the necessary nutrients, as well as the minor nutrients whose roles we don't yet know in plant growth. Just like our bodies, plants and animals will be healthy and not require medicine if they are properly cared for and fed a well-balanced diet.

BIBLE BEEF

For the most part, using chemicals, artificial fertilizers, antibiotics, and other drugs is a new phase in farming and animal husbandry. This has only recently been practiced just like giving medications to humans is a part of modern medicine. Herbs, tinctures, salves, teas, poultices, and various health giving foods like garlic, wine, and olive oil were used in Bible times as medications. The herds of oxen were small and a herdsman stayed with them at all times, therefore, each animal could be personally attended to without having to give all the animals the treatment. The cow was being domesticated around 6100 to 5800 B.C. in Turkey and Macedonia. Dairy cows were kept around 3,000 B.C. Sheep and goats were domesticated as early as 8920 B.C. in Iraq and Rumania.[9] These animals were not raised on antibiotics, drugs, growth hormones, or fractionated foods. They were raised on real food, water, grains, fodder made from various grasses and greenery from plants that they foraged themselves.

SERVING SIZE

A serving size of beef or other animal protein is considered to be 3 or 4 ounces, not the 16 ounces of the nutritional breakdown below. This would give a 4 ounce serving 400 calories and 37 grams of fat.

NUTRITIONAL VALUES

Beef carcass, choice grade, trimmed to retail level (100 grams)
   25.1 g total fat
   12 g unsaturated fatty acids
   13.1 g saturated fats

Beef, porterhouse steak, choice grade (1 pound)
 1,603 calories
 60.8 g protein,
 148.8 g fat
 0 carbohydrate
 33 mg calcium
 559 mg phosphorus
 9.0 mg iron
 213 mg sodium
 973 mg potassium
 300 I.U. vitamin A
 0.26 B1
 0.55 mg B2
 14.6 mg B3[10]

Veal, loin cuts, raw, with bone (1 pound)
 681 calories
 72.3 g protein
 41 g fat
 0 carbohydrate
 41 mg calcium
 734 mg phosphorus
 10.9 mg iron
 253 mg sodium
 1,157 mg potassium
 0 I.U. vitamin A
 0.53 mg B1
 0.96 mg B2
 24.2 mg B3[11]

Veal, loin chop, lean, cooked (3 1/2 ounces)
 421 calories
 35.9 g fat
 1.1 g polyunsaturated fatty acids
 90 mg cholesterol
 22.7 g protein
 0.14 mg B1
 0.21 mg B2
 4.7 mg B3
 44 mg sodium
 314 mg potassium
 6 mg calcium
 16 mg magnesium
 187 mg phosphorus
 2.90 mg iron[12]

COOKING RULES

All protein foods should be cooked on medium or medium/high heat. Meat should be broiled 6 inches from the broiler unit whether it is gas or electric. This will take a longer time to cook, but the nutritional values will be preserved and the meat will not be tough and stringy. High heat tends to make the meat sinews contract and tighten up. They become hard to eat and the nutrients run out onto the pan leaving just the tough parts to be eaten.

If you have any questions about how long to cook protein foods there is a simple answer. Use a meat thermometer. This can be used with any animal protein foods, even fish. When properly used a thermometer takes the guess work out of cooking times.

Generally, meat should be baked or roasted at 325°F. It should never be precooked in some way such as browning or searing. This tends to toughen the muscles and cause the juices to run out leaving the meat dry and, possibly, stringy. Generally, I allow 20–30 minutes per pound for medium beef, pork, lamb, and veal and fully cooked fowl. I usually time for 20 minutes per pound and using a meat thermometer remove the meat at the appropriate time. It is suggested that roasts be allowed to "rest" for 10-15 minutes after being removed from the oven to finish cooking and facilitate cutting. For more details on cooking meats see *The World's Oldest Health Plan Recipe Companion.*

MEAT AND CANCER

Studies done at the Lawrence Livermore National Laboratory found that well-cooked hamburgers could contain as many as 6 chemicals that cause mutations, chromosome damage, and possible cancer. Arthur Miller, head scientist at the U.S. Department of Agriculture research laboratory in Philadelphia, in 1986 said that many studies have shown traces of unidentified mutagens in other well-done muscle meats including beef cuts other than hamburger, pork, chicken, and fish with spines, but not in shellfish or organ meats. It is best to eat meat not well-done. It is healthier and it tastes better. Meat should always be at least pink when eaten. If the beef was grown under healthy balanced conditions and stored at the proper temperature there should be no problem with salmonella or bacteria of any kind. James Felton, a biomedical scientist, presented a paper to the American Association for Cancer Research in May of 1986 that pointed out that the high rates of colon cancer in the

United States might be directly linked to the high consumption of meats, especially improperly cooked meats. In Bible times meat was boiled or broiled. But it might have only been eaten 5 or 6 times a year, not 5 or 6 times a week.

COOKING PROTEINS

Salt should never be added to meats that are baked, broiled, or roasted. Adding salt can draw moisture out of the meat, making it stringy and less tender. Salt can be added, if desired, to soups or stews while cooking so that the flavor of the meat will be absorbed by the broth. This will give more flavor to the finished product. Adding lemon or tomato to soups or stews helps to break down the sinewy parts of the meat making them more tender. Adding acid or foods containing vitamin C can also help with the absorption of the iron in the meat. Adding lemon, lime, vinegar, or tomatoes to a broth of bones and water being made into a stock can help to break down the bones in such a way that the calcium in the bones will be more bioavailable in the stock. (I feel, however, that it is best to get calcium from plant sources.)

HEALTH SOUP

A soup made from raw or roasted bones, garlic, lemon or tomato, roasted barley, small amounts of fresh chemical free meat, and carrots simmered for several hours will be very healthful, even if only the broth is taken. This will contain iron, calcium, pro vitamin A or Beta carotene, B vitamins, carbohydrates, protein, amino acids, and the mysterious health-giving properties of garlic. Other vegetables could be added after the stock is made and simmered lightly, adding more nutrients. I like to add an onion stuck with whole cloves and a leaf or two of bay laurel. Chopped fresh parsley makes an excellent garnish sprinkled over each serving. This is an excellent food to give someone who is ill to help regain his or her strength without overtaxing the body.

Stuffed Peppers

6 medium or 4 large	sweet bell peppers, red, green, or yellow
1 Tbsp.	virgin olive oil
2–3 cloves	fresh garlic
1 lb.	ground beef, veal, or lamb or a mixture
	grinding black pepper

3 large	eggs
2 cups	already cooked brown rice
2 Tbsp.	corn starch
2 tsp.	ground cumin
1 Tbsp.	soy sauce, tamari, or shoyu
1 Tbsp.	ground basil
1 tsp.	ground oregano
28 oz. can	tomatoes in their own juice
1/4 –1 tsp.	cayenne pepper or other type chile pepper

Slice tops off peppers, remove seeds and veins and discard. Trim bottom a little to allow them to sit flat if needed. Heat olive oil in skillet or large frying pan over medium heat. Chop onion and garlic coarsely and sauté in oil. Add meat when onions turn transparent, stir and cook until no longer red. Cool and mix with black pepper, eggs and rice. Blend remaining ingredients in blender. Fill peppers with the rice mixture to level with the top or a little less to allow for expansion. Set them in a glass, pyroceram, or other casserole dish* with a lid if possible. Pour about 2 tablespoons of the sauce over each pepper, pour the remaining sauce into the dish at the base of each pepper. Cover and bake in a 375°F oven for one hour or more or until peppers are soft and sauce thickened.

Serve the peppers with some of the thickened sauce over them with a dark green salad and yellow vegetable. These peppers are especially wonderful if each person is served two peppers, one red and one green. Very small stuffed peppers can also serve as an appetizer or party fare on a buffet.

*Do not use a metal pan unless it is stainless steel. Use aluminum foil to cover a glass dish as long as the foil doesn't touch the food.

The best part of this recipe is that regular meat and potato eaters love this recipe since it is so traditional. It is an excellent way to eat more grains and vegetables and still have meat.

This same recipe can be adapted to stuffed cabbage leaves, grape leaves, or squash. It works very well with a large zucchini. Remove the center of a zucchini, leaving about a 1/2 inch wall. Chop the pulp up and mix it with the filling. Pile it high in the hollow zucchini, cover with sauce and bake in a casserole as above.

Meat Loaf

2 Tbsp.	butter or virgin olive oil
1 large	cooking onion
2 large cloves	garlic
4–5 medium	mushrooms, wiped clean
2 stalks	green celery*
1/2 tsp.	dry mustard powder
3–4 sprigs	fresh parsley, finely chopped
3 pieces	dry whole grain bread, rolled into crumbs
1 lb.	low fat ground round
1 lb.	tofu, drained
2 tsp.	soy sauce, tamari, or shoyu
3 tsp.	dried basil
2 tsp.	dried oregano
1 tsp.	Worcestershire sauce, optional
1/4 tsp.	cayenne pepper sauce
6 oz.	tomato paste (remove 1 Tbsp. for sauce)
2 Tbsp.	corn or arrowroot starch
1 tsp.	soy sauce, tamari, or shoyu

Heat butter or olive oil over medium/high heat and sauté chopped onion, garlic, and mushrooms until they begin to change color. Add finely chopped celery and continue to cook until onions are transparent. In a large bowl mash with potato masher or your hands mustard powder, parsley, bread crumbs, tofu, meat, soy sauce, oregano, basil, Worcestershire sauce and pepper sauce, add onion mixture. Lightly oil or butter loaf pan. Spoon in meat mixture and smooth top with back of spoon. Bake in 350°F oven for 1 1/2 hours. Serve with sauce, dark green salad with grated carrots, and baked potato, whole grain noodles, or brown rice.

Sauce

1 Tbsp.	tomato paste
2 Tbsp.	corn or arrowroot starch
1 tsp.	soy sauce, tamari, or shoyu
1 1/2 cups	water or tomato juice

Mix together in sauce pan and heat over medium/high heat, stirring constantly, until thickened. Three to four thinly sliced or chopped mushrooms can also be added while cooking, if desired.

Slice meat loaf into 4 or 6 servings. Place each slice on a plate and spoon over a few tablespoons of sauce. Add a baked potato, with tofu sour cream instead of dairy sour cream or butter if you want to keep this lower in fat and cholesterol, and salad or serve the salad in a separate bowl or plate. Steamed broccoli and carrots or zucchini and carrots or yellow squash also go well with this.

*Celery is a green vegetable. Always try to get the greenest ones you can. Celery used to be "bleached" by piling soil around the developing stalks to prevent the sun from getting to it. The same kinds of things were done to Belgian endive and asparagus to make them whiter. This defeats the purpose of eating a green vegetable. The green is where the nutrients are in green vegetables.

Beef And Tempeh Pie
(filling)

2 Tbsp.	butter
3 Tbsp.	virgin olive oil
1/2 lb.	beef stew meat or round steak, diced fine
1/2 lb.	tempeh, any variety*
1 small	cooking onion
2 cloves	garlic
5–6	mushrooms
4 Tbsp.	whole wheat bread flour
2 small	potatoes OR
2 medium	carrots
2 stalks	green celery
2 tsp.	ground cumin
2 cups	water
2 Tbsp.	dry red wine, optional
1/2 cup	frozen or fresh peas
1/2 cup	frozen or fresh corn OR
1 cup	frozen chopped mixed vegetables
3 tsp.	dried marjoram or savory
4–5 sprigs	fresh parsley, chopped
1/2 tsp.	sea salt, optional
several grindings	dried black pepper

This can be made in a deep dish casserole. If you have one that goes on the stove top and in the oven use it for the cooking and baking. If your casserole only goes in the oven use a deep skillet to cook the filling then put it in a casserole and cover with the pastry.

Heat the oil and butter over medium heat until it is melted, foams up and subsides. Cut the tempeh in small cubes about 3/4 inch square and begin to brown, stir often. Add the meat cut in the same size pieces after the tempeh begins to brown a little. Coarsely chop the onions and add them, stir. Slice the mushrooms and add them, stir. Finely chop or press the garlic and add it, stir. Add the flour, stir. Cut the potatoes in cubes about 1/2 inch add and stir. Continue to stir to keep the flour evenly distributed. When flour is toasted, about 5 minutes, add the water. Stir until mixture begins to thicken. Add cumin, celery, wine, and cook until thickened. Remove from heat and stir in remaining vegetables and herbs. Stir and set aside. Or put into casserole dish. Preheat oven to 425°F. Make crust and place on the top. Bake for 12 minutes then reduce the temperature to 375°F and continue to bake for 45–50 minutes or until crust is lightly browned.

(crust)

1 cup	whole wheat pastry flour
1/3 cup	butter
1/4 tsp.	sea salt
3 Tbsp.	milk

Sift flour and salt together. Cut in butter. When mixture is like coarse meal add the milk and mix in with a fork. Gather dough into a ball and roll out to the size of your casserole dish, allowing a little extra room to make a nice edge. For more instructions on making pie dough see Chapter V— Special Treats.

Serve with green salad. Serves 4–6. Or more depending on how big you make it. This is very flexible. You can add more vegetables to serve more people. Select from: sweet potatoes, squash, lima beans, zucchini, yellow summer squash, broccoli, cauliflower (I would steam it a little first), green or yellow beans (add last), turnip, parsnip, leek, or cooked beans such as pinto, garbanzo, romano, navy, or black eyed-peas. Any combination of veggies can be used, other kinds of meats can be used such as lamb, veal, chicken, or turkey.

*Tempeh is a soy bean product sold frozen or fresh at Oriental stores or natural food stores. It often comes in original soy bean and many new varieties such as with peanuts, other grains, or sea vegetables. See Chapter III—Our Daily Proteins under Soy Beans for more information. This is a version of a dish my grandmother used to make called steak and kidney pie. She even had a pie bird. A pie bird is something you put in the pie to hold the crust up off the filling more information. This is a version of a dish my grandmother used to make called steak and kidney pie. She even had a pie bird. A pie bird is something you put in the pie to hold the crust up off the filling so it doesn't get soggy during baking. Real pie birds have an open bottom and mouth so that steam escapes from the pie filling. Real ceramic pie birds can be purchased at most gourmet cookware shops. My grandmother used a heavy ceramic egg cup that she used only for this kind of pie. She would invert it in the filling before adding the crust. (An egg cup is used when eating a soft-boiled egg and is a small footed dish just large enough to hold one boiled egg on its end. The shell is then taken off the top, the top cut open and the egg eaten, either with a spoon or toast fingers that are dipped into the yolk.) Be sure that it is ceramic and not plastic or you will have a big mess.

Beef And Tofu Pie

Make **Beef And Tempeh Pie** recipe and substitute cubes of very well drained tofu for the tempeh. They can be added at the same time as the beef if very well dried. This will have more of the texture of steak and kidney pie.

SHEEP, LAMB, AND GOAT

Now, my son, listen carefully and do what I tell you: Go out to the flock and bring me two choice young goats, so I can prepare some tasty food for your father, just the way he likes it. Genesis 27:8-9 (NIV)

Kids were eaten on special occasions such as above. In this case it was goat kids, but it also could be lamb or sheep kids. The kids being the young animals, rather than the large older animals. Sheep and lamb are eaten in North America and the British Isles. Goat is eaten in many other places including the West Indies, but is not as common as lamb. Passover or Easter time is the time when goat and sheep kids are most likely to be eaten for special festivities. In Ontario I met many farmers who raised goats for the many ethnic markets of the larger cities, especially at Easter. Eating lamb or goat kid in a special festival in the spring is a custom older than the Christian religion. There is always an article in the local paper every year saying that goat meat is going to become popular because it is so healthful and readily available. It never seems to happen.

NUTRITIONAL VALUES

Goat, raw (3 1/2 ounces)
165 calories
9.4 g fat
18.7 g protein
0.17 mg B1
0.32 mg B2
5.6 mg B3
11 mg calcium
2.20 mg iron

Lamb–loin chop, cooked (3 1/2 ounce)
302 calories
22.5 g fat
0.9 g polyunsaturated fats
70 mg cholesterol
23 g protein
0.17 mg B1
0.27 B2
6.5 mg B3
49 mg sodium
466 mg potassium
10 mg calcium
20 mg magnesium
193 mg phosphorus
3 mg iron

Lamb Stew

For each 4 persons to be served use 1/2 pound lamb stew meat, 1 cup pot barley, 2 tablespoons virgin olive oil, 1 onion, 2–4 cloves fresh garlic, 1–2 quarts water, and vegetables. Cut the lamb into very small pieces. Sauté the barley in the oil until it starts to turn golden, then add the chopped onions, lamb, and garlic, stir to coat all with oil and ensure even browning. When the barley is browned add the water. Then begin to add vegetables of your choice and cook until the barley is as soft as you like it. This could take one hour or as many as 5 or 6 hours. I always add chunks of carrot, potato, celery, and turnip. Let this cook for an hour or more then add seasonings and simmer for as long as you wish. This can be cooked in a slow cooker overnight on low or all day. Be sure to add enough water if you are leaving it unattended. I would start with 2 quarts and add more as needed. The barley will swell and absorb the water as long as it is cooking. The vegetables will contribute some of the liquid to the barley as well. When it is almost cooked add seasonings such as fresh parsley, or fresh or dried rosemary and vegetables that take less cooking time like green beans, peas, corn, kale, broccoli, turnip greens, or pea pods. If you want to add curry powder of some kind this can be added during the sautéing of the barley for the best flavor.

Meat Stews—The kind of stew eaten by the Hebrews had very little meat, just enough for flavor, and lots of grains and vegetables. It was served in a large soup plate. You can serve the same kind of meals of stew with very little meat with a garnish of chopped parsley. You can also add a handful of arame or hijiki sea vegetables while it is cooking to add minerals and a salty taste. If it is not salty enough, soy sauce can be added at the table. Leftovers can be reheated and served as stew or, with more water added, as soup, or even as gravy on rice, noodles, or toast.

FISH

And while they still disbelieved for joy, and wondered, he (Jesus) said to them, "Have you anything here to eat?" They gave him a piece of broiled fish, and he took it and ate before them. Luke 24:41-43 (RSV)

Fish is one of the main animal source foods eaten in the Middle East. There are 50 different types of fish mentioned in texts dating from before 2300 B.C.[13] There are 40 species found in the inland waters of the Near East, 22 of which are peculiar to Palestine and Syria, and of these 14 are known only to the Jordan river system.[14]

FISH FOR BREAKFAST

Jesus said to them, "Come and have breakfast." Now none of the disciples dared ask him, "Who are you?" They knew it was the Lord. Jesus came and took the bread and gave it to them, and so with the fish. John 21: 12,13 (RSV)

Fish was eaten at most times of day, but not on a regular basis, although it was eaten more often than red meats. Fish was eaten for breakfast as you can see in the quote above. It still is in the Middle East, the British Isles, and along the coasts of North America and other countries where fishing is a main industry. The Sea of Galilee was the center of a large fishing industry during New Testament times. Commerce in fresh and dried or salted fish was carried on with the known world.

Fish was used in a sauce somewhat like the Worcestershire sauce that we have today. The little fish were pickled, spiced, salted, and allowed to ferment into a very strong brine that was included in many sauces. A very small amount of this "garum" went a long way. The intestines and all parts of the fish were used. The best garum was made from fish livers only that were allowed to dry in the sun before being made into the sauce.[15] This allowed vitamin D to form and provided a very high nutritional content of vitamins A and D. Many people drink spoonfuls of cod liver oil daily for extra vitamins so fish liver sauce isn't so strange to us.

Anchovies were known to the Middle East as far back as 3000 B.C. Many of our foods contain the flavoring of anchovy like Worcestershire sauce and Caesar salad dressing. Caesar salad dressing is made with a small quantity of anchovy, egg yolks, virgin or extra virgin olive oil, fresh garlic, salt, pepper, lemon juice, and sometimes, a dash of cayenne pepper sauce or Worcestershire sauce. Grated Parmesan cheese is generally added once the dressing is mixed well. This is served on romaine lettuce with whole grain croutons This could even be a recipe from turn of the millennium Rome.

Sprat, horse-mackerel, mackerel, and shrimp were also eaten as well as anchovies.[16] Salmon, sardines, anchovies, and mackerel are all high in Omega 3 EPA. We will talk more about this later in the chapter.

Fish were eaten broiled, boiled, salted, dried, pickled, and in Rome they were often highly spiced with fresh green herbs such as mint, rue, green coriander, cumin, raisins, lovage, caraway, wild thyme, raisin wine, onions, saffron, prunes, vinegar, and oil. Then they were cooked, most likely in the oven or broiled. An entire chapter in *Apicius, Cookery And Dining In Imperial Rome,* was devoted to fish recipes. Pickled fish roe, served with cream and honey in a separate dish was very popular. Fish roe are the unlaid eggs from the female.

In the New Testament broiled fish is described as the fish having been placed on the coals and the blackened parts removed before eating. This sounds like a specialty of Cajun cooking: blackened fish.

OMEGA-3 OMEGA-6

Omega-3 and Omega-6 are essential fatty acids, this means that the body can not manufacture them, they have to be ingested. Nonessential fatty acids are made in the body from whatever foods are eaten. Essential fatty acids (EFA) are essential in the cell membranes to allow all materials to be transported into and out of the cells. Without the needed EFA the membranes will become stiff and slow down the normal processing in the cells. Some of the classically recognized disorders that result from a deficiency of either Omega-3 or Omega-6 fatty acids are: skin problems such as itching, flaking, peeling, hair loss; headache accompanied by fatigue, restlessness, confusion, and general weakness; easy bruising, pain, inflammation, and swelling of the joints; infertility, abortion, and kidney problems.[17]

The essential fatty acids are also known to convert cholesterol to bile salts to emulsify fats and make them digestible thereby allowing the body to get rid of cholesterol smoothly and efficiently. Without EFA in the body, the cholesterol attaches to a saturated fat molecule and becomes the dangerous kind of cholesterol we hear so much about, low density lipoprotein.

EFA are also converted into prostaglandins that regulate nearly every body function. Prostaglandins affect the functioning of the brain, heart, kidneys, liver, reproductive organs, skin, the immune system, and all healing.[18]

The main sources of Omega-3 are torpedo shaped dark fish such as albacore tuna, anchovies, bluefish, herring, mackerel, pilchard, rainbow trout, salmon, sardines, and sprat; oils extracted from nuts, seeds, or grains grown in northern climates such as walnut, soy, chestnut, hazelnut, wheat germ, pumpkin seed, and linseed; and beans grown in northern climates such as navy, kidney, pinto, soy, red, and Yankee beans.

THE TURNING POINT IN OUR HEALTH

Dr. Donald Rudin in his book *The Omega-3 Phenomenon,* has stated: "Three things have caused the reduction of EFA consumption: (1) a change in flour-milling technology, (2) a turn toward beef as a primary protein source, and (3) the introduction of hydrogenated vegetable oils." It is the reversal of these three things that *The World's Oldest Health Plan* hopes to restore to the world and thereby help millions of people regain the vibrant health that once was enjoyed by all people.

FISH AS MEDICINE

Poultices of fish brine were used for rheumatism. It seems to me that since garum was made from fish liver exposed to the sun, there must have been many medicinal tonics made from fish livers as well.[19]

NUTRITIONAL VALUES

Anchovy (3 fillets, canned, 12 grams)
    21 calories
    2.3 g protein
    1.2 g fat
    0.7 g polyunsaturated fatty acids
    20 mg calcium
    25 mg phosphorus.

Cod (1/3 ounces, broiled)
    162 calories
    26.1 g protein
    5 g fat
    170 I.U. vitamin A
    0.08 mg B1
    0.10 mg B2
    2.8 mg B3
    105 mg sodium
    386 mg potassium
    29 mg calcium
    260 mg phosphorus
    0.90 mg iron.

Atlantic Herring (raw, 3 1/2 ounces)
    176 calories
    17.3 g protein
    11.3 g fat
    2.0 g polyunsaturated fatty acids
    85 mg cholesterol
    110 I.U. vitamin A
    0.02 mg B 1
    0.15 mg B2
    3.6 mg B3
    256 mg phosphorus
    1.10 mg iron.

Mackerel–Atlantic (canned, 1/2 cup)
    192 calories
    20.2 g protein
    11.7 g fat
    460 I.U. vitamin A
    0.06 mg B1
    0.22 mg B2
    6.0 mg B3

194 calcium
287 phosphorus
2.20 mg iron.

Mackerel–Pacific (raw, 3 1/2 ounces [100 g])
159 calories
21.9 g protein
120 I.U. vitamin A
8 mg calcium
274 mg phosphorus
2.10 mg iron

Roe–raw—carp, cod, herring, haddock, pike, shad, (3 1/2 ounces)
130 calories
24.4 g protein
2.3 g fat
1.5 g carbohydrate
360 mg cholesterol
14 mg vitamin C
0.10 mg B1
0.76 mg B2
1.4 mg B3
0.60 mg iron

Sockeye Salmon (canned, 2/3 cup)
171 calories
20.3 g protein
9.3 g fat
36 mg cholesterol
230 I.U. vitamin A
0.04 mg B1
0.16 mg B2
7.3 mg B3
522 mg sodium
344 mg potassium
259 mg calcium
29 mg magnesium
344 mg phosphorus
1.20 mg iron

Sardines–Pacific in brine (canned, 3 1/2 ounces)
196 calories
18.8 g protein
30 mg fat

760 mg sodium
260 mg potassium
303 mg calcium
354 mg phosphorus
5.20 mg iron

Sardines–Pacific in soy oil (1 can, 105 g)
380 calories
180 g protein
34 g fat
140 mg cholesterol
0.01 mg B1
0.30 mg B2
7.4 mg B3
80 mg sodium

Tuna–Albacore (canned in water, 6 1/2 ounces)
237 calories
51.5 g protein
3.5 g fat
1.3 g polyunsaturated fatty acids
64 mg cholesterol
110 I.U. vitamin A
0.06 mg B1
0.09 mg B2
22.8 mg B3
0.68 mg B6
2.58 mcg B12
6 mcg folic acid
0.14 mg pantothenic acid
865 mg sodium
478 mg potassium
9 mg calcium
59 mg magnesium
0.92 mg zinc
0.074 mg manganese
405 mg phosphorus
2.21 mg iron
0.110 mg copper[20]

COOKING RULES

Fish should be cooked on medium or medium/high heat. It should be just cooked, not dried out or tough. Fish, when properly cooked, will not smell "fishy" while cooking. Adele Davis, the mother of modern nutrition, used to say that if you went somewhere for dinner and you smelled fish when you arrived, you should leave right away because the fish had been cooked too long or on too high a temperature, and it would be indigestible. Fish should be purchased fresh whenever possible. Often frozen fish has been coated with preservative so it is best to ask the fishmonger where you shop if it has been frozen or to let you see the box it came in to see if it has been treated. Purchasing a whole fish and having it filleted or cut into steaks is the one way of knowing if the fish is untreated.

A fresh fish will have eyes that are alert, not cloudy. Pressing on the eyes should cause them to pop back up. If not, the fish is not fresh. The gills should be pink and the skin should not be slimy.

Poached Fish

Fish can be poached by placing the fish in a broth and lightly simmering the liquid, covered, until the fish is done. The time will depend on the thickness of the fish. Poaching liquids are prepared and fully cooked before adding fish. The most popular one contains minced carrots, celery, onions, garlic, white wine, bay leaves, black pepper corns, and a slight amount of red chilies. This should be simmered for 15–20 minutes or until the vegetables are very soft. The bouillon is then strained, pressing all the liquor out of the veggies. This is used to poach the fish. The vegetables are discarded since all the nutrients are in the broth. Slices of lemon can also be added or used in place of the white wine.

A rack can be used that will allow the fish to be removed from the poaching liquid easily. If that is not available you might use several layers of cheese cloth. Place the cloth in the pan with enough hanging over the pan to fold over the top of the fish and roll up to give a handle for removing the fish. Add the fish, bring the edges of the cloth together above the fish, roll the two ends down like a paper bag, and pour in the poaching liquid. Remember to add a little more liquid to compensate for the cloth soaking it up.

Herb Poached Fish

Use large sprigs of fresh herbs like tarragon, dill, thyme, chervil or basil. Place them in the water and bring slowly to a simmer. Add the fish and cover, simmer until done. Enough water should be used to cover the fish when it is in the pan.

Steamed Fish

Fish can be steamed very easily. I always use a Chinese bamboo steamer for fish. It only takes a few seconds to do fillets or steaks since steam is so much hotter than other methods of cooking. The Chinese method of steaming a fish is to place an oval plate with the fish on it onto a small rack in a steaming wok, cover and steam. Often herbs are added to the fish along with soy sauce, ginger, spring onions, and sesame oil.

Steamed Fish Meal

Marinate fish fillets or steaks in a mixture of freshly pressed ginger and garlic, soy sauce, white wine or lemon juice, and enough water to make a thin sauce. For two you would use a 1/2 inch piece of ginger, 2 teaspoons tamari, 2 tablespoons wine* or 1 tablespoon lemon or lime juice, 2–3 tablespoons water.

Using a bamboo steamer steam vegetables while fish is marinating. I start with cauliflower, broccoli stems, and carrot first cut into even size pieces. When they are soft I add green beans or celery and the fish. Just as the beans begin to turn a brighter color I add broccoli florets. The fish generally takes five minutes to cook, more if it is thick. It should be moist. The leftover marinade is then thickened by adding 2 tablespoons of corn starch and 1/2 cup water and bringing to a boil and cooking until thickened, about 2–3 minutes.

To serve, place veggies on a plate in a semi-circle on one half of the plate. Alternate the colors or arrange the colors into a rainbow effect. Put the fish in the center of the crescent and pour the sauce over it. Sprinkle with finely chopped fresh parsley.

*The steaming or boiling will generally drive off any alcohol in the wine.

Baked Fish

Fish can be baked in a covered casserole dish with a small amount of moisture added. Lemon baked fish would be fillets layered with slices of fresh lemon or lime on top and bottom. This can be done either covered or uncovered. Use a thermometer to determine when the fish is done. With some fish it might be necessary to insert the probe when you think the fish is almost done and verify the cooking time.

My favorite is to use a foil package to cook fish. This allows you to layer fish fillets with herbs, veggies, or lemon slices. We enjoy red snapper with tomato slices, basil, and thinly sliced zucchini. Another favorite is very thinly sliced potato, butter, perch or trout, finely chopped parsley, and thinly sliced yellow summer squash. Use your own imagination to prepare variations that suit you. Baking time in a 350°F oven will be about 20 minutes with veggies added or 15 minutes without.

Barbecue Fish

Fish and herbs with lemon and/or butter can be done on the barbecue following the instructions above. Fish and veggies can also be done on a grill. It is also possible to broil fish on a grill, generally a special basket is used to hold the fish or sea food. Tomato based barbecue sauce can also be used.

Middle Eastern Broiled Fish
(For each person to be served)

1/4 lb.	boned fish
1 Tbsp.	virgin olive oil
1 tsp.	freshly squeezed lemon juice
1/4 tsp.each	basil and oregano
1/4 clove	freshly pressed garlic or more to taste

Mix seasonings together and brush on fish. Broil 6 inches away from heat source, turning once and brushing with the seasonings frequently. The length of time for cooking will depend on the thickness of the fish, type of fish, temperature of fish when placed in broiler, and efficiency of the broiler. A meat thermometer will give an accurate reading of when the fish is done. Place the probe in the center of the thickest part (not touching a bone). The fish should be soft, not dry, and just past the point of being pink inside. Almost any fillet can be used for this. It is especially nice with bass, sea bass, perch, cod, haddock, tuna, splake, or trout.

CHICKEN AND OTHER FOWL

. . . How often I have longed to gathered your children together, as a hen gathers her chicks under her wings . . . . Matthew 23:37b (NIV)

The domestic hen was common in the Mediterranean by the 5th century B.C., almost every Athenian had one. Records indicate that thrushes and partridge were part of the Greek diet then, and many people kept geese, quail, pigeons, ducks, and peacocks, as well.[21]

EGGS

If a son asks for bread from any father among you, will he give him a stone? Or if he asks for a fish, will he give him a serpent instead of a fish? Or if he asks for an egg, will he offer him a scorpion? Luke 11:11,12 (NKJV)

Of course, there were eggs, since you can't have a chicken without an egg. Young Hebrew boys were often given this problem to figure out during their instructions: "Could an egg be eaten that was laid on the Sabbath by a hen that didn't know the law against working on the Sabbath?"[22]

Apicius, the great Roman chef of the time around the birth of Jesus, is credited with inventing the omelet and the soufflé, and some even say the cheesecake. All of these dishes use eggs, so it is obvious that eggs were being eaten during New Testament times. Eggs were used as binders in many Roman recipes that included vegetables and grains. They even had a kind of bread pudding that used eggs, honey of some kind, old bread, milk, raisins, and spices. Often eggs were used to bind together some of the stuffings for roasted pigs, hares, and other animals as well as the stuffings for many different kinds of stuffed baked or deep fried vegetables.

The Romans even had special plates for serving hard boiled eggs. Generally they were like our deviled eggs. The dishes were deep and had special hollow places for the eggs, just like we do today in hard-cooked egg plates. They were made of metal, probably pewter. The eggs were cradled by the hollowed out sections so they wouldn't slide around the plate while being served.

PERFECT PROTEIN?

In this century eggs have been considered to be "perfect protein" and were the basis for judging the quality of all other protein foods. The PER (protein efficiency ratio) was the measurement that determined how well the body would use the protein. This was generally determined by feeding the protein to rats. If they thrived, then the PER was considered to be acceptable. Eggs were perfect and all other protein was judged to be perfect, or less perfect, depending on how well rats thrived. I guess they loved eggs, the perfect food for rats. Rats didn't thrive very well on beans, not even soy beans, so they were considered to have a very low PER and were not considered "complete protein." (This is how it was described to me at a scientific convention in 1980.)

In 1979, however, Scrimshaw and Young of the Massachusetts Institute of Technology found a new way of determining the PER of foods. Instead of feeding it to rats and seeing how they thrived, they fed the foods to humans and measured the output of nitrogen in their urine. And, low and behold, the output from soy beans showed that they did contain complete protein after all. Soy beans had lower amounts of one amino acid than animal protein generally had. This was methionine and was used by rats to grow tails and hair on the tails. Now I don't know about you, but I don't have a tail nor hair that might even be construed as growing on one. This research revolutionized the way we think about protein.

COMPLEMENTARY PROTEINS

Until the late 70's, the best idea was to mix proteins so that the amino acids were "balanced" by the amino acid contents. A grain that was low in lysine would be mixed with a bean that was high in it, thus making complete protein. This was very useful to vegetarians at the time. But with the discovery by Scrimshaw and Young, it meant we could eat soy protein and have "complete protein." The pioneer in the complementary protein system, Francis Moore Lappé, used the old way of determining the PER. Her work was very valuable, even revolutionary at the time, and still somewhat necessary if we are using beans other than soy beans.

PROTEIN FOR HUMANS

Eggs are acceptable for humans to eat. Beans, grains, and other vegetables are much better sources of energy, as the latest work done by Dr. T. Colin Campbell is showing. If you enjoy the occasional egg, it is fine, the same with fish, chicken, and other animal foods. Just don't make them the main protein source in your diet. These animal proteins are very high in fats of varying kinds that we are now seeing can contribute to loss of vitality, health, and well-being.

Sure I eat eggs, now. For many years I was a very strict vegetarian and did not eat eggs, meat, fish, chicken, or even gelatin. And I felt OK. I also exercised very heavily. But the rigidity of this type of diet was not easy, since I was developing recipes for a tofu company that insisted I include animal products in some of my recipes. It was very difficult to eat out as well. This began my research on the perfect balance that I call the World's Oldest Health Plan.

COOKING RULES FOR CHICKEN AND EGGS

All protein foods should be cooked on medium heat, as I have said before. Eggs are no exception. If you fry an egg, which I hope you never do, it should never be crispy or lacy around the edges. This means that it has been cooked on too high a heat and it will be very difficult to digest. This causes stress in the body and the body responds by raising the cholesterol levels in the blood. By cooking an egg on gentler heat, it lowers the chances of it causing health problems in the body. A poached, coddled, soft scrambled, or soft boiled egg, is the best way to eat eggs. When eggs are firm boiled they should be placed in water the same temperature as the egg to start. The recipe for poaching and/or boiling eggs is below.

Chicken is best when broiled 6 inches away from the heat source, poached, or baked (roasted). Baked chicken should be cooked at 325°F. Use a meat thermometer to determine when it is done. The general rule is to bake it about 20–30 minutes for each pound of chicken. This will give a digestible, juicy, delicious chicken. There is no need to add anything, or grease up the bird before cooking. The only thing you might consider is piercing the breast in the fat places with a knife or fork after the bird has been roasting for about an hour. This releases the fat to the pan so that you eat only the meat. If you are using a chemical free bird that has been raised in a certified farm on grains and vegetables and has no added drugs or chemicals, you will have a safe meal. If you are using a commercially raised bird, you must use a thermometer to determine when it is done to be sure that it is heated through and any salmonella that might be present in the bird is fully destroyed.

When eating eggs it is best to also eat lots of vegetables with them. This is why most of the recipes I do call for vegetables in or with the eggs.

Soft Boiled Eggs

A soft boiled egg is generally cooked for 3 or 4 minutes. Place room temperature eggs into lightly boiling water using a large spoon. Gently lower them into the water so that they don't crack. When the water returns to the boil begin to time the eggs. After the time is up remove the eggs and pour out the water, replacing it with cold water. Lift the eggs out and serve. They can be served upended in an egg cup or cracked open into a bowl with a small amount of olive oil, salt, and pepper. Often I serve eggs this way with fresh parsley and a clove of pressed garlic added. Eggs can be cooked for 3, 4, 5, or even 6 minutes. Allow extra time if the eggs are cold. Cold eggs tend to contract and crack when placed in boiling water. It is better to put them in a small bowl and heat them up with hot water for a few seconds before adding to boiling water. Often the use of a slotted spoon when adding eggs to boiling water will help slowly heat up the eggs and prevent cracking.Often I steam an egg in the shell near the end of the cooking time for a plate of steamed vegetables. I love this for breakfast or lunch. I start with potatoes and carrots, sometimes beets, then add onion, garlic, celery, green beans, or broccoli. I add the egg before the broccoli, since the egg takes 4–5 minutes to steam and the broccoli a little less. I top this with virgin olive oil and butter combined and a grating of fresh black pepper.

To break a soft cooked egg into a bowl, cool it with cold water for a minute to be able to handle it. Then using the back of a knife blade gently crack the egg around the middle. Using both thumbs open the shell and allow the half with the yolk to empty into the bowl. Use a spoon to scoop out the remaining egg. Put the shells into the compost or give them to the birds.

Firm Cooked Eggs

Place the eggs into water the same temperature as the eggs, being sure to cover the eggs thoroughly. Put the pan on medium heat and bring just to a boil. Reduce the heat to as low as it will go and continue to cook eggs for 15–20 minutes. Remove from heat, drain, and cover with cold water for up to 10 minutes. Change the water so that the eggs cool off rapidly. Refrigerate or remove shells immediately. If the eggs are very fresh it might be difficult to remove the shells easily so buy your eggs a few days before you want to make firm cooked eggs. (If you buy your eggs from a supermarket or chain store and you are buying a brand that is not locally produced the chances are great that they are not that fresh.) A fresh egg is one that has just been laid within the last day or two.

Poached Eggs

Use a non-stick fry pan or lightly oil the bottom of another pan. I use a cast iron pan with a slightly rounded bottom and sides. Four is about the maximum that should be done at once. Put water into the pan, enough to cover the eggs. On a medium heat bring the water to a simmer, keep it simmering. Add one teaspoon of apple cider vinegar, this keeps the egg from spreading. Add the eggs one at a time. After the eggs have begun to set up and look slightly cooked, you might want to run the spatula gently under each egg to be sure that it is not sticking. The eggs might float up when you do this, that is OK, actually that is great. If you cover the eggs to hurry the process, you might cause the water to boil up and spoil the eggs. If the eggs are not cooking as fast as you would like, use the spatula to flip the simmering water onto the yolk. As soon as you put the eggs in start the toast. When the toast is done and buttered, the eggs should be done or almost done. Place the egg on the plate after draining it on the spatula for a few seconds. Then use a paper or cloth towel to soak up the excess water. If you are serving the eggs on the toast you don't need to butter the toast.

Scrambled Eggs

3 large	fresh eggs
1 Tbsp.	cold water
3 sprigs	fresh parsley, finely chopped
1 Tbsp.	butter
1 Tbsp.	olive oil or canola oil
1/4 small	cooking onion or green onion chopped
1 large clove	fresh garlic
4	mushrooms
1/8	sweet red or yellow bell pepper

Beat eggs, parsley, and water together and set aside. Heat butter and oil together over medium/high heat. Chop onion, garlic, and mushrooms and sauté in oil butter mixture. When they are limp add the red peppers, stir. When the vegetables are just soft add the eggs. Stir once and leave them. Allow the eggs to begin to set. Then lift the outer edge and allow the runny uncooked eggs to run onto the hot pan. Continue to do this until the eggs are cooked. Turn over if needed to finish cooking. Serves 4. Serve with a garnish of sprouts, salsa, or chile sauce and whole grain toast.

I always add seaweed to the eggs like arame or hijiki because we love it and because the sea vegetables contain so many minerals. Many other veggies can be used in this simple recipe. Pre-cooked veggies can be used as well. Try broccoli, zucchini, grated carrots, sweet potato, green or yellow beans, spinach, mustard greens, or any fresh or dried herbs, tomatoes, etc.

Eggs scrambled with onion, garlic, and mushrooms with fresh dill and smoked salmon added with the eggs are a treat for royalty. This would be enough fat and protein for the entire day's worth. Steamed or baked vegetables with lemon juice or a simple sauce made without butter would be good for the other meals this day. Soup without fat that included beans would be good or a meal of a fruit salad or even low fat beans on whole grain noodles or toast could round out a day and keep the fat down.

Omelets

4 large	fresh eggs
1 1/2 Tbsp.	cold water
2 Tbsp.	unsalted butter
grinding	black pepper

Beat eggs with a fork or whisk until mixed, then add water and pepper and beat until fluffy. Heat omelet pan on medium heat, add butter and when it finishes foaming up add eggs. After 10–15 seconds stir with the flat of a fork once or twice around the pan. Cook undisturbed for another 5–6 seconds. Lift up the edge of the omelet to let any remaining raw egg run onto the hot pan. When set up fold in half using omelet pan or spatula. Serves 2. Serve with dark green salad or vegetable like broccoli or mustard greens.

When I was a college student my friend Linda Lou Tyler and I used to make omelets by separating the eggs and beating the whites until they were almost stiff. We then folded the yolks and herbs into the stiff whites and cooked them. We made a filling of various vegetables and spices which we put in the middle of the fluffy eggs when partially cooked. She had a special pan that had two kidney shaped halves hinged together. We would put the egg mixture on either half and cook until almost set. Then close the pan with the filling on one side, covered with cheese. This made both halves hold together. The pan was then turned over when needed to cook both sides. I haven't seen one of these pans for years. This was, of course, a suburban convenience pan of the 50's, not a real French style omelet pan. It was sure fun to do this. We usually made this for dinner in the evening, not breakfast. A green salad was served.

Cheese Omelet

Make the basic omelet above and add 2–3 tablespoons of grated cheese just before folding over. Strong cheeses such a cheddar or aged Swiss are good. If using cheese add finely chopped fresh parsley to the eggs or with the cheese. Low fat cheese will work just fine here.

Filled Omelets

Add heated filling to half of the omelet and fold over. Left over veggie gravy, stir fried veggies, lentils, or steamed veggies can be added. See Chapter II—Our Daily Bread under Vegetable Gravy for instructions and ideas.

Egg Salad

3	firm cooked eggs
1/4	small onion, finely chopped OR
2	green onions including tops, finely chopped
4 sprigs	fresh parsley, finely chopped
1/8	red or yellow pepper, cut in slivers
2 stalks	green celery, thinly sliced or finely chopped
6	black olives, sliced
	mayonnaise to taste

Mix ingredients well. Serves 4. Serve on whole grain bread with lettuce and sprouts. Green olives can also be used. A quarter teaspoon curry powder can be mixed in for a different taste, this eliminates the need for added salt. Any vegetables can be added to this like green beans, pea pods, English peas, broccoli or cauliflower, all raw or lightly cooked. Serve this as a salad plate with cold steamed vegetables and dark green lettuce.

This can also be mixed with a can of water packed tuna. This should be enough to serve 6 or 8 people. To reduce some of the cholesterol and saturated fat you may use half eggs and half firm tofu very well drained and cut into small cubes. In this case add a little extra seasonings as the tofu tends to absorb the seasonings. Tofu mayonnaise can be used for a lower fat dressing.

CHICKEN COUGH

In the early '70s I was visiting with a neighbor who raised chickens. He raised broilers in a large building that had a conveyor belt of food running through the middle of the room and water feeders placed around in different areas. He raised 60,000 at a time in this one room. He had just changed to a new feed that made the chickens attain the required weight to qualify as broilers in a week less than his old feed. This means that he would be making more money off his crop so he was very elated. I asked to see the bag the feed came in. You can imagine my surprise when I read the first ten or so ingredients. They were all medications, the next 6 or 8 were nutrients, and the last four ingredients were grains. Each medicine was for a different reason, they were just to prevent certain diseases from striking the flock. This was standard practice, give the medication to all of the animals whether they need it or not and you will not have to worry about illness ruining your crop. I was horrified.

But that wasn't as bad as the "chicken cough." One of the medications was in the feed to prevent chicken cough. When I asked him what that was he replied that often chickens cough for no reason, sort of like clearing their throat. It is not the symptom of any illness or disease, he told me, but it sure was annoying when you were trying to sleep at night and 60,000 chickens were all coughing. So they added something to keep the farmer from staying awake at night because the chickens coughed. This is not my idea of good crop management. I was brought up with the expression: "If it ain't broke, don't fix it." And this seemed like a flagrant fixing of something that wasn't broken. I would never take medication for something that I never had any suggestion of contracting, why should my chickens do this? Or any foods I eat, for that matter. Maybe they don't do it anymore.

Firm Cooked Eggs

Place the eggs in a pan and cover with water the same temperature as the eggs. Put on medium heat and bring to simmering. Simmer for about

5 minutes*. Turn the heat off and leave for 20 minutes. Cover with cold water until chilled. Then store in the refrigerator or peel and prepare them.

*You could simmer them for up to 20 minutes as long as the eggs don't rock or the water bubbles break the surface.

NUTRITIONAL VALUES

Chicken–roasted with skin (3 1/2 ounces)
> 239 calories
> 27.3 g protein
> 13.6 g fats
> 3.0 g polyunsaturated fatty acids
> 3.8 g saturated fatty acids
> 88 mg cholesterol
> 161 I.U. vitamin A
> 0.06 mg B1
> 0.17 mg B2
> 8.5 mg B3
> 0.40 mg B6
> 0.30 mcg B12
> 5 mcg folic acid
> 1.03 mg B5
> 82 mg sodium
> 223 mg potassium
> 15 mg calcium
> 23 mg magnesium
> 1.94 mg zinc
> 0.020 mg manganese
> 182 mg phosphorus
> 1.26 mg iron
> 0.07 mg copper

Egg (1 large, soft boiled)
> 79 calories
> 6.1 g protein
> 5.6 g fat
> 0.7 g polyunsaturated fatty acids
> 1.7 g saturated fatty acids
> 274 mg cholesterol
> 260 I.U. vitamin A
> 0.04 mg B1
> 0.14 mg B2
> trace B3
> 0.06 mg B6
> 0.66 mcg B12

24 mcg folic acid
0.86 B5
69 mg sodium
65 mg potassium
28 mg calcium
6 mg magnesium
0.72 mg zinc
1.04 mg iron[23]

REFERENCES

1. Hastings, James (Ed.), *Dictionary of the Bible*, Charles Scribner's and Sons, New York, 1963, p. 300.

2. Miller, Madeleine S. and J. Lane, *The New Harper's Bible Dictionary*, Harper and Roe, New York, 1973, p.189.

3. Tannahill, p. 57.

4. Perlmutter, Cathy, "Just Try It For A Week," and "Reverse Heart Disease Naturally," Dr. Ornish's Intensive Healing Diet, Prevention Magazine, May 1990, Vol. 42, No. 5, pp. 51–81.

5. Brody, Jane E., "Huge Study of Diet Indicts Fat and Meat," New York Times, May 8, 1990, pp. B5, B6.

6. Physicians Committee for Responsible Medicine, personal interview with Virginia Messina, M.P.H., RD., April 27, 1990.

7. Vine, W.E., *An Expository Dictionary of Biblical Words*, Thomas Nelson, Nashville, 1971, p. 400.

8. Vine, p. 400.

9. Tannahill, p. 40.

10. *USDA Handbook, 456*, p. 24.

11. *USDA Handbook, 456*, p. 168.

12. Pennington & Church, p. 105.

13. Tannahill, p. 61.

14. Miller, pp. 194–195

15. Apicius, p. 22.

16. Tannahill, p. 97.

17. Rudin, Donald O., and Clara Felix, *The Omega-3 Phenomenon*, Avon Books, New York, 1987, p. 18.

18. Rudin, pp. 19–23.
19. Bouquet, A.C., *Everyday Life in New Testament Times,* Charles Scribner's and Sons, New York, 1954, p. 97.
20. Pennington and Church, pp. 68–70.
21. Bailey, Albert Edward, *Daily Life in Bible Times,* Charles Scribner's and Sons, New York, 1943, p.255
22. Tannahill, pp. 83, 49.
23. Pennington and Church, pp. 69, 119.

VII

Drink Up
Water, Juice, Wine, Beer, & Teas

Water

The servant hurried to meet her and said, "Please give me a little water from your jar." Genesis 24:17 (NIV)

There came a woman of Samaria to draw water. Jesus said to her, "Give me a drink." John 4: 7 (RSV)

We can live for 20 to 40 days or more without food, but for only a few days if we have no water or other liquids to drink. This is true of peoples everywhere, we all need to drink to live. Even animals need water to drink. Water is needed to grow plants, wash clothes and dishes, prepare food, and clean our bodies. Water is an essential component in life. It is even more important in areas where there is very little water to drink like in a desert, on the ocean, or in areas where the water is in short supply or is polluted.

Since water is so essential why do we pollute it with industrial, farm, and home wastes? A healthy lifestyle takes these things into consideration. This is why so many municipalities now have a central water supply and common sewage removal systems. This eliminates each family needing a well and/or septic tank for sewage recycling. Imagine if you lived in a large city like Denver, Chicago, or New York and had to go to the corner to draw water from the neighborhood well. This would certainly be a way of meeting your neighbors a few times a day! It might also be a place for feuding and fraud. How lucky we are to be able to just turn on the tap and have moderately pure water come out, depending on where you live, of course.

There were times recounted in the Bible of feuds at the well, segregation at the well, poisoning of the well, and so forth. Would we be any different if we had this kind of water supply? Even now many states don't want to supply water to other states who have none or very little, preferring to save it for themselves. Some states see selling water as a way of earning money, a cash crop if you will. Many times flooding occurs because a dam or water reservoir is opened by man or natural causes. Water is very important for life and death in our world today just as it was in Bible times.

And he answered him, "Let it [a fig tree] alone, sir, this year also, til I dig about it and put on manure." Luke 13:8 (RSV)

We saw in the preceding chapter that it takes more water to raise animals than it does to raise grains. The pollution of the water supply by the animal runoffs is also great. In this arena vegetable and grain farmers are not totally innocent either. Much of the ground water pollution comes from the artificial chemicals that are used on crops, such as insecticide, fertilizer, and weed killers. A more natural method of farming is needed to save the water supply. This poses a problem since the most commonly used natural fertilizer has been animal manure. Without animals there will be no manure.

GREEN MANURE

There are other manures that can be used, such as green manure. This is a nitrogen-rich crop that is grown on the land and then dug in to compost and add nutrients back into the soil. This method of composting has been used for thousands of years around the world. It is safer because all the nutrients come from the land and go back to the land. The roots of the crops used go very deep and bring the deep nutrients to the plant and thus to the surface of the soil. Once they are plowed in, they are made available for the next crop grown. The refuse of the crop can also be composted with other vegetable matter to be put back into the soil. Other organic matter, such as grass clippings, tree trimmings, and sawdust made from tree trimmings can also be used as a fertilizer or mulch.

SEA VEGETATION MANURE

Many natural fertilizers are made from sea vegetation and minerals removed from the sea water. Some even include ground sea animals as well. These mineral-rich products are a great way to harvest crops that can be used for growing plants without harming the environment by the harvesting or the use as manure. There are many allusions to the use of sea vegetation as crop food in Bible times, but we haven't found any definitive research that says that they did.

OUR OWN GARBAGE

The best system would reuse all the organic garbage, grass clippings, tree trimmings, and farm crop refuse composted into viable organic fertilizer. This could also include papers that have non-lead print on them and would give a place to recycle the huge volume of papers that we now bury in land fills or burn.

HOW MUCH WATER SHOULD WE DRINK?

The general consensus is that we should drink at least a quart of water a day. During a weight loss program the water should increase to at least 2 quarts a day. If the weather is very hot or dry water should be taken in in direct proportion to the amount lost either through perspiration or urination. During heavy exercise water should be drunk to replace the fluids lost to prevent dehydration and sore muscles. Often during exercise minerals or some form of complex sugar like juice also should be taken to prevent muscle cramping. When hiking, running, or bicycling water should also be handy to drink to replace lost fluids. During extreme heat and intense exercise it might be necessary to also add a small amount of salt to the water as well as complex sugars. This will prevent dehydration, muscle cramping, and headaches. Water rich vegetables like lettuce, watercress, parsley, and celery are good to eat when engaging in these kinds of activities, for the water and the minerals that are necessary to replace the nutrients lost during the activity. Vitamin C rich fruits and fruit juices are necessary for preventing headaches as well as supplying the essential sugars that are needed.

In hotter climates like the Middle East and India, people wear clothes that keep them covered. They are often well-covered, with layers of clothing. This helps to prevent water loss through evaporation directly from the skin as well as to prevent sunburn that might weaken one as well. The outer layers of clothing act as a cooling agent by allowing evaporation of the moisture on the outer layers only, actually preventing excessive perspiration.

The newer clothes for bicycling have layers of material that actually "wick" the perspiration away from the body to prevent chafing from the friction of damp clothes moving against the skin.

A cyclist always carries at least one water bottle from which he constantly drinks to replace the lost fluids.

During any type of athletic event, whether it is football or running, there is always water available for the participants to replace lost fluids and prevent exhaustion.

WHAT ABOUT ICE WATER?

Drinking ice water is often not advised since it can cause a shock to the stomach which might prevent proper digestion or even cause stomach cramps. There are those natural health practitioners who feel that ice water can even cause constipation, but this is only a theory. However, if you drink ice water (or any iced drinks) and suffer from constipation, you might want to eliminate the ice cold drinks for several weeks and see if there is any improvement. Ice water is not as cooling in the summer as room temperature water or even hot tea which will bring on a slight perspiration that will then evaporate causing the body to cool. Natural cooling comes from evaporation, this is why it is essential to replace the fluids lost in hot weather. The body will expend a lot of fluid to keep itself cool and this can cause weakness or exhaustion if it is not replaced.

Juice

I would give you spiced wine to drink, the juice of my pomegranates.
Song of Solomon 8:2c (RSV)

Juice also was a popular drink in Bible times. Most of the juice came from fruits as we mentioned in Chapter V—Special Treats under fruits. The most popular juices were fig, grape, pomegranate, date, plum, mulberry, pear, and cherry. This list reads almost like the labels in our modern supermarket or natural food store juice section.

Juice is a very concentrated sugar product, it is very sweet! It is not complete! Juice is missing the fiber, pulp, skin, and pectin of the whole fruit. When you drink apple juice, for example, you drink about 2 or 3 apples' worth of juice in one glass. This is a very high caloric intake compared to just eating one apple. There are more benefits to eating the fruit whole than to having juice only. So many of the health-giving properties of fruits exist mainly when the whole fruit is eaten.

I suggest that juice should always be diluted about 1 part juice to 3 parts water just as it was in Bible days. This will reduce the calories and sugar while still having the benefits of the vitamins and complex carbohydrates. Children should never be allowed to drink straight juice for this reason. It can give them too much concentrated sugar and make them a little overactive. It can also do damage to the teeth and the teeth that are forming. A baby should never be allowed to sleep with a bottle of juice of any kind, or milk either for the same reason. The sugars will damage their teeth. Drinking undiluted juices can encourage a taste for sweets that might be hard to break in later years and lead to obesity, sugarholism, or even alcoholism.

Wine

When the wine was gone, Jesus' mother said to him, "They have no more wine." John 2:3 (NIV)

In Bible times the most popular juice drink was wine. There were six different kinds of wine drunk: sweet, sour, mixed, foamed, spiced, and fragrant. Mixed wine was generally mixed with water, not necessarily mixed with other types of wines.[1] Wine was drunk almost daily by most people, even at breakfast. Wine was generally diluted 1 part wine to 3 parts water for everyday use. Wine is mentioned at least 230 times in the Bible, not including winepress or wine cellars. Water of all kinds is mentioned about 385 times. It seems that water and wine were very popular as drinks during Bible times. They were also considered necessities of life.

WINE MAKING

Wine was fermented in vats that were smeared inside and out with resin. It was filtered into goatskins or pigskins if it was for domestic consumption. If it was to be exported it would be put into a clay amphora.

Various methods were popular to keep wine for long periods of time:

1. Adding a brew of herbs and spices which had been mixed with condensed sea water and matured for several years.
2. After 1,000 B.C. a liquid resin that was mixed with vine ash was added to grape juice before fermentation.
3. Wine-filled jars were often kept to mature in the same lofts where wood was seasoned and meat was smoked.

WINE FROM GREECE AND ITALY

Wine was an important cash crop for both domestic and export consumption. Italian vineyards often produced over 2,000 U.S. gallons of wine per acre. By 121 B.C. Italian vintages became popular like the Opinian and Falernian. These were exported to all the known world. From 3000 B.C. to 1000 A.D. Roman gourmets often imported wine from Jura. As early as 3000 B.C. Greeks exported olive oil and wine to Rome and the Middle East. Greece had been known as the home of fine wine since the fifth century B.C.[2]

WINES OF THE ISRAELITES

Wine was made from figs, dates, grapes, and pomegranate juice. There was also a type of "honey" wine that may or may not have had fruit juice in it. Since this "honey" came from bees, figs, dates, and carob pods, it is rather confusing to tell the difference. Wine was thought of as the universal drink.

SPICED WINE

Wine was spiced with many different spices and herbs. Among these were myrrh, cassia *cinnamomum cassia*, and cinnamon *cinnamomum zeylanicum*. Spiced wine was most often kept on ice until it was drunk.[3]

WINE AS MEDICINE

No longer drink only water, but use a little wine for the sake of your stomach and your frequent ailments. 1 Timothy 5:23 (RSV)

Wine was used with oil on wounds as we learned in Chapter V—Special Treats–olive oil. Wine was mixed with purple aloes as medicine. Wine mingled with myrrh was used as a pain killer. Some people believe this is why Jesus refused the wine and myrrh in Mark 15:23. He didn't want to take a pain killer.

BANQUETS AND BANQUET HOUSES

He has taken me to the banquet hall, and his banner over me is love. Song of Songs 2:4 (NIV)

Banquet, banquet hall, and banquet house mean "drinking" in both Hebrew and Aramaic. Drinking was the main purpose of a banquet.[4] Drinking always took place at feasts as well.

OVERINDULGENCE IN WINE

Be not among winebibbers, or among gluttonous eaters of meat; for the drunkard and the glutton will come to poverty, and drowsiness will clothe a man with rags. Proverbs 23:20,21 (RSV)

Noah was the first tiller of the soil. He planted a vineyard; and he drank of the wine, and became drunk, and lay uncovered in his tent. Genesis 9:20,21 (RSV)

Do you not know that the wicked will not inherit the kingdom of God? Do not be deceived: neither the sexually immoral nor idolaters nor adulterers nor male prostitutes nor homosexual offenders nor thieves nor the greedy nor drunkards nor slanderers nor swindlers will inherit the kingdom of God. 1 Corinthians 6:9, 10 (NIV)

Although wine was a highly-favored drink, being a drunkard was not favored at all. During the Passover meal four glasses of wine were to be drunk. Even children drank highly-diluted wine. This was not considered enough to make one drunk. Perhaps if it were diluted 1 to 3 with water it might not be enough to cause drunkenness. People who are used to drinking wine daily would often have 3 or 4 glasses of wine in a day. In order to become drunk one would have had to consume a very large quantity of wine. Often feasts would go on for days, so this was why the large amount of wine. Perhaps the wine was not as strong, or perhaps they worked off the effects of the alcohol by walking, dancing, and moving about more than we do. They would have been eating so that could have slowed down the action of the alcohol.

The sweeter a wine, the more intoxicating it is. The more sweet wine one drinks, the greater the aftereffect. Sweet wine can throw off the sugar in one's system and make one want more just from the sugar. Often a hangover comes from the sweetest wines more than the very dry ones.

In many wines there is another problem that is a modern one. That is the addition of chemicals that might cause allergic reactions. Chemicals can be used to bring on fermentation, stop it, settle the wine, filter it, and so on. The chemicals and/or the yeast are often the cause of problems from drinking wine. This can be determined by a visit to an allergist, a clinical ecologist, or other natural health practitioner.

Personally speaking, I have lost the taste for drinkng wine or spirits of any kind. I prefer to drink the wine of worshipping my Lord at the throne of grace.

WINE IN COOKING

Wine is used in cooking to give a special flavor to the food. Generally the alcohol is burned off so only the flavor is left. Wine is added to casseroles, soups, stews, and even cakes and puddings.

A small amount of wine, say a tablespoon, to four servings of food will give a special flavor that will not require the addition of salt to the food. This might be helpful if you are trying to cut down on salt. Each serving will have less than a teaspoon of wine, with the alcohol cooked off.

STRONG DRINK

Wine is a mocker, strong drink a brawler; and whoever is led astray by it is not wise. Proverbs 20:1 (RSV)

There are over 22 references to strong drink in the Bible. One source defines strong drink as made from the wine-grounds, dates, and honey. This might be something like brandy or fruit liqueurs.[5] Another source describes strong drink as barley beer.[6] This is another of those gray areas. The Bible mentions strong drink and yet we are not sure what it is. Each scholar has his or her own interpretation of what that means.

Beer

Beer was known as the favorite drink of the Philistines, not the Israelites. Sumerians consumed a large quantity of beer as did the Romans. During the Neolithic revolution in Egypt there was mead, wine, and beer being drunk.

In 1989 Professor Solomon Katz, an anthropologist specializing in nutrition at the University of Pennsylvania, along with Fritz Maytag, the owner of a San Francisco natural brewery, brewed a Sumerian beer. The recipe was part of a Sumerian hymn to the goddess Ninkasi, written in cuneiform on a clay tablet that dates back to 1800 B.C. The ingredients included dates and loaves of yeasted barley bread. Often the brewery was in the same room as the bakery. Solomon Katz believes beer may be the cornerstone of civilization and has argued that ancient man turned from hunting to farming to raise grains for beer. Why else would people domesticate a cereal grain that has so little nutrition, he postulates, unless it was for a source of fermented sugar for making beer?

It is known that 40% of the Sumerian grain yield was used for beer production. Ordinary temple workmen received a daily ration of 2.2 US pints of beer a day. Senior dignitaries received five times as much and often used it as currency. In Sumeria there were 8 types of beer from barley, 8 types from wheat, and 3 types from mixed grains.[7]

The Sumarians' successors drank date wine. They had to, the soil had been soured due to improper growing of barley, and other grains would not grow there. There are many times in history where improper growing or irrigation techniques ruined the soil and crops could not be grown. This has happened in most of the areas around the Mediterranean Sea from the earliest recorded time until the present. It has also happened in many other places in the world.

Egyptians drank a beer known as "hag" that was made from red barley of the Nile. Egyptians had many different beers that were brewed from a variety of spiced sprouted grain breads.

Women usually brewed beer in Egypt and sold it from their houses. Here we have the record of women owning and running businesses. People are always saying that women became "liberated" in the 1960's, when ancient Egyptian women owned businesses. The Code of Hammurabi which was dated just before 1750 B.C. mentions these ale houses. In 1400 B.C. an Egyptian papyrus warns people not to get drunk by saying:

"Do not get drunk in the taverns in which they drink beer, for fear that people repeat words which may have gone out of your mouth, without you being aware of having uttered them." [8]

WOMEN AND ALCOHOL

On August 4, 1988 The New England Journal Of Medicine published the results of a study done with 87,526 middle-aged female nurses. They were asked questions regarding their general health and their alcohol consumption. After four years it was determined that "among middle-aged women, moderate alcohol consumption decreases the risks of coronary heart disease and ischemic stroke, but may increase the risk of subarachnoid hemorrhage." [9] Perhaps the moderate consumption of alcohol, along with eating high amounts of vegetables, pasta and whole grains, olives and olive oil, and low amounts of meats and animal fats is the success of the Mediterranean diet.

Teas

TEAS IN THE BIBLE

Teas or infusions of herbs were used in the Bible as healing medicines. Dill was used for flatulence, mint for calming and stomach problems, cumin was used as a carminitive (an agent to relieve gas in the intestines or stomach), rue was used for medicinal purposes along with thyme and marjoram. The list of digestive teas is impressive: parsley, celery seed, dill, asafetida, caraway, and ginger. Rosemary, hyssop, rue, and polygonium were used for stomachache or other pains in the belly. Maidenhair fern tea was used against tape-worm. Pellitory root was used for toothache.[10]

Spices were used for (1) seasonings, (2) making cosmetics and unguents, (3) for sacred incense, and, (4) preparation of bodies for burial.

Teas are mentioned in medical texts of the time as medicinal, but there are no references to teas being drunk on a regular basis. The current thinking on the subject is similar. Use herbs for medicinal purposes and cooking purposes. Do not drink herbal teas of the medicinal type unless it is needed. Mint tea is common fare in all of the Middle East now and mint was available as far back as recorded time so, perhaps, they used mint tea. Many people drink mint tea on a daily basis and it is acceptable. All cooking herbs can be made into teas to be drunk on the odd occasion, not on a daily basis lest they be useless when needed for medicine.

For more information on the medicinal and cosmetic uses of herbs, spices, and oils see *The World's Oldest Health Plan, Diets, Poultices, And Medicines.*

WHAT ABOUT COFFEE AND TEA?

Coffee and tea were not popular drinks during Bible times, so far as we know. Coffee is grown in parts of Africa now, so it is possible that coffee was available. Coffee is very popular in Greece, Turkey, and Italy. This is espresso or other dark roast coffee. These have less caffeine, but they still do have it.

Caffeine is an addictive drug. It is considered to be as dangerous as cocaine and amphetamines, except that it is less powerful. This drug has a cumulative effect. You can take moderate doses before you notice that it is doing something to you. By then you are hooked! It is in coffee, and in various forms in tea, cola, chocolate, and some non-prescription drugs such as pain killers, headache preparations, cold remedies, and "stay awake" pills.

Caffeine can give a wide variety of symptoms. One to two cups of coffee a day (50–200 mg) can lead to increased alertness and decreased drowsiness. More than that or doses over 200 mg can produce "caffeinism" which results in headaches, tremors, nervousness, irritability, and sleep disturbances. Caffeine causes narrowing of the blood vessels which makes the heart work harder to pump the blood through.

Dr. David Rowland of the Canadian Nutrition Institute often remarks that if coffee were to be sent through the Food and Drug Administration for approval as a safe food that it would be rejected and listed as a drug for which a prescription would be needed.

Please reevaluate your caffeine intake. Daily consumption of caffeine can be dangerous to your health.

What Can I Drink?

It is good to drink pure water every day, at least a quart or two. Drink diluted fruit juices or water with a squeeze of lemon or lime in it, or even mint tea.

WHAT SHOULD I AVOID?

Do not take anything that will harm your body. After all, your body is the temple of God. What things can harm us? Anything containing caffeine, alcohol, or large amounts of sugar or synthetic sweeteners. This means coffee, colas, beer, wine, hard liquor, chocolate drinks, soft drinks, diet soft drinks, or even milk might have to be avoided.

HOW CAN I TELL?

Since research has shown that all the drinks mentioned can be harmful in some way we should avoid them. I would suggest if you take any of these things that you go off them for 2 weeks. If you feel worse in the first 3 or 4 days, you may be having "withdrawal" from the substance. This means that you are addicted, and that is definitely harming your body. If after the first full week you begin to have more energy, feel more alert, look younger, and can concentrate better, you will know that these drinks might have been giving you trouble.

Certain drinks can be very subtle. I once took a client off milk when I worked in a clinic. She came in after two weeks saying that she had started to get a cold. She said she realized she needed more protein and went back on the milk and her stuffy nose cleared up. How subtle her mind was. In reality, she was having withdrawal from the milk in the form of congestion. Most people have heard that "milk makes mucus" so it is obvious that my client didn't get rid of the mucus by drinking milk, she stopped the reaction of the withdrawal. She went home and went off all milk products. After two weeks of strange symptoms she began to feel better than she ever had in her life.

If you drink certain things every day, you might start by reducing your consumption to less and less. You may be amazed at how much better you will feel without the caffeine, sugar, and alcohol.

REFERENCES

1. Bailey, p. 184.
2. Tannahill, pp. 54, 77, 78, 94.
3. Bouquet, p. 73.
4. Hastings, p. 87.
5. Bailey, p. 185.
6. Buttrick, Vol. 4, p. 448.
7. Tannahill, p. 63.
8. Tannahill, p. 64.
9. "A Prospective Study of Moderate Alcohol Consumption and the Risk of Coronary Disease and Stroke in Women," Meir J. Stampfer, M.D., Graham A. Colditz, M.B., B.S., Walter C. Willett, M.D., Frank E. Speizer, M.D., and Charles H. Hennekens, M.D., The New England Journal Of Medicine, Vol. 319, No. 5, August 4, 1988, pp. 267-273.
10. Daniel-Rops, Henri, *Daily Life in the Time of Jesus*, Hawthorn Books, Inc., New York, 1962, p. 369.

VIII
The Secrets Of Good Health
How Far is it to Jerusalem?
The Breath of Life
Spiritual Exercise

How Far Is It To Jerusalem?

When the Lord learned of this, he left Judea and went back once more to Galilee. Now he had to go through Samaria. So he came to a town in Samaria called Sychar, near the plot of ground Jacob had given to his son Joseph. John 4:3,4,5 (NIV)

Jesus and his disciples started at Cana and went to Capernaum, about 18 miles, then they went to Jerusalem, another 85 miles. After the Passover and the visit from Nicodemus, Jesus and his disciples went to the land of Judea, or into the open spaces from the city where his disciples were baptizing. Then they went into Galilee to the city of Sychar, which could have been another 30 to 50 miles. This didn't take a few hours. One thing we do know is that there were no buses, trains, or airplanes. They had to walk, maybe some of them rode on donkey carts, but not very many. They covered at least 135 miles. How long has it been since you walked 135 miles? Walking was the main means of transportation in Bible times. Oh sure, some had horses or donkeys, some had carts, or chariots, but most people walked. Walking is a very natural thing to do. It is one of the first ways we learn to get anywhere. Then comes running, biking, skating, etc.

The people who lived in Bible times didn't go to the gym to get exercise. Their daily life was mostly exercise. Walking was just one of the many things that required strength, endurance, and total fitness. They didn't have washing machines, automatic stoves, or electric light switches.

In the September/October 1981 issue of Biblical Archaeology Review magazine an article titled "Housewares and Recipes from 2000 Years Ago" shows photographs of actual pots and pans and a stove from a first century kitchen. The stove is a large mud or adobe structure built into the wall and resting on the ground. It is about the height of our modern stoves and looks to be about twice as long. It has three openings over which pots were set. There is a larger opening near the floor for making the fire and adding more fuel. Behind the burner openings are 4 or 5 indentations about the size of cereal bowls that were used for herbs and spices and various cooking tools that were to be used during cooking. Many of the frying pans and soup pots were made of earthenware and coated with pitch. This would make them very heavy even before food was put in them. The average cook would have to lift pots and pans that weighed probably three or four times what we lift today. Almost everything they did then took a lot of physical strength. Can you imagine doing the entire washing for a family of four by carrying it on your head down to some central location or the river to wash it? Then spending hours rubbing, wringing, and rinsing it in the river? Then hauling the wet, heavy, clothes back to your home to hang it out to dry? This is probably more exercise than most North Americans do in a week. Add to this everything else that "takes a lot of work" like hauling in fuel, building fires to cook, weaving clothes, making pots, etc. I will add that some of the things listed were hired out and done by someone else, just as we might have a cleaning person, send our clothes to the laundry, or have someone cook for us.

When you think about it, it is really true that we get less exercise than most other generations or many of the people still living in developing countries. The best way to recover supple and strong bodies is to begin getting exercise by starting easy: **Walk**.

HOW TO WALK

Walking should be a natural thing, but many people need to relearn how to do it right for it to be the most beneficial. It is best to wear shoes that have a rounded heel to cushion your heel impact and allow your foot to roll. The sole of your shoe should be able to bend. Look around in stores and catalogues for "walking" shoes.

Start by standing straight, feet together, toes pointing straight ahead, knees slightly bent. Lift up the right foot by bending the knee a little and lifting the foot. Place it in front of you, toes still pointing straight ahead, with the heel on the ground first. Rock up onto the ball of your foot; at this point the left foot should be preparing to step forward by the heel coming up. Your knees should be still slightly bent. When your right foot comes forward, your left hand should also swing forward as a balance. Keep the motion of rocking beginning with the heel and rocking onto the ball of your foot.

So much for the feet, knees, and hands. But that isn't all! There is also the involvement of your hips, tummy, and shoulders, head, neck, and jaws. When you are standing straight before you start to walk measure the plumb line. If you could drop a plumb line down inside your body from the head it should fall to the floor, straight or plumb. Of course we can't really do that so we will have to measure in the next best way. Your ankles, knees, hips, and shoulders should all be in a straight line, directly over each other. Look in a mirror front, side, and back to see if you are standing straight. When you begin to walk you may feel that your hips are leading by a fraction of an inch or so. Feel yourself in a relaxed manner stretching as tall as possible while you are walking.

Your jaw should be parallel to the floor or ground. This will prevent any neck problems. Your jaw should also be relaxed. That means that your lips are lightly closed, but your teeth are not touching or clenched. Your tongue should be inside your mouth and resting on the floor of your mouth, flat.

When you walk do not allow your feet to rock to the side. This could throw your back out or cause you to fall, not to mention injuring your ankles and toes.

Walk gracefully and rhythmically, breathing in the same way. Do full deep breathing while you are walking. This will exercise all your internal organs and help to prevent sluggishness. Deep breathing while you exercise will also help to keep you relaxed.

When you walk upstairs it is very important that you do measured, deep breathing. This will give you the oxygen you need to do the physical work. You will arrive at the top of the stairs refreshed instead of being tired. Use every movement you make to exercise your body. Many Jewish sects prohibit working on the Sabbath; they can't use a stove, make bread, or drive a car. They have to walk to services and to friends' houses. It seems that they think of walking as not working. At least one day a week they get exercise by walking.

START SMALL

Follow the practices of the ancient and modern Hebrews by walking to worship. Walk on Saturday or Sunday as often as you can. Then branch out and begin walking more. I have a client who tells me that he parks at the far end of the parking lot and walks the extra distance to the store when he goes shopping. This is a good start. Take the stairs as often as you can. Where I live most of the buildings have no second floor, therefore no stairs. The first thing I do when I go somewhere else is climb the stairs. It is pure joy to be able to walk or run upstairs. I have always tried to do this as my exercise, but now it is a thrill.

Several years ago I was so ill I couldn't walk. I developed crippling asthma from the sulphur in the well water in our house and it took nearly two years to figure out what was wrong with me. When we moved into that two story house and I ran up and down the stairs several times a day, I felt like a child with a new toy. After a year I could barely walk on level ground. Now that we have moved away from the sulphur, and through constant prayers, I have been healed. I walk up and run up stairs as often as I can find them. What a thrill when a teenager once asked me to slow down on the stairs because he couldn't keep up. This may sound amusing when you read this, unless you too have been affected in some way so that you can't walk. The best way to regain your strength is to do it. Do it more and more every day until you are strong.

Exercise, especially walking, is helpful to improve health when you have fatigue, arthritis, headaches, stress problems of any kind, lower back problems, stiff muscles, overweight, underweight, addictions, smoking problems, poor digestion, diabetes, constipation, hypoglycemia, insomnia, and osteoporosis, actually the list is endless. Exercise can help you feel better and improve your health. If you have any major, or even minor illness, please ask your doctor if walking is right for you. There might be some other reason why you need to take it easy when you start to do an exercise program. Walking was the main way people got exercise in Bible times, and it is a good way for us to begin to get exercise too.

SPEED WALKING OR RACE WALKING

Very fast walking around a track, the mall track, or on the streets is a variation of the above type of walking. First, you move much faster than regular walking. Your hands and arms do not swing. The elbows are bent so that your forearms are nearly parallel to the ground or floor. Your hands are held chest high in front of you. During speed walking the elbows alternate going back and forth in the same way they would go if you were running. The fists generally stay in front of your body. Because of the speed of the feet and legs, the hips seem to wiggle. This is OK, they should do this.

Still do slow, regulated, deep breathing. Start by counting the inhalation and exhalation. Start with a count of eight in and eight out. Then gradually increase it to 10, 15, 20, even 30 in and out. Oxygen is needed for all kinds of relaxation, so the more you get while exercising, the easeir it will be to relax and get the most benefit out of the time spent.

WALKING AND DEEP BREATHING

The best way to deep breathe is to use your breathing muscle. It is called the diaphragm. Place your open hand over your tummy at the waist, palm in. Breathe normally. Do you feel your hand moving? You should if you are using your diaphragm to breathe. Still breathing normally, place your open hand palm down over your chest. Do you feel it moving? It should only be moving slightly if you are resting. The major movement during breathing is at the waist. Your hand should be moving in and out at your waist as you inhale and exhale. This is where the diaphragm is.

The diaphragm is a muscle that dissects the body. If we were sawed in half below the ribs (don't try this, look in a book) one half of the body would have skin covering it like the skin on a drum. This is the diaphragm. It looks like a bowl. When you breath out (exhale) it looks like an inverted bowl as it gently presses all the dead air out of the lungs. When you breath in (inhale) it looks like a shallow bowl as it drops down below your waist to allow fresh air to be drawn into the entire area of your lungs. This movement of the diaphragm muscle also is helpful to exercise all your internal organs. I have heard of people reversing constipation by starting exercise with deep breathing. We have ribs to protect our lungs. So you have lungs under all the area where the rib cage is. When you use the full capacity of your lungs you will feel better, look better, have more energy that when you don't.

WHAT ELSE IS THERE ABOUT WALKING?

Walking is a weight-bearing exercise so it helps you to make calcium available to your muscles and bones. This is good news if you have osteoporosis. You can do a walking program and start to overcome it. Walking helps increase your oxygen so that you will have healthier skin, hair, nails, and better circulation. It has been known to burn fat. Walking and deep breathing can exercise the heart, lungs, kidneys, intestines, and liver, thus overcoming any sluggishness of these organs. Constipation will often go when walking is done on a daily basis. You might find that your posture improves and you begin to look younger when you walk daily. Many people find that walking increases the HDL (good cholesterol) and reduces the LDL (bad cholesterol). You will sleep better, be less anxious, and more able to withstand stress. You will just feel better in all ways if you walk more.

The Breath Of Life

Then he said to me, "Prophesy to the breath, prophesy, son of man, and say to the breath (or wind or spirit), Thus says the Lord God: Come from the four winds, O breath, and breathe upon these slain, that they may live." So I prophesied as he commanded me, and the breath came into them, and they lived, and stood upon their feet, an exceedingly great host. Ezekiel 37:9,10 (RSV)

In Ezekiel breathing is compared to the wind or the spirit. I can't say that if you deep breathe you will be filled with the Holy Spirit. I can say that if you deep breathe, you will be more alive, feel better, and have more energy.

Place your hand on your tummy again, palm facing in. Use your hand to press into the empty cavity as you exhale. Now, using the diaphragm muscle, inhale. Draw the air into your hand and push it out with the strength of the muscle. Exhale and push your hand in again. Inhale and push your hand out. Don't just use the diaphragm to push your hand, use the expansion of the diaphragm to do the work as you draw in the air and fill the floor of your tummy. When you inhale your ribs should expand out, when you exhale they should contract in. Did your diaphragm feel like a soup plate when it was relaxed? When you exhale, your diaphragm looks like an inverted serving bowl, pushing the air out of your lungs. Does it feel like this when you exhale? When you inhale your diaphragm feels like a bigger bowl than when it is relaxed.

If you want to see where the diaphragm is look at a small child who has just finished running. His little diaphragm will be working hard, his little tummy moving in and out. Look at a dog or cat when they pant. They are using quick movements of the diaphragm.

In the beginning you might want to practice firming up your breathing muscle by inhaling and exhaling through a drinking straw. This will give you a resistance that will make you have to use your diaphragm to breathe. Smokers do this all the time when they take a "drag" on a cigarette. Many times when people need more oxygen they yawn. Many people experience fatigue when their blood sugar drops. A good way to combat this is to do deep breathing or brisk walking. This will bring up the blood sugar levels and the oxygen levels giving you more energy.

WHY OXYGEN?

Oxygen is essential for relaxation of the muscles. When there is fear, fright, anxiety, or anger the breathing is shut down and we begin to do shallow breathing. This is part of the "fight or flight" syndrome. Heavy exercise requires lots of oxygen, fast, and is accomplished by quick, but shallow, breathing. We are talking about running several miles at a very fast pace. Or very quick starts to get away from an attacker. Whenever we allow our body to do the fight or flight response without good cause or the required running or heavy fighting, we cheat ourselves out of oxygen by doing shallow breathing. This lack of oxygen prevents us from relaxing. People who are in the habit of living off stress, especially those who drink coffee, colas, other forms of caffeine, smoke cigarettes, or take pep pills or diet pills, or cause stress in their body by not eating or eating too many sweets, often develop the habit of shallow breathing. This prevents them from relaxing and keeps them hooked on the things that they think are helping them relax. Deep breathing through exercise can stop this circuit of stress, stimulation, addiction, fatigue.

DO NOT BE ANXIOUS

Therefore I tell you, do not be anxious about your life, what you shall eat or what you shall drink, nor about your body, what you shall put on. Is not life more than food, and the body more than clothing? Look at the birds of the air: they neither sow nor reap nor gather into barns, and yet your heavenly Father feeds them. Are you not of more value that they? And which of you by being anxious can add one cubit to his span of life? . . . therefore do not be anxious . . . your heavenly Father knows you need them all. But seek first his kingdom and his righteousness, and all these things shall be yours as well. Matthew 6:25, 26, 27, 31a, 32b, 33 (RSV)

If we are to not be anxious, we must learn to stop doing the fight or flight response and by making a conscious effort to stop worrying and let God take care of everything.

If something goes wrong, stop and turn it over to God. Sit down, if you can, take a few slow deep breaths and pray that God will take this from you. Say something like "I turn this incident (name it) _____ over to you today. I ask for your forgiveness. Thank you God for saving me from all wrongdoing and anxiety. Thy will be done. Amen."

Continue to do slow deep breathing so that your body will be calm and relaxed. Sometimes you might have to do this a few times before your body gives it up, other times you might feel the peace that this brings immediately.

For physical training is of some value, but Godliness has value for all things . . . . 1 Timothy 4:8 (NIV)

As much as I believe in exercise and deep breathing (Physical training), I also believe that it is important to do spiritual training (Godliness). Never neglect your spiritual training even for exercise.

Spiritual Exercise

Do you not see that whatever goes into the mouth passes into the stomach, and so passes on? But what comes out of the mouth proceeds from the heart, and this defiles a man. For out of the heart come evil thoughts, murder, adultery, fornication, theft, false witness, slander. These are what defile a man; but to eat with unwashed hands does not defile a man. Matthew 15:17-20 (RSV)

There is more to health and healing than food and drink. All kinds of emotions, whether begun in childhood or adulthood, can affect the body and mind. Anger and fear can come from blood sugar problems which can generally be reversed by changes in dietary habits. Medical science is now showing that anger and fear can create the blood sugar fluctuations as well. Many times the things we allow ourselves to think can affect the way our body reacts and make the difference between good health and not so good health. Sometimes the things we say can also affect our body and our health.

After all that has been said in this book about food, nutrition, and health, I can now say that the Bible also warns us that food is not all there is and that living a good life is better for our health. "What comes out of the mouth," the things that we say in daily life that are not pure, are defiling to us. This lets us know that what we say is very important. Sometimes in supermarkets, shops, and parks I overhear conversations or diatribes, such as angry words, name-calling, or the like, that may be more damaging to the person saying them than the other person. Who is hurt more, the sayer or the hearer? In many cases it is the sayer who is hurt more. How often have we said something and wished we hadn't said it? How many times has this gnawed away at our insides? Some of the great faith healers and medical doctors report that many times they have found that people with cancer are people who are harboring anger and hatred for somebody or something, or even for themselves. These emotions actually begin to turn on the person holding onto them. Some people have found health through forgiving the person with whom they are angry, and by giving up the anger towards them.

Put to death therefore what is earthly in you: fornication, impurity, passion, evil desire, and covetousness, which is idolatry. On account of these the wrath of God is coming. In these you once walked, when you lived in them. But now put them all away: anger, wrath, malice, slander, and foul talk from your mouth. Do not lie to one another, seeing that you have put off the old nature with its practices and have put on the new nature, which is being renewed in knowledge after the image of its creator. Colossians 3:5-10 (RSV)

It is possible, through much work and prayer, to give up the kind of actions and reactions that are spoken of in this passage. There are many books written on personal growth. Even the 12 Step programs such as in Alcoholics Anonymous touch on a new life where you give up the old ways that might be causing you inner pain. Almost every system for personal growth and healing deals with changing what you say to others and what you say to yourself. Our words are important and can be powerful. Sometimes the words we mean the least can often have the most affect on us.

The apostle Paul said, "I die daily." He died daily to the old nature; he had to think about it every single day! Giving everything over to God, giving Him the control of our lives is something we must do daily.

Many people pray daily: *lead us not into temptation, but deliver us from evil.* Do we really mean that we are willing to make the effort to stop doing these things by resisting the temptation to gossip, yell at someone, become angry, doing things to someone else because they did you wrong?

IT'S NOT MY FAULT

I sometimes hear people say that whatever is wrong with them is not their fault because it is hereditary. I have always held that what was hereditary was a way of life that was passed on. Yes, we do inherit the tendency to certain diseases of body, mind, and soul, but it is up to us to see that we do not succumb.

No, it's not your fault if you were given hereditary tendencies to certain diseases, temptations, or weaknesses. But it is your fault if you don't seek help for these things. Even if your parent(s) did not resist the temptation of alcohol or other drugs, you have the choice. You can follow in his (her) footsteps and be weak, or you can ask God to help you resist. The World's Oldest Health Plan is a three-part health program: diet, exercise, prayer and forgiveness. Following the diet will allow your body to be healthy so that exercise and forgiveness are possible. In grade school we used to say: "A healthy body is a healthy mind," and I still believe it.

IS IT SIN?

Sin is defined in *An Expository Dictionary of Biblical Words* by W.E. Vine (Thomas Nelson Publishers) as "missing the mark," or, in the Old Testament usage, "a painful burden or difficulty; a toilsome, exhausting load of trouble and sorrow which the offender causes for himself or others." The use of sin as a verb is defined as meaning "to transgress, cross over, pass over." The American Heritge Dictionary (Dell) defines sin as "1, a transgression of a religious or moral law and 2, a serious offense or fault."

HOW DO WE TRANSGRESS?

In Old Testament times there were many moral and religous laws that were considered essential for people to follow. Such a law is washing one's hands before eating. We do this for hygenic reasons, for them it was required by law to be done on certain occasions. It was considered that someone had "sinned" if he had not done this. The religious laws known as "The Ten Commandments" were also laws to be followed. If anyone didn't do this he transgressed or committed an offense.

Most faiths have religious and moral laws that need to be followed. How often have we heard the report that in some place a person caught stealing had his hand cut off. This is their way of dealing with a person who has transgressed the law (sinned). Stealing is considered to be a big offense in most faiths. In the Bible, it is one the Ten Commandments. In the East Indian belief they don't just say "You shall not steal!" They take it a step further and describe what that means. Missionaries who have worked in India have told me that to interrupt someone while he is talking is considered stealing. Say you have just had something happen to you that was exciting. As you begin to tell a friend, he cuts you off, saying he has had the same thing happen to him and it is no big deal. You are crushed, even angry. He has stolen your moment of feeling good, of excitement. He has committed the "sin" of stealing. The Ten Commandments in the Bible leave it up to each of us to decide what is and is not stealing. This is why "sin" or missing the mark of being perfect is hard to interpret. Is it OK to steal from a big corporation and not a little mom and pop store? Is it acceptable to bear false witness by cheating on our income taxes?

Society in North America is getting away from the Judeo-Christian ethic found in the Bible and is turning more toward humanistic interpretations of what is right and wrong. In the last 20 years in my practice as a nutrition consultant I have seen more and more people in pain because they have refused to accept the possibility of sin. They have no way of being healed from these types of transgressions. They tell me they don't want to feel guilty about anything they do. Guilt is there for a purpose. It lets us know that we have transgressed the laws set up by God. We can then be healed from the pain of the guilt by asking for forgiveness and turning away from the transgressions.

NEW TESTAMENT LAWS

One of the teachers of the law came and heard them debating. Noticing that Jesus had given them a good answer, he asked him, "Of all the commandments, which is the most important?" "The most important one," answered Jesus, "Is this: 'Hear, O Israel, the Lord our God, the Lord is one. Love the Lord your God with all your heart and with all your soul and with all your mind and with all your strength.' The second is this: 'Love your neighbor as yourself.' There is no commandment (law) greater than these." Mark 12:28-32 (NIV)

If I love my brother I will not be angry with him. If I love myself I will not be angry with myself. It is very simple. If I love God with all my heart, soul, mind, and strength, I won't have anything left to hate with, or slander with, or be angry with.

Love is patient and kind; love is not jealous or boastful; it is not arrogant or rude. Love does not insist on its own way; it is not irritable or resentful; it does not rejoice at wrong, but rejoices in the right. Love bears all things, believes all things, hopes all things, endures all things. . . . So faith, hope, love abide, these three; but the greatest of these is love. 1 Corinthians 13:4-7, 13 (RSV)

Better is a dinner of herbs (vegetables) where love is than a fatted ox and hatred with it. Proverbs 15:17 (RSV)

SINS OF OTHER GENERATIONS

Then the Lord came down in the cloud and stood there with him and proclaimed his name, the Lord. And He passed in front of Moses, proclaiming, "The Lord, the Lord, the compassionate and gracious God, slow to anger, abounding in love and faithfulness, maintaining love to thousands, and forgiving wickedness, rebellion and sin. Yet He does not leave the guilty unpunished; He punishes the children and their children for the sin of the fathers to the third and fourth generation." Exodus 34:5-7 (NIV)

This has come to be known as generational sin, the sins of the father being passed down to the children.

Many times habits or action patterns such as anger, violence, lying, etc. are passed on to the children. This can be from learned or unlearned behavior. These actions were once considered transgressions of the moral laws of common courtesy. Many times diet has a role to play in this. If parents are given to eating foods that encourage them to be hostile or volatile, their children learn that this is the proper way to behave because they haven't seen otherwise. They will continue this pattern by eating the same foods. If parents are angry, abusive, unrational and unloving, their children will learn that this is the proper way to behave and mimic it themselves. They might even think that they have no choice in their actions. They might even feel that it's not their fault, because their parents acted this way and so must they.

Unless the children change their ways of eating, speaking, and living they will be forced to carry the same sins as their father. It might be essential to break the generational ties with faults of past family members to be able to live a free life. There are some faults (sins) such as anger, adultery, lust, and so on that we might not even know about that a family member could have committed in his or her youth. This could be holding us open to temptation that we cannot resist on our own. This is the time that you need some help by calling the minister, priest, or elders of the church to come and break the ties to all generational sins in your family. It could be something as common as divorce, anger, abortion, or alcoholism, or it could be murder, theft, adultery, or even witchcraft.

There are many books in Christian bookstores on breaking the ties, often they are called something about healing the family tree or breaking the bonds of generational sin. This generational sin is often the very same thing as hereditary tendencies. Once you break the ties to the sins in your family tree you can be free to have self-control in a way that was never available to you before. Temptation will be easier to resist when you are only resisting the temptations that come to you. When you are weakened because somewhere in your family tree a father, uncle, grandmother, or other person succumbed to temptation and has passed it down to you, you will not be able to resist. No diet alone can make us strong enough to withstand this.

And the prayer offered in faith will make the sick person well; the Lord will raise him up. If he has sinned, he will be forgiven. Therefore confess your sins to each other and pray for each other, so that you may be healed. The prayer of a righteous man is powerful and effective. James 5:15-16 (NIV)

Many churches are now offering "reconciliation" times for those who wish to meet with an elder, prayer team, or priest to reconcile his or her heart to God when they have strayed from following the laws set up by God in the Bible. It used to be called confession, confession of your sins. Many churches have a ministry of healing that is there for the members to come to for prayer and healing. How long has it been since you recognized a sin (fault) in yourself, confessed it to a friend, priest, minster, elder, or pastor, prayed about it, been forgiven, and then let it go? It is possible to recognize a way that you have "missed the mark." Just look at the things you feel guilty or bad about. It is very simple to call this "sin" and then to ask to be reconciled to God by your own admission of having sinned.

START NOW

You have heard that is was said to the people long ago, 'Do not murder, and anyone who murders will be subject to judgement.' But I tell you that anyone who is angry with his brother (without cause) will be subject to judgement. Matthew 5:21 (NIV)

Make a list of the sins above and in Matthew 15 and Colossians 3. Keep the list with you. Each day check yourself to see if you have committed a transgression against God, your neighbor, or yourself.

Ask yourself, "Did I tell a lie? Did I say something slanderous about someone? Did I get angry with my neighbor? Or the person in front of me in traffic? Or my child? Or the government? Or the gas company? Did I hurt my body by getting angry? Was this loving to my neighbor or to myself when I blew up at him? Has my anger hurt my liver? My adrenal glands? My heart? Am I Type 'A' personality? Type 'Anger,' that is?" If you want to see how different emotions affect your body read *None of these Diseases* by S.I. McMillen, M.D.

WHAT SHALL I DO?

Repent therefore, and turn again, that your sins may be blotted out, that times of refreshing may come from the presence of the Lord. . . . Acts 3:19 (RSV)

Recognition of sin (faults), confession of sin, repentance or turning away from sin, and then asking for forgiveness can relieve you from all your burdens. This is the beginning of the road to health, health of body, mind, and soul (spirit).

WHAT ABOUT FEAR AND ANXIETY?

Anxiety, stress, fear, these are not things for us to endure. How many times have we heard that angels always say: "Fear not," or "Be not afraid." This should give us the idea that we should have no fear. And we will have no fear when we learn to trust God completely for everything. We also have to do our part and keep our body healthy with the right foods, right liquids, right attitudes, right trust.

Therefore I tell you, do not be anxious about your life, what you shall eat or what you shall drink, nor about your body, what you shall put on. Is not life more than food, and the body more than clothing? Look at the birds of the air: they neither sow nor reap nor gather into barns, and yet your heavenly Father feeds them. Are you not of more value than they? And which of you by being anxious can add one cubit to his span of life? . . . Therefore do not be anxious, saying, "What shall we eat?" or "What shall we drink?" or "What shall we wear?" For the Gentiles seek all these things; and your heavenly Father knows that you need them all. But seek first his kingdom and his righteousness, and all these things shall be yours as well. Therefore do not be anxious about tomorrow, for tomorrow will be anxious for itself. Let the day's own trouble be sufficient for the day. Matthew 6:25-27,31-34 (RSV)

Anxiety, worry, or being anxious, as mentioned above, is not within God's plan for us. Righteousness, which was formerly known as rightwiseness, is the Greek word *dikaiosune*. It means the character or quality of being right or just. In this passage it means the sum total of the requirements of God. It also means purity of heart and rectitude of life. (*An Expository Dictionary of Biblical Words*, W.E. Vine, Nelson)

I take this to mean that we need to take care of our body, mind, and spirit, but we should not get anxious over it. God knows what we want and need and he will provide what he thinks we need. God is in charge and no matter what we do or say, we cannot guarantee perfect health if he is not willing to agree. We can only do that which is ours to do, and let God do that which is his to do. **Don't Worry! Fear Not!** Let us forgive others their issues against us and ask for forgiveness for ours.

HOW MUCH SHOULD I DO?

Peter came up (to Jesus) and said to him, "Lord, how often shall my brother sin against me, and I forgive him? As many as seven times?" Jesus said to him, "I do not say to you seven times, but seventy-times seven." Matthew 18:21, 22 (RSV)

This could take forever! Yes, that is exactly what Jesus must have meant. Do it, keep doing it, still love your brother, do not get angry with him, confess when you do, ask for and receive forgiveness when you lapse into anger. Love your brother and love God. This should bring you **Peace.**

Peace I leave with you; my peace I give you. I do not give to you as the world gives. Do not let your hearts be troubled and do not be afraid. John 14:27 (NIV)

The World's Oldest Health Plan is a plan taken from the Bible that tells us how to have the best health possible. We can learn to have healthy bodies with nutrition and exercise; healthy minds and bodies with forgiveness, peace, and love.

Index

Books by Starburst Publishers
(Partial listing—full list available on request)

The World's Oldest Health Plan — Kathleen O'Bannon Baldinger

Subtitled: *Health, Nutrition and Healing from the Bible.* Offers a complete health plan for body, mind and spirit, just as Jesus did. It includes programs for diet, exercise and mental health. Contains foods and recipes to lower cholesterol and blood pressure, improve the immune system and other bodily functions, reduce stress, reduce or cure constipation, eliminate insomnia, reduce forgetfulness, confusion and anger, increase circulation and thinking ability, eliminate "yeast" problems, improve digestion, and much more.

(trade paper-opens flat)   ISBN 0914984578   **$14.95**

Dr. Kaplan's Highway To Health — Eric Scott Kaplan

Subtitled: *A Guide to THINNING and WINNING.* A comprehensive guide to the formulas and principles of: FAT LOSS, EXERCISE, VITAMINS, SUCCESS and HAPPINESS. It emphasizes *Maximum Metabolism* through diet modification—fat and carbohydrate modification, coupled with exercise and the removal of sugar, stimulating the body to utilize stored and dietary fat for energy. Dr. Kaplan will teach you a natural approach to food combinations—what you can eat in quantity and what foods such as sugar, white flour and salt to modify or eliminate so *you can eat more and weigh less.*

(trade paper)   ISBN 091498456X   **$14.95**

Stay Well Without Going Broke — Gulling, Renner, & Vargas

Subtitled: *Winning the War Over Medical Bills.* Provides a blueprint for how health care consumers can take more responsibility for monitoring their own health and the cost of its care—a crucial cornerstone of the health care reform movement today. Contains inside information from doctors, pharmacists and hospital personnel on how to get cost-effective care without sacrificing quality. Offers legal strategies to protect your rights when illness is terminal.

(hard cover)   ISBN 0914984527   **$22.95**

Allergy Cooking With Ease — Nicolette M. Dumke

Subtitled: *The No Wheat, Milk, Eggs, Corn, Soy, Yeast, Sugar, Grain, and Gluten Cookbook.* A book designed to provide a wide variety of recipes to meet many different types of dietary and social needs, and, whenever possible, save you time in food preparation. Includes: Recipes for those special foods that most food allergy patients think they will never eat again; Timesaving tricks; and Allergen Avoidance Index.

(trade paper-opens flat)   ISBN 091498442X   **$12.95**

Books by Starburst Publishers—cont'd.

The Low-Fat Supermarket — Judith & Scott Smith

Subtitled: *A Guide to Weight Loss, Cholesterol Control and Good Nutrition for the Entire Family.* A comprehensive reference of over 4,500 brand name products that derive less than 30% of their calories from fat. Information provided includes total calories, fat, cholesterol and sodium content. Organized according to the sections of a supermarket. Your answer to a healthier you.

(trade paper)   ISBN 0914984438   **$10.95**

Off The Floor . . . and Into Your Soup? — Charles Christmas, Jr.

A shocking account of what goes on behind the scenes at many restaurants–high class or not. Author looks at the restaurant itself, its employees, and the food that is served to the customer. He also reveals the practical jokes, and more, that kitchen employees do to each other, and the not-so-kind things they do to patrons.

(trade paper)   ISBN 0914984381   **$7.95**

Alzheimer's—Does "The System" Care? — Ted & Paula Valenti

This book reveals a *unique observation* as to the cause of Alzheimer's and the care of its victims. It also tells the story of the Valenti's personal care homes and their fight with the health bureaucracy.

(hard cover)   ISBN 0914984179   **$14.95**

A Woman's Guide To Spiritual Power — Nancy L. Dorner

Subtitled: *Through Scriptural Prayer.* Do your prayers seem to go "against a brick wall?" Does God sometimes seem far away or non-existent? If your answer is "Yes," *You* are not alone. Prayer must be the cornerstone of your relationship to God. "This book is a powerful tool for anyone who is serious about prayer and discipleship."—Florence Littauer

(trade paper) ISBN 0914984470   **$9.95**

Purrables — Alma Barkman

Subtitled: *Words of Wisdom from the World of a Cat.* This book was derived from the antics of the family cat, Sir Purrcival van Mouser. The author has taken anecdotal material used in a weekly humor column and combined it with Scriptural truths from the book of *Proverbs.* **Purrables** is an inspirational self-help book with a unique slant. Sir Purrcival van Mouser draws the reader into consideration of spiritual truths as they apply to everyday living. In each *Purrable* the theme is brought into focus by a verse from *Proverbs.* The humorous behavior of the cat is used to draw a parallel with our own experience or attitude, and the application is summarized by an appropriate proverb. **Purrables** especially appeals to anyone who loves a cat and would therefore enjoy reading truth from a different *purr*spective.

(trade paper)   ISBN 0914984535   **$6.95**

The New American Family   —Artlip, Artlip, & Saltzman

Subtitled: *Tools for Strengthening Step-Families.* American men and women are remarrying at an astounding rate, and nearly 60% of the remarriages involve children under the age of eighteen. Unfortunately, over half of these remarriages also end in divorce, with half of the "redivorces" occuring within five years. **The New American Family** tells it like it is. It gives examples and personal experiences that help you to see that the second time around is no picnic. It provides practical, good sense suggestions and guidelines for making "your new American family" the one you always dreamed of.

(trade paper)   ISBN 0914984446   **$10.95**

Purchasing Information

Notes

Notes

Notes

Notes

Notes

Notes